Flourishing

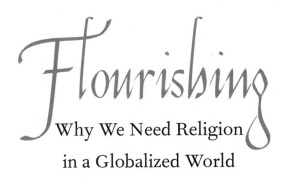

Flourishing
Why We Need Religion in a Globalized World

MIROSLAV VOLF

Yale
UNIVERSITY PRESS
New Haven and London

Published with assistance from the Ronald and Betty Miller
Turner Publication Fund.

Yale University Press books may be purchased in quantity for
educational, business, or promotional use. For information,
please e-mail sales.press@yale.edu (U.S. office) or sales@
yaleup.co.uk (U.K. office).

Designed by Sonia L. Shannon.
Set in Fournier type by Integrated Publishing Solutions,
Grand Rapids, Michigan.
Printed in the United States of America.

ISBN 978-0-300-18653-6 (cloth : alk. paper)

Library of Congress Control Number: 2015942789

A catalogue record for this book is available from the British
Library.

This paper meets the requirements of ANSI/NISO Z39.48–
1992 (Permanence of Paper).

10 9 8 7 6 5 4 3 2 1

For Jessica

Contents

Preface

*F*lourishing is the title of this book. It stands for the life that is lived well, the life that goes well, and the life that feels good—all three together, inextricably intertwined. I use the term interchangeably with "the good life" and "life worth living." It evokes an image of a living thing, thriving in its proper environment: a tree "planted by streams of water, which yields its fruit in its season" and whose leaves "do not wither" (Psalms 1:3), a sheep lying "down in green pastures" and walking "beside still waters" (Psalms 23:2), an "eagle, with great wings and long pinions, rich in plumage of many colors" (Ezekiel 17:3). Though these images may strike some as too pastoral for fast-track modern lives, most readily embrace the idea they represent: the good life consists not merely in succeeding in one or another endeavor we undertake, whether small or large, but in living into our human and personal fullness—that, in a word, is a flourishing life.

The image is compelling, but many, especially the young, have a sense that humanity is doomed to languishing, stuck "in the valley of the shadow of death" (Psalms 23:4), in the "land of deep darkness" (Isaiah 9:2), even if they don't use the words of psalmists and prophets to express the sentiment. Ours are certainly not the darkest of all times, but I can understand the pessimism. Climate changes wreaking devastating impacts on the environment; likely global pandemics; great and growing discrepancies in power, wealth, and skill;

emerging artificial intelligence menacing humans with redundancy; the global reach of barbaric terror burning and beheading enemies and destroying artifacts of our great civilizations—these and other threats place an ashen mantle of melancholy on many. Though we can identify threats, each threat is also an unknown, a "known unknown," as it is sometimes called, placing before us an uncertain future; and we are haunted by a sense that these might be just the first scrawny cows of the Pharaoh's dream (Genesis 41), to be followed by more—"unknown unknowns," perils of which we aren't yet even aware. Some are paralyzed by the thought of the world coming to a full stop, with all human life extinguished, as in Lars von Trier's *Melancholia*. Others fear a postapocalyptic, dystopian future—urban wastelands and deserts with survivors locked in conflict, fumbling to lace together the shreds of their own humanity and civilizational ties. Even in the absence of such nightmarish scenarios, in the world as it stands today, too many of us believe that human lives are and will forever remain bereft of meaning, caught in a pointless dance of light and darkness as if in a segment of some random cosmic lightshow. If you are a pessimist of this sort, "flourishing" will seem to you a wistful word, an impossible dream from a "la-la land" world.

The two most potent images of human flourishing in the Western cultural traditions come from the Bible, from the opening chapters of its first book and from the final chapters of its last. One is an image of the verdant garden, beautiful and nourishing, a habitat for humans to "till and keep" and a temple in which to converse with their God (Genesis 2). The other is of a universal city that has become a temple, "the new Jerusalem" on a "new earth," rich in the glory and honor of nations and utterly secure (Revelation 21). For those who embrace them, these images aren't mere dream-clouds, floating around in the sky of religious fancy. They are part of a grand narrative arc starting with world's creation and ending with new heavens and the new earth, of which the Hebrew Bible and the Christian Scriptures tell;

and both, the grand arc and the visions of flourishing, are rooted in convictions about the reality of the One who dwells in inapproachable light. The promise of these visions of flourishing is a prize jewel in the treasury of the Christian faith, one of its best gifts to the world. Adherents of other religions and secular humanists perhaps use different images, but their own faiths offer a similar pledge of hope.

Von Trier's *Melancholia* ends with two sisters and a child huddled in an improvised temple made out of slender and sparse sticks as the bright light of a world-annihilating asteroid approaches. Is this an image of a leap of faith into the light? Or is it a symbol of the absurdity of religion in the face of the unconquerable darkness that is, ultimately, this universe itself? Von Trier leaves us guessing. In a sense, in this book I am leaving that question open as well. Are the convictions that underpin religious visions of human flourishing true, or are they beautiful but deceitful stories, celestial echoes of the fragility and meaninglessness of the lives of those to whom they promise protection and flourishing? How do they stack up against secular accounts of reality claiming to be based on hard science? If religious convictions and visions of flourishing are true, are all of them true? If only one religion is true, which one is and why?

These are important questions—and I completely bypass them in this book. Instead, I focus on the claim that gives these questions their importance in the first place and demands that we wrestle with the issue of their truth or falsity. The claim is this: far from being a plague on humanity, as many believe and some experience, religions are carriers of compelling visions of flourishing. In this book, I highlight key elements of these visions in world religions, sketch why they are needed in a globalized world, and explore how religions can advocate and embody them peacefully and in concert while taking seriously the claims to truth they make.

Acknowledgments

Since the roots of this book lie in the Faith and Globalization seminar conducted at Yale University in the fall semesters of 2008–11, I must first thank my co-teachers. I am grateful to Prime Minister Tony Blair, with whom I taught the first three iterations of the course, for pulling me in to work on the topic and for the vigorous Thursday morning discussions we had as we were preparing for the afternoon sessions. I owe much to Philip Gorski, a colleague from the sociology department with whom I taught the fourth iteration of the course, especially for opening my eyes to complexities of secularization and of the relation between nationalism and violence. In 2010 I gave a version of the course as a summer seminar for junior faculty at Calvin College. Three years later an early draft of this book served as the basis for a seminar for international young diplomats and scholars of religion and politics organized by the American University in Kosovo, the Kosovo Ministry of Foreign Affairs, and the Tony Blair Faith Foundation. At all three places I was blessed with wonderfully inquisitive and insightful participants from around the world representing a variety of academic disciplines.

I lectured on the topics in this book at many academic institutions and conferences across the globe. I list here only a sampling of the cities in which the events took place, in alphabetical order: Adelaide, Australia; Beijing, China; Boston, Massachusetts (Annual Prophetic Voices Lecture at Boston College); Bucharest, Romania (ITP Annual

Lectures at Theological Pentecostal Institute); Buffalo, New York (Joseph J. Naples '41 Conversations in Christ & Culture Lecture and Performance Series at Canisius College); Dallas, Texas; Edinburgh, United Kingdom (Cunningham Lectures at the University of Edinburgh); Georgetown, Washington, D.C.; Holland, Michigan; Hong Kong, China; Houston, Texas; Macon, Georgia (Harry Vaughan Smith Lectures at Mercer University); Marburg, Germany; Melbourne, Australia (Hughes-Cheong Lectures at Trinity College); Osijek, Croatia (Annual Lectures at Evangelical Theological Seminary); Pasadena, California (Payton Lectures at Fuller Theological Seminary); Sarajevo, Bosnia and Herzegovina; Seoul, South Korea; Seattle, Washington; South Bend, Indiana; Sydney, Australia; Taipei, Taiwan. I am grateful to the organizers of the events at which I spoke as well as to colleagues and audiences for engaging with my arguments. I have learned from their questions, resistances, and suggestions more than I knew then and, I am sure, more than I am aware of even now.

Three sets of scholars read and discussed with me a draft of the entire book, except for the introduction and the epilogue. The first discussion was organized by Daniel Chua, professor in the Department of Music at the University of Hong Kong, in May 2013. In addition to Chua himself, this lively interreligious and interdisciplinary group was comprised of Uzma Ashraf, Ng Wai Hang, Sik Hin Hung, Chan Jianlin Jianlin, Gareth Jones, Louie Kin, David Palmer, Conan Pengyin, Simone Raudino, Kang Phee Seng, Benny Tai, Ang Sze Wei, Louie Kin Yip, Esther Yau, Wendy Yuen, and Liang Yuanyuan. The second set met just prior to the 2013 annual meeting of the American Academy of Religion in Baltimore for an excellent dinner and intense conversation that was generously funded by my friend Phil Love, a member of the advisory board of the Yale Center for Faith and Culture and a theologian in his own right. At the gathering—which was better than a symposium, with less wine than Socrates used to drink and, I am certain, better food—were José Casanova, Willis Jenkins, Charles Mathewes, Joerg Rieger, and Mona Siddiqui. The scholars in the third set, who were generous enough to set aside an entire day, including an evening at Le Petit Café, in December 2013, were all my Yale colleagues: Nayan Chanda, Philip Gorski, Zareena Grewal, Jennifer Herdt, Kathryn Lofton, Aleksandar Santrač, Kathryn Tanner, and Linn Tonstad. The things I learned from all three of these groups would be too long to list in these acknowledgments. Many of these scholars, especially Kathryn Lofton, Mona Siddiqui, and Linn Tonstad, have pressed me to make more explicit my own convictions and the stance I take, which resulted in the two texts now bookending the volume, the introduction and epilogue. Chapter 3 was originally presented as a paper at the God and Human Flourishing consultation on respect, one in the series of consultations I have organized at the Yale Center for Faith and Culture. I am grateful to Alonzo McDonald of the McDonald Agape Foundation for funding the event and to the participants for critical and constructive feedback: Alon Goshen-Gottstein, John Hare, Jennifer Herdt, Gilbert Mailander, and Michael Peppard. In addition to these three groups of scholars, Monica Duffy Toft of Oxford University offered comments on a draft of chapter 1, Tobias Faix and Tobias Künkler of Marburger Bildings - und Studienzentrum on chapters 1 and 2, and Daniel Philpott of the University of Notre Dame on a draft of chapter 5.

As I was painfully aware from the moment I contemplated teaching the course to the moment I finished the last line of the epilogue, the topic of this book is too big for an individual scholar. The diverse contributions I received from colleagues, audiences, and students across the globe were indispensable to the completion of the project. I have also sought specific advice from experts on religious traditions other than Christianity. I am grateful to three good friends from those traditions who were generous with their time: Anantanand Rambachan, professor of religion at St. Olaf's College (Hinduism); Dr. Alon Goshen-Gottstein of the Elijah Institute, Jerusalem (Judaism); and HRH Prince Ghazi bin Muhammad, professor of philosophy and chief advisor for religious and cultural affairs to HM King Abdullah II of Jordan (Islam). I have received generous help on Confucianism from Joseph A. Adler, now retired professor of East Asian religions at Kenyon College. On occasion I departed from their expert advice, so none of them should be blamed for any blunders the book may contain with regard to these religions.

Throughout teaching, researching, and writing, I have received help from many able teaching and research assistants. Neil Arner, Lisa Tepper Bates, Scott Dolff, Osman Haneef, John Hartley, Natalia Marandiuc, Jeff Morris, Christiana Peppard, and John Super worked as teaching assistants, with Neil Arner, nicknamed Neil the Magnificent, doing with splendid efficiency and skill the lion's share of the initial intellectual and pedagogical work needed to get the Faith and Globalization course going. Yeehyun Chun, Karin Fransen, Brad Gable, Janna Gonwa, John Hartley, and Jordan Kassabaum worked as researchers, all except for John Hartley in the last phase of writing. In addition to serving as the coordinator of research and a critical reader in that last phase, Matt Croasmun wrote a brief on agency of systems, a short section of which was incorporated into the introduction.

Two research assistants must be singled out; they are amazing human beings and wonderful scholars and I am deeply grateful to them. Justin Crisp helped shape the introduction, wrote two notes on Confucianism in chapter 2, and did extensive research for chapter 3, especially on the Augustine/Locke/Proast debates and for the sections "Toleration" and "Respecting Other Religions." He also prepared briefs on aspects of the thought of José Casanova, Reiner Forst, and Maurice Merleau-Ponty and aggregated all the feedback received from the discussion groups in Baltimore and at Yale. Ryan McAnnally Linz, my doctoral student who has worked with me on various projects for six years now and has become more a dialogue partner than a research assistant, deserves to be mentioned last because he contributed most. He helped form the argument of the introduction; in chapter 1 he conducted research for the sections "Religions, Markets, and the Affirmation of Ordinary Life" and "The Difference Religions Make"; in chapter 2 he helped with "Ways of Living Ordinary Life" (including writing the lengthy footnote on Augustine) and "Malfunctions and Contentions" (including the decision of where to place the section in the chapter); in chapter 3 he did research for "World Religions and the Freedom of Religion" and "Apostasy and Conversion" (a section we debated a lot); he helped with the argumentative shape of chapter 4 as a whole and contributed significantly to the section "Incompatible or Not?"

Most of these researchers received their suppers for their extraordinary singing thanks to the generous support of the advisory board of the Yale Center for Faith and Culture; the board members are an exceptional group of people without whom this book and many other projects embraced by the center wouldn't be possible. One "outside" supporter of the Yale Center for Faith and Culture contributed substantially to funding my research: my friend Warner Depuy, who encouraged the William H. Pitt Foundation and its president Robert G. Simses to support financially work on this book. I am grateful to him, to the foundation, and to the advisory board of the center for their generosity.

I wrote most of the book in the course of one sabbatical and finished editing it in the course of another. I am grateful to Yale University and to two Yale Divinity School deans, Harold Attridge and Gregory Sterling, for setting me free from teaching responsibilities. At crunch times, when deadlines were looming, my good friend Skip Masback, the managing director of the Yale Center for Faith and Culture, not only administered the institution, including research activities, with his extraordinary skill but did so without one single time knocking on the door of my writing cave (actually, an office down the hall). It is truly a gift to have him as a collaborator. My editor Jennifer

Banks, copy editor Robin DuBlanc, and the rest of the team at Yale University Press were all an author, especially a nonnative writer, could possibly hope for; I am grateful for their skill and passion for the project.

Flourishing is dedicated to Jessica Dwelle, my wife, a woman of razor-sharp intellect and extraordinary sensibility. Our courtship began in the fall of 2010 around the time when I started thinking about writing the book. Its crafting is intertwined with the wonder of our love.

Flourishing

Introduction

The roots of world religions[1] and globalization reach back nearly as far as the recorded history of humanity itself. Today, each of these two complex and multidimensional phenomena encompasses the entire planet and appears in a myriad of diverse local incarnations.

The phrase *religions and globalization,* two nouns separated by a conjunction, may suggest that the two are merely external to each other: religions are outside of globalization processes, reacting to them in various ways—rejection, affirmation, ambivalence, withdrawal, aggression—and globalization is outside of religions, displacing them, energizing them, transforming them—pushing, for instance, against their otherworldliness or the predilection for nonegalitarianism or intolerance that marks some versions of them. That wouldn't be right, though; truly, the conjunction in the phrase binds the two nouns together. Religions and globalization aren't two neighbors, each living in its own home separated by a tall wall, alternately cooperating, competing, or quarreling. The world religions are part of the dynamics of globalization—they are, in a sense, the original globalizers and still remain among the drivers of globalization processes—and globalization is part of the dynamics of religions, their moral and doctrinal self-articulations, their cultural and political formations,

1

and their intergenerational and missionary dissemination. Globalization is *within* religions and world religions are *within* globalization.

The goals of this book are to shed light on how religions and globalization have interacted over the centuries and to suggest what their relationship ought to be in the future. Unless we understand these two powerful phenomena in their relation to each other, we will neither know what is happening to us and to our world nor be able to act responsibly in it. More than anything else, with the possible exception of technological innovation, globalization and the great world religions are shaping our lives—from the public policies of political leaders and the economic decisions of industry bosses, investors, and ordinary employees, through the content of the curricula in our colleges and universities, all the way to the inner longings of our hearts. As I explain succinctly in the epilogue, the main thrust of my argument is that a vision of flourishing found in the quarreling family of world religions is essential to individual thriving and global common good.

When we want to get a sense of something big and complex, we step back, squint a bit to shut out distracting details, and take in its outline. This, roughly, is what I have done here. Specialists in diverse fields and subfields dealing with various aspects of religions and globalization may be frustrated that I haven't paid more attention to the "details"—that I have not attended to some important features of the phenomena, that I have neglected an intense scholarly conversation about a particular issue, that I haven't paid sufficient attention to all relevant figures from the past, and so on. But as I see it, we sorely need synthetic, integrative, and action-guiding knowledge, and the inescapable price of having it in an age of intense subspecialization is a kind of "amateurism." I ask specialists among my readers to squint with me for a while as they consider the relation between religions and globalization, and then examine the charcoal sketch I offer here, considering its merits as just such a sketch (and I request that, before making judgments, they read the extensive endnotes in which I offer justification for many of my positions!). If they still strongly disagree, I urge them to articulate a similarly integrative and normatively inflected alternative of their own.

In sketching the basic contours of the relation between religions and globalization, I've simplified my task in a variety of ways. For instance, with regard to globalization, I have concentrated on its economic and political dimensions and the implicit visions of human flourishing embedded in them, touching globalization's other crucial dimensions—ecological, technological, and legal—only on the margins. And with regard to religions, I've zeroed in on those that have been, inadequately, called "secondary" or "world" religions, and of these, primarily on Buddhism, Confucianism, Hinduism, Judaism, Christianity, and Islam. I have left aside religions that are equally inadequately designated as "primary," "indigenous," or "local." Local religions have their own, mostly unhappy, history with globalization as well as their own contribution to make to its reshaping, especially when it comes to globalization's relation to local natural habitats and the planet as a whole.[2] But someone else will have to take on that story.

The book, more a programmatic essay than an academic monograph, traces its origin to the Faith and Globalization course that Prime Minister Tony Blair and I taught for three semesters at Yale University (2008–10). But I bring to the book more than just the expertise of a professor. A Westerner and a Christian, I write about the subject from a particular vantage point and with a set of deep commitments, from a place where globalization processes and a version of a world religion intersect in a single life. Perhaps it is important to give a brief account of my vantage point and my commitments before delving into the exploration.

I was born in a country that dissolved at "the end of history." When I first heard the phrase, popularized by Francis Fukuyama at the end of the Cold War,[3] I thought: "Last time I checked, history was still going strong." I felt it was speeding up, in fact, pulled by our dreams and fears, and leaving in its trail an impressive array of achievements as well as desolate landscapes and human habitations, lives enriched with knowledge and technological advances as well as people crushed in the cogwheels of global economic machinery, discarded and forgotten under the sands of time. The country of which I am writing, Yugoslavia, was in the Balkans, and in 1990s the region continued to produce more history than it could consume, to use Winston Churchill's famous and supercilious remark about that part of the world. After "the end of history" wars were still fought and won or lost, governments were formed and dissolved, economic systems were altered, cities were destroyed and rebuilt, children were born and died, and dreams were—what? What *was* the history of the countless dreams to which the marriage of hearts and eyes had given birth?

For Fukuyama, of course, "the end of history" meant neither that time had stopped and eternity had begun nor that human beings suddenly lost interest in writing about the past. Instead, he used the phrase to describe the world historical change that he argued occurred with the fall of the Berlin Wall. That event symbolized for him the "end point of mankind's ideological evolution and the universalization of Western liberal democracy as the final form of human government."[4] Fukuyama was wrong about the end of history—also about *his* kind of end of history. Even though a particular form of liberal democracy is an integral part of the position I advocate here, it would be a grave mistake to consider any kind of liberalism—or any kind of system, for that matter—the end point of humanity's "ideological evolution." Liberalism is too ambivalent for such closure, with failures of major proportions shadowing its impressive successes,[5] and human lives and history are too dynamic and unpredictable to stick with liberalism. History did not end when the hammers hit the Berlin Wall.

But something did end in November 1989. It was the rivalry on the world stage between two major projects of globalization, two ways of living in the world seen as a single, integrated reality. One was communist, commenced with the Bolshevik revolution in the twentieth century and marked by a totalitarian or authoritarian state and a planned command economy; the other one was capitalist, commenced with the Age of Discovery in the fifteenth century and marked, mostly, by a democratic political order and a free market economy.[6] The communist project of globalization lost—definitively, I think; the capitalist project won, for now.

People suffered under communist globalization; I know it from firsthand experience, having grown up in the former Yugoslavia. A powerful state robbed us of civic freedoms, forced us into mergers of "unity and brotherhood" in the name of goals we didn't share, disregarded our dreams of "eating fruit from our own vine and fig tree and drinking water from our own cisterns," as the prophet of old put it (Isaiah 36:16), despoiled the environment, and trampled on freedom of religion and the right to live our lives as we saw fit. Without exception, majorities in all European nations and ethnic groups that were roped into the project of communist globalization welcomed the triumphant capitalist globalization. They longed for freedom, democracy, and human rights, for a market economy and prosperity.

Each of Yugoslavia's constituent parts established itself as a separate democratic state with a capitalist economy. Simultaneously, the majorities in these constituent parts sought to reassert their own ethnic and religious identities,[7] which had been suppressed by the ideals and political realities of the unitary state inspired by Marx's global vision.[8] Some of them fought bitter wars in the 1990s, partly with the help of transnational ethnic networks that sent both money and soldiers to the homeland.[9] Western Europe had little understanding of the separatist aspirations of these peoples, engaged as it was in development of greater integration after the end of the Cold War. But the two processes, the unification of Europe and the dissolution of Yugoslavia, were also connected: communal self-assertion shadowed increasing regional integration.

After the war, each of the newly founded states sought integration into the European Union, itself a major force in capitalist globalization. But the prospect of integration into the European Union triggered negative reactions as well, fears about the loss of national sovereignty and the erasure of cultural identity, anger about forced buyouts and the imposition of unfair economic conditions undermining local industries, frustration about the growing disparity between rich and poor and the crumbling of social services, and—a thread running throughout all of these—people's uncertainty about their ability to realize dreams of flourishing as individuals and communities.

For the people of these states, as for most people on all continents, capitalist globalization rouses ambivalent feelings: it is both full of rich possibilities and brimming with uncertainties and dangers. I've experienced this double-faced character of capitalist globalization both from the perspective of its dominant core states (the United States and Germany) and from the point of view of the smaller and more fragile nations (Croatia). Both of these settings have confirmed my conviction that we should neither simply celebrate capitalist globalization nor simply denounce it.

I was born into a faith—well, not actually born into it. My parents belonged to a religious community made up of what the great Harvard philosopher and psychologist William James called "twice born" people, born once of earthly parents and the second time of the heavenly Spirit. They believed that all human beings required new birth because they've severed themselves from the Source of true life, and they were convinced that a religious community is a voluntary association (what Max Weber called a "sect") that you join after you've been born the second time, not a "family" or a "culture" into which you are slotted just by arriving into this world (what Max Weber called a "church").[10]

Despite his fierce anger against God for letting him, an innocent man and a socialist, suffer in a communist labor camp, my father, at the time a teenager on the brink of death, embraced faith in God—as he tells the story, it was God who embraced him—and ended up a Pentecostal believer. The family into which I was born was a faith island, an austere but beautiful and nurturing social microenvironment. With my first cry as a newborn, I learned that not all forms of religiosity are "religions" in the pejorative sense—mind-shutting and freedom-trampling cultural edifices used as instruments of social control.

The Pentecostal movement started some forty years before my father's conversion, in Los Angeles, 6,318 miles as the crow flies away from the camp where he was forced to carry sacks nearly twice his own weight on his back. Pentecostalism's founder was William Seymour (1870–1922), a black man and the son of former slaves; he was in charge of the multiracial and multiethnic original congregation from which Pentecostalism spread worldwide.[11] Seymour's faith became my father's faith because a Slovenian migrant worker had converted in the United States and, nudged by the Great Depression, sailed over the Atlantic on a return voyage to spread the good news. Today, there are about 279 million Pentecostals on all continents, comprising 12.8 percent of all Christians. Moreover, Pentecostal spirituality has influenced at least as many Christians in other Christian denominations, including Catholics and Episcopalians, bringing the total number of Pentecostal and Charismatic Christians to about 585 million, or 26.7 percent of all Christians.[12] Within a single century, the faith of a downtrodden black man from the New World had engulfed the entire globe, shaped the lives of more than half a billion human beings, and garnered the sympathies of prominent religious leaders like Pope Francis.[13] Closer to home, it literally delivered my father from death and made him into a new man.

Yugoslavia was an overwhelmingly Catholic and Orthodox country with a Muslim minority. In the aftermath of World War II, the communists persecuted all religious communities and, in their own spheres of cultural dominance, the Catholics and the Orthodox persecuted the "sects" like Pentecostals, known regionally under the nickname "yellow faith." (The name was an echo of the much more horrible persecution of the Jews, who were at least since AD 807 often forced to wear clothing marked with yellow.) Notwithstanding their profound differences, communists and the two major religious groups shared a deep conviction that a close tie must exist between religion/ideology and political society.[14] You were politically "in" if you belonged to the religion/ideology that defined the "social sacred"; you were "out" if you didn't.[15] The communists and the leaders of dominant religious groups were in agreement that the "sects" were out; they broke the ties between religion/ideology and political society. For the sects, allegiance to the one God of all people meant that no political or ethnic group could be excluded from belonging to any particular religious community and that the state should neither seek legitimation from nor offer special treatment to any single religious group; religion and politics are distinct cultural systems. Though my father never articulated even the rudiments of a political philosophy, as a Pentecostal he stood implicitly for a vision of the relation between religion, politics, and ethnic identity in stark contrast to the one dominant not just in the former Yugoslavia but in the entire history of humanity. Although he would never have put it this way, his political stance was pluralist rather than exclusivist, akin to the stances formulated by the English Baptists of the early sixteenth century and later, in an attenuated way, by John Locke.[16]

Pentecostals are known for their love of transcendence—for interest in miracles, prophecies, and visions. My parents prayed intensely, even speaking in strange tongues as they did so; they often heard God speaking to them and experienced miracles God performed. Yet they were not "otherworldly," eager to escape this world for a mystical union of blessed souls with God. They prayed (and worked) for health, wealth, fertility, and longevity, the key components of natural flourishing that most people desire. For them, the salvation of the soul was only one half of the gospel; the other half was the health of the body.[17] At their worst, Pentecostals invoke God to open for them the gates to the paradise of conspicuous consumption, a practice my parents disapproved of intensely. At their best, they emulate Jesus, who prayed at night and during the day healed the sick and fed the hungry. My parents aspired to make God the source and goal of their lives and the power through which they acquired, enjoyed, and distributed the goods of ordinary life to those less fortunate than themselves.

Over the years I have inched myself into the Episcopal Church, but important impulses in my parents' faith, some widely shared among Christians, have remained with me. I consider God's relation to human beings and human beings' relation to God to be the condition of possibility for human life and flourishing in all dimensions. I believe that faith and politics are two distinct cultural systems but that an authentic faith is always engaged, at work to relieve personal suffering as well as to push against social injustice, political violence, and environmental degradation.

The Pentecostals among whom I grew up not long after World War II were revolutionaries, but the kind armed with the gospel of peace rather than AK-47s. Members of a minuscule and oppressed group, they were hoping for a new world order, a *radically* new world order: "a new heaven and a new earth" (Revelation 21:1). The Messiah—the same Jesus Christ who died on the cross in first-century Palestine, was raised on the third day and ascended into heaven—will return in glory and the kingdoms of this world will "become the kingdom of our Lord and his Messiah, and he will reign for ever and ever" (Revelation 11:15). They did not sing these words with as much sophistication as choirs in grand cathedrals do when resounding the "Hallelujah Chorus" from Handel's *Messiah*—but they *believed* them. They awaited, literally, "the end of history" as we know it, making their own variety of the centuries-old Jewish, Christian, and Muslim hope, a this-worldly religious hope, that was later first drained of any semblance of materiality and transposed into timeless eternity and then secularized into mundane global utopias, like Marx's communist society or, in a way, Fukuyama's liberal democracy.[18]

But why did they wait for this new world rather than rolling up their sleeves and working to bring it about? There is something not quite right with this question. It assumes that waiting and working are opposed. They aren't, as I will note shortly. You can work while you wait. Still, they waited, hoping for something more than what humans alone could achieve. Why? First, for them the only end of history worth hoping for wasn't a mere reformist or even revolutionary transformation of global political and economic systems. The end of history was full-fledged "salvation," freedom from death, evil, and suffering and freedom for abiding love, beauty, and truth. Second, they waited because a marginal community made up of men who had survived the violence of war or the torments of labor camps and women who had endured rape or mourned fallen sons and husbands had a hard time believing that a political and economic system would ever be designed that wouldn't crush the most vulnerable. All kings and kingpins, democratically elected or not, were suspect, as they were all out to fatten their own bank accounts and wallow in luxury while the poor, subjugated and dispossessed, lived in misery. So marginal people like my parents waited for the "King of kings and the Lord of lords" to come and set the world aright (Revelation 19:16).

Though it seems passive and impotent, "waiting" was the right stance to take, provided you properly understood it. I didn't think so as a teenager, but I think so now, having been a student of one of the great

theologians of the second part of the twentieth century, Jürgen Moltmann. Early in his career, Moltmann, a political theologian rather than
a mystical one, started distinguishing between two kinds of futures, *futurum* and *adventus*. Futurum is the future for which present causes are
a sufficient explanation, the future with which the present is pregnant
and to which it gives birth; adventus is the future coming from outside
of time and space as the fulfillment of God's promise.[19] The end of
history is future as adventus, not as futurum, he argued; you cannot
bring it about by replacing a wrong world system with the right one or
by tinkering with the state of the world as you might with a sputtering
machine to make it purr. The end of history comes when *God* comes.
Christians have always called this the "second coming" of Christ.

The Christian faith makes the immodest claim that globalization—
the present state of interconnectivity and interdependence in the world,
the whole process that led to it, and the capitalist market working in tandem with the "spirit of insatiability" that today mainly drives it—is just
one moment in the grand arc of history that starts with creation and
ends with the new creation. God created the world in the beginning
out of nothing (*ex nihilo*); God will create a new world at the end out of
the old one (*ex vetere*).[20] Both of these creations are God's acts; humans
weren't around for the first, and it is beyond our powers to bring about
the second. Hence we pray: "Come, Lord!" And we wait.

But what does it *mean* to wait? Waiting for something contrasts to
making something happen. Many people today experience religion—
or religion other than their own—as an irrational force seeking to impose itself on the unwilling. The history of religions, including that
of Christianity, gives them justification. But if waiting is essential to authentic Christian faith, then imposition is inappropriate. Not trying
to create on one's own what God's coming will bring about, say, by
"Christianizing" the world, is central to the character of the faith.[21]
This is the passive side of waiting.

Waiting also has an active side. The coming of God consists of two parts: the second coming, when God brings about the end of history, and the first coming, when God enters history. The life of Jesus Christ, the God who has come and who is coming, exemplifies what we do as we wait. We are born, and new possibilities open up for us and for the world;[22] we hear a voice from heaven in the depths of our being, calling us to love God above all things and to love our neighbors as ourselves, and our lives are turned around;[23] we celebrate and enhance what is good in us and around us, we repair what is broken and ameliorate what can be perfected; and occasionally we pull back from what is intractably toxic and evil (in line with the dark prophecy of Dietrich Bonhoeffer, whom the Nazis killed in the Flossenbürg concentration camp: "It will be the task of our generation, not to 'seek great things,' but to save and preserve our souls out of the chaos, and to realize that it is the only thing we can carry as a 'prize' from the burning building").[24]

Waiting for the Christ who will come in glory and echoing in our everyday acts the Christ who came in humility, we are to be neither idle nor coercive but always engaged.[25]

This book is about world religions and globalization. Every time I taught the course on this subject at Yale, one or another student would ask, "But what about nonreligious faiths?" They had in mind varieties of secular humanism, like the communist humanism of Karl Marx or the evolutionary humanism of Julian Huxley, or some smorgasbord variety of humanistic nonreligious faith.[26] Some students, secular in their worldview, felt excluded in a course about *religions* and globalization. Others believed that the thrust of the course was misguided because they saw religions mainly as obstacles to progress, forces for ill, and believed that moral orientation must come from secular visions of human flourishing. So why in this book, as in the course, do I leave aside secular humanist perspectives and engage only world religions? One reason is because religiously inspired zealous violence and irrational foot-dragging are major problems in a highly interconnected and interdependent world. Religions are a global problem requiring sustained attention. But religions aren't just a problem. They are also an indispensable part of the solution. That's the second reason why I concentrate on religions, a more important one than the first.

Arguably, world religions are our most potent sources of moral motivation and deliberation. They are also carriers of visions of the good life, which billions have found compelling throughout history and still find compelling today. Central to these visions is the paramount importance of transcendence, of the invisible realm, of God—but not as a mysterious power outside the world. Relation to that transcendent realm fundamentally shapes how we understand and relate to our world and ourselves.

Consider first the nature of the world. Christians, to stay with the example of my own faith, believe that God is the Creator: "I believe that God has made me and all the creatures," wrote the Protestant reformer Martin Luther (1483–1546) in his *Small Catechism*. To claim that God made "all creatures" isn't to dismiss on the authority of an ancient holy book the findings of modern physical cosmology and evolutionary biology; it is to relate to oneself and to the world in a certain way, as a gift, for instance, rather than merely as a particular form of matter and energy. Imagine an object you very much like, say, a well-designed and skillfully crafted fine leather wallet with a texture you can't resist touching. Think of yourself, first, in a store examining it as you contemplate whether to purchase it and, second, holding it in your hands after receiving it as a gift from a lover to commemorate your first date. It is the same object, and yet it isn't: the love between you and your lover is part of how you experience the object, enhancing your appreciation and enjoyment of it. The first is world as cosmos; the second is world as creation.

Consider now human beings as God's creatures. The most important thing about us isn't that God created us; God created bacteria as well. It is that God created us *for relationship with* God.[27] God isn't an add-on to our already completed being. As I will argue in chapter 2, we are oriented toward God in the very fabric of our being, even before our will comes into play. We call ourselves "religious" if we embrace and articulate orientation toward God and see the world as more than just a sum (however conceptualized) of its components; we call ourselves "secular" if we don't. But the fact of the orientation isn't influenced by what we call ourselves or by anything we do, just as the reality of the world as creation isn't altered depending on whether we experience it as a divine gift or not.

The Christian faith is not alone in making such a claim. Other world religions, unlike varieties of secular humanism, for which nothing but the world can be the case,[28] have their own versions of a claim that there is more to the world than its physicality and that human beings are oriented toward God. The reason is simple. As I will argue in chapter 2, world religions assert that reality is made up of "two worlds," a transcendent one and a mundane one, and they see human beings stretched between these two worlds. For world religions, the key to the good life in the mundane realm is in the transcendent realm. With secular humanism they debate the *existence* of a transcendent realm; among themselves they debate the *nature* of the transcendent realm (for instance, whether it is personal or not) and the character of the relation between the transcendent and the mundane realms (for instance, whether this relation is noncompetitive or close to dualistic). Still, they all agree on the paramount importance of the transcendent realm for human existence, for the character of the experienced world, and for the good life. This conviction lies at the heart of the stances world religions take toward globalization.

For me as a Christian, the course of world history—including the shape, direction, and significance of globalization—is ultimately decided in the contest of desires in people's hearts: for the God "above" this world (and therefore for the world as God's creation) or for the idols of this world (and therefore, ultimately, against the world). Two great commandments shape my stance toward globalization. In response to a lawyer's question about which commandment of the Jewish law was the greatest, Jesus said: "'You shall love the Lord your God with all your heart, and with all your soul, and with all your mind.' This is the greatest and first commandment. And a second is like it: 'You shall love your neighbor as yourself'" (Matthew 22:37–39, citing Deuteronomy 6:5 and Leviticus 19:18). Together, the two commandments, which Christians have learned from the Jews and, arguably, share with Muslims,[29] express both the primacy of the transcendent realm (love for God) and the centrality of the mundane realm (love of neighbor). Approaching globalization normatively, I ask the following questions:

- In what ways might globalization impede or make possible love for God? The concerns here are about (1) *religious freedom* (under the conditions of a given form of globalization, what space do people have to worship God privately and publicly as their conscience directs?) and (2) *idolatry* (to what degree does globalization "flatten" the world and reinforce the human desire for false gods?).
- In what ways does globalization impede or make possible love of neighbor? The concerns here are about (1) *human capacities and virtues* (under the conditions of a given form of globalization, how well is each person able to develop his or her capacities as created in the image of the God of love and employ them so as to better love God and neighbors?) and (2) *conditions of life* (what kinds of social, economic, and ecological effects does a given form of globalization have on the most vulnerable citizens of the globe?).

Put slightly differently, life marked by love for God and neighbors, flourishing human life, is the end; globalization is a means, valuable insofar as it enables us to achieve that end.

With globalization it is a bit as it is with our daily work: we work in order to make flourishing life possible, but things are at their best when we also flourish as we work, when working doesn't undermine flourishing but enacts it. So, globalization is valuable secondarily to the extent that through participating in its processes we enact ends that it ought to serve. Then again, it may also be that the workings of the global system run *counter* to genuinely human ends, in which case our assessment of globalization would have to be adjusted accordingly. Indeed, in the long development of global markets and communication networks, especially during the period of colonization, millions of human lives were damaged or sacrificed. Many ends achieved were and still remain salutary, but the processes themselves were oppressive and deadly. Today, too, while millions benefit from globalization, many suffer under it as well.

Lives flourishing and loved and lives languishing and despised—bread, water, and friendship given to the most vulnerable and these valuables withheld from them—would both have to figure in assessing globalization. I believe that we should assess world historical processes in a way analogous to the way we should assess our own lives. Caught in the frenzy of living, we often forget what truly matters. Facing death, we sometimes get clarity. As there are no pockets in a burial shroud, what matters little to us when we are about to depart is how much we have acquired, whether of material possession, fame, power, or experiences. Instead, what matters is how much we have loved and have been loved in return, how much we have helped others to thrive and lead meaningful lives. As a Christian, who believes that Jesus Christ is the measure of true humanity, the incarnation of love for God and others, my normative assessment of globalization boils down to this: it is good to the extent that it helps me and others participate in the character and mission of Jesus Christ, and it is deficient to the extent that it doesn't. Representatives of other religions would replace the name of Jesus Christ with that of the Buddha, Confucius, Muhammad, or some other sage, saint, or moral ideal. But for all of them, I submit, globalization would be assessed as a means for living out authentic humanity as defined by those sages.

Perhaps a comment on the relation between the character of our lives (echoing in our own way Jesus Christ) and the circumstances in which we live (globalization insofar as it makes possible or hinders our lives having that character) is appropriate here. I believe that it is possible to align desires, commitments, talents, and efforts with God as revealed in Jesus Christ no matter what situation we find ourselves in.[30] In a letter to Christians in the ancient imperial city of Rome, the Apostle Paul wrote: "We know that all things work together for good for those who love God, who are called according to his purpose." "If God is for us," the apostle continues, "who is against us?" Those who are loved by God and who love God are ultimately unassailable by "hardship, . . . distress, . . . persecution, . . . famine, . . . nakedness, . . . peril, . . . or sword" (Romans 8:28, 31, 35). But to be unconquerable by circumstances isn't necessarily to be indifferent to them. Life marked by such negative experiences isn't life as it should be, isn't flourishing life.

Social arrangements can both help life go well for people and plunge them into misery. Such arrangements—for instance, global trade agreements or global environmental regulation—can be embodiments of love for God and for neighbor if they are fair and attentive to the basic needs of the most vulnerable, or they can be embodiments of the self-seeking and indifference of the powerful and therefore incarnations of contempt for God, neighbor, and ourselves. If we love God, who "brings down the powerful from their thrones, and lifts up the lowly," and who "fills the hungry with good things" (Luke 1:52–53), we will lift up the lowly ourselves and fill the hungry with good things. Ultimately unassailable by circumstances, we will then work to change them, to make God's and our love incarnate in them. At the end of history, after the work of the millennia will have been done and the traffic on all the interconnected pathways of a globalized world as we know it will have ceased, the gold of our love for God, neighbor, and ourselves will be purified in the fire of the divine judgment of grace, whereas the chaff of our nonlove, no matter how creative and productive it happened to have been, will burn away (see 1 Corinthians 3:10–15).

These are my commitments and this is my hope, nourished by the Christian faith I embrace and forged in the crucible of the circumstances in which I lived. This is where I stand as I write about faith and globalization.

I have just sketched a set of sturdy Christian convictions informing my perspective. But this book is about the relation between *religions* and globalization, not just Christianity and globalization. Before I state its main purpose and thesis, I need to explain how religions other than my own figure in the proposal.

As is evident from the preceding comments, I have rejected one possible approach. I could have tried to shed the particularities of my own faith and culture and to survey the landscapes of multiple religions and globalization processes impartially, as if I were a mechanical drone with no biases or interests of my own. But the "view from nowhere" is impossible; drones always fly at somebody's behest and for somebody's interest. Creatures of time and place, we all think, speak, and write from our own vantage points, and we do so even when we seek to imaginatively inhabit the worlds of others and learn from them. Yet when thinking about world religions and globalization, we inescapably make claims about things that concern all people, their beliefs and practices, and our common life on the planet. This brings authors of books like mine into a predicament:

the works are particular but must make universal claims. How have I dealt with this conundrum? Simply: from the place where I stand, I have proceeded to make universal claims about a planetary process called globalization and about other religions.

You might think, then, that I have offered here simply a Christian take on religions and globalization, one religion's account of the relationship between the two as well as of the relationship among religions in the context of globalization. Without addressing global realities specifically, I have done something of the sort in *A Public Faith*—a book about the public role of faith written by a Christian, for Christians, and using predominantly Christian sources, and a book in which I forged a Christian vision in conversation with non-Christians, both religious and secular.[31] The present book is different. It contains a dual proposal: how people with Christian convictions should relate to other religions and to globalization *as well as* how adherents of other world religions should relate to one another and globalization. It is about how all of us, Christians and non-Christians, in all our quarrelsome diversity, can live under the common global roof. For such a dual proposal, it would not have sufficed to articulate a vision based on Christian sources and enriched in dialogue with others, a customary procedure of those who, like me, reject the "view from nowhere." In addition, I had to show *how and why adherents of other world religions have reasons rooted in their own deep convictions to embrace or at least take seriously my proposal*. Doing these two things simultaneously is the gist of the third way that I am forging in this book. In effect, I am saying to the adherents of world religions, "What I offer here is a Christian proposal, but I can point to ways in which you as a faithful adherent of a different world religion could be committed to its main elements; if I am correct, this will help us get along and live better in our common world."

This third option involves a risk. Adherents of other religions may feel that I am seriously misunderstanding their convictions, that I am interpreting them in a nineteenth-century fashion, peering with my prim eye through a Christian monocle. I believe the risk is worth taking, considering the alternatives: either each religious community has to suppress its deepest commitments as we shape our common life (secular exclusion of religion) or each religious community strives to impose its vision of our common life on all others (imposition of a single religion to the exclusion of all others along with varieties of secular ways of living in the world). Moreover, we can mitigate the risk. There is no need to repeat today nineteenth-century imperialist readings of other religious traditions. In the twenty-first century we can easily imagine a common table around which all world religions living under a common global roof can engage in public debate or plan their joint projects on equal terms. This book would be the document I would bring to the discussion at the global common table—my construal of the features of my own Christian faith and of corresponding features of other world religions that underpin a vision of how world religions can constructively relate to globalization and to one another in a single interconnected and interdependent world. I hope that adherents of other religions will come up with their own analogous proposals. And then we will debate and readjust these proposals about our mutual relations as well and not just our respective visions of human flourishing and their social, political, and legal implications.

In chapter 2 I have noted six key formal common features of world religions—exemplified in each in distinct ways and to various degrees as well as prioritized differently. My claim is not that all versions of all religions have these features, but that world religions *can be interpreted* to have these features and that their own prominent adherents have interpreted world religions as having them. My suggestion is that these features provide a framework for negotiating relations among religions, including their partly competing and partly overlapping visions of the good life, as well as supply a structure for working out our common engagements with globalization processes. The six features together aren't the universal core of all world religions; I don't think there is such a core. Neither are they key elements of some proposed future single global religion; I don't think such a religion will in fact ever emerge.[32] Each world religion is distinct and will likely remain distinct in the ways it understands these common features, each makes partly overlapping claims to truth, each offers distinct alternative accounts of a life worth living, and each in its own way generates the loyalties and motivates the behavior of its adherents. Nevertheless, these features help make it possible for the religions to set up a political framework for common life, to act in common or, when they cannot, to negotiate their differences in peace.

Standing where I do, what was my goal in writing this book? For sure, I wanted to increase our understanding of the relation between world religions and globalization, as I noted earlier. After all, I am an academic and, quite apart from that vocation, I don't like driving in fog, which is what living feels like if we don't understand. Understanding lifts the fog so we can avoid crashing. I want to do more than just avoid crashing, though. I also want to know where I am headed and which roads, with all their twists and turns and seeming detours, will take me there. Visions of flourishing—those visions we have articulated for ourselves as well as those that remain inchoate but are embedded in our institutions and social practices and sedimented in the deeper regions of our souls—set the direction, so we know where we are headed.

This book is about world religions, globalization, and accounts of human flourishing, or visions of the good life. Economics, politics, cultural habits, and social ethics all come into play, but visions of flourishing are at its center. My main thesis is simple. I can state it in the words that, according to the Hebrew Bible, Moses said to the children of Israel at the end of forty years of wandering in the wilderness and the words that Jesus, weakened after forty days of fasting in the wilderness, hurled at the Tempter in self-defense (Deuteronomy 8:3; Matthew 4:4): "One does not live by bread alone, but by every word that comes from the mouth of the Lord." The greatest of all temptations isn't to serve false gods, as monotheists like to think. The greatest of all temptations, equally hard to resist in abundance and in want, is to believe and act as if human beings lived by bread alone, as if their entire lives should revolve around the creation, improvement, and distribution of worldly goods. Serving false gods—or turning the one true God into a mere bread provider, which amounts to the same thing—is the consequence of succumbing to this grand temptation.

When we live by bread alone, there is never enough bread, not enough even when we make so much of it that some of it rots away; when we live by bread alone, someone always goes hungry; when we live by bread alone, every bite we take leaves a bitter aftertaste, and the more we eat the more bitter the taste; when we live by bread alone, we always want more and better bread, as if the bitterness came from the bread itself and not from our living by bread alone. I could continue with the analogy, but you get my point: living by "mundane realities" and for them alone, we remain restless, and that restlessness in turn contributes to competitiveness, social injustice, and the destruction of the environment as well as constitutes a major obstacle to more just, generous, and caring personal practices and social arrangements.

Trying to live by "bread alone" kills both us and our neighbors.[33] "Alone" is a key word in the biblical passage and in my thesis: bread *alone* (or, perhaps, bread *above all*). For we all live *also* by bread, and without bread all of us are dead. Still, without the divine Word we shrivel even when we are in overdrive, we fight and destroy, we perish. The Word is the bread of life, and it gives abundant life, as it is suggested in the Torah and written in the Gospels (Deuteronomy 8:1–20; John 6:35, 10:10).

Globalization is a complex phenomenon with many dimensions and multiple successive historical forms. As I will argue in chapter 1, both in its discarded communist form and in its presently dominant capitalist form, globalization is principally (not exclusively) about "bread," about a particular kind of enhancement of ordinary life. It proceeds as if the Word were not the source of abundant life and keeps our sights fixed on multiplying the bread. World religions, on the other hand, stand explicitly for the Word or, more precisely, for varieties of competing understandings of the Word. One might expect that the world religions would nudge us to forget daily bread and flee into divine realms of feasting on the pure Word. That does happen, but not often, not today. The great temptation to which world religions frequently succumb is to devolve either into mere instruments of procuring bread or into weapons in worldly struggles, which are largely about bread as well.

Before enumerating my subsidiary theses, perhaps it is important to say a word about how I understand "agency" with regard to globalization and world religions. In my description, globalization and world religions appear as both objects of human agency and as agents exerting influence upon human beings; correspondingly, human beings appear as both shapers of globalization and of religions and as objects of globalization's and religions' influence. In my judgment, the relationship between individuals and social formations is dialectical. As Peter Berger and Thomas Luckmann note in *The Social Construction of Reality:* "The product acts back upon the producer. . . . *Society is a human product. Society is an objective reality. Man is a social product.*"[34] Awareness of the feedback loop among human beings, world religions, and globalization helps us understand what is at stake in the discussion of religions and globalization. On the one hand, globalization and world religions impinge powerfully on human lives, including their character and agency, and do so for good and for ill. On the other hand, individuals and small communities can shape religions and globalization processes, say, by participating in reform and renewal of religions and engaging in global redesign projects on local and global levels.

The kind of complex push and pull I just described that globalization and world religions exert forms the backdrop for the book's key subsidiary theses. I defend them in part 1.

- Though religions often legitimize violence and sometimes impede the progress of science and technology, they are not mere sand in the cogwheels of globalization processes, as some nonreligious people fear.
- Because they articulate visions of flourishing, at whose center is the ultimate attachment to the divine, world religions are not mere lubricants for the cogwheels of globalization, as others believe.
- Globalization will be able to contribute to "improving the state of the world" only if visions of human flourishing and moral frameworks shape it.
- Even though market-driven globalization is mostly about "bread," it need not be a force merely undermining higher spiritual life and pulling people to live by bread alone, as many religious people fear.
- Provided they are managed well, globalization processes can be a means of achieving goals that are consonant with authentic human flourishing, such as uniting humanity and ensuring that the lives of all go well (for instance, by expanding individuals' capacities, improving health, or removing drudgery from lives).
- Globalization can help free world religions from troubling alliances with particular communal identity and politics and nudge them to rediscover their genuine universality.

These theses, including the main one, are controversial. Many world leaders and public intellectuals consider world religions a disease in need of treatment rather than a medicine able to cure anything least of all the maladies of globalization in its current form. Though many things may be wrong with globalization, critics of my thesis might concede, isn't it true that it unites humanity in a network of interdependence while world religions divide people into discrete groups and set them at odds? In part 2 I argue that world religions, though often agents of division and strife, have internal resources to foster political pluralism, cultures of respect, and reconciliation.

- Sturdy religious commitments to transcendent goals need not breed intolerance but can and do underwrite tolerance and even respect for people of other faiths or of no faith at all.
- Religious exclusivists—those who believe that their religion alone is true—need not advocate authoritarian or totalitarian forms of government but can be, and historically have been in some cases, active political pluralists.
- World religions are not "by nature" violent; being tightly associated with political power and functioning as markers of identity, the main reason why they become violent, is "unnatural" for world religions. World religions have been and can continue to be agents of reconciliation and promoters of just peace.

I believe that the convictions expressed in the theses above are all true of the Christian faith and its relation to globalization; more precisely, I believe that the Christian faith can be and has been plausibly and authentically interpreted in such a way that all this can be said to be true of it. I believe that my theses hold true for other world religions to the best extent that I, an outsider, am able to interpret them. Do I therefore think that world religions are all equally true? How could they be, when their claims often differ? Do I think that they all lead people equally well to reach the ultimate human destiny? How could they, when their conceptions of the ultimate destiny differ markedly?

Each world religion is not simply one thing but comes in many, many forms. What I say above is not true of *all* the varied embodiments of the Christian faith in the world today; it's not even true of most of them. As it travels in time and space, the Christian faith needs regular realignments with its own deeper truth; such realignments are termed reformations. Christians, too, and not just their convictions, will need to keep realigning themselves to the authentic versions of their faith; these realignments are termed renewals. I exhort us as Christians to reform and renew our faith so as to lead lives worthy of the calling to which we have been called (Ephesians 4:1). If we don't, the Christian faith may well turn out to be a curse to the world rather than a source of blessing—an embodiment of the fall into the temptation to live by bread alone rather than a means of resisting it, a faith insufferably self-righteous and arrogantly imposing itself on others to control and subdue them, a source of strife over worldly goods rather than a wellspring of confident humility, creative generosity, and just peace.

It is my hope that all world religions, each in its own way, can and will keep returning to their best selves through reformation and renewal. As they do, they will argue about many things, but above all about visions of human flourishing, of the good life—about which "Word" articulates transcendence appropriately, about the kind of "bread" we need, and about the relation between "bread" and "Word." But if they commit themselves to reformation and renewal, their arguments, no less than their positive convictions and practices, might turn out to be a blessing to the world. Attuned and responsive to one another and to globalization processes as each articulates the truth about human flourishing as it sees it, world religions might then become shapers of globalization for humanity's good. Heaven knows, globalization in its current state needs it.

Part One

I

Globalization and the
Challenge of Religions

Globalization Then

On February 22, 1848, Paris city officials canceled a fund-raising banquet in support of universal suffrage and thereby ignited the first revolution with a global reach. Two days later, the French king Louis-Philippe fled the city. The flames of the revolution spread quickly and widely, driven by the winds of rising food prices, depressed economic conditions, and radicalized political attitudes. Most of Europe was soon affected by what came to be known as "the Springtime of the Peoples." The revolution even made a transatlantic voyage and reached as far as Brazil and Colombia.

A day before the revolution broke out, two German philosophers-cum-activists, both under thirty, published in London a short text in which they described globalization better than anyone before them and, for at least a century, better than anyone after. The word itself never shows up in the text. It couldn't have. According to *The Oxford English Dictionary, globalization* was first used in 1930 and gained wide currency only after the end of the Cold War in 1989, after the demise of the Soviet Union and other states inspired by the communist vision.[1] Though the word didn't exist in 1848, globalization itself was progressing rapidly. The two young men had keen eyes to see and deft pens to articulate the radical changes occurring on a planetary scale. Their names were Karl Marx and Friedrich Engels. The title of their essay, composed mainly by Marx, was *The Communist Manifesto,* a booklet destined to become a kind of secular "sacred text" to millions.

Consider the following six key passages from the *Manifesto*'s treatment of globalization. As you read, focus on the content of the description of planetary transformations and disregard for a moment that the description is a step in an argument for an alternative globalization, the communist globalization, a single, technologically highly advanced world system of global prosperity and freedom in which individual and communal interests have become identical. The key elements of the global order identified in the *Manifesto* in the nineteenth century remain the central features of globalization in the twenty-first century.

- "Constant revolutionizing of production, uninterrupted disturbance of all social conditions, everlasting uncertainty and agitation distinguish the bourgeois epoch from all earlier ones. All fixed, fast-frozen relations, with their train of ancient and venerable prejudices and opinions, are swept away, all new-formed ones become antiquated before they can ossify. All that is solid melts into air, all that is holy is profaned."[2]
- "Modern industry has established the world-market, for which the discovery of America paved the way. This market has given an immense development to commerce, to navigation, to communication by land. . . . The need of a constantly expanding market for its products chases the bourgeoisie over the whole surface of the globe. It must nestle everywhere, settle everywhere, establish connections everywhere."[3]
- "The bourgeoisie has through its exploitation of the world-market given a cosmopolitan character to production and

consumption in every country. . . . All old-established national industries . . . are dislodged by . . . industries that no
longer work up indigenous raw material, but raw material
drawn from the remotest zones; industries whose products
are consumed, not only at home, but in every quarter of the
globe. In place of the old wants, satisfied by the productions
of the country, we find new wants, requiring for their satisfaction the products of distant lands and climes."[4]

• "And as in material, so also in intellectual production. The
intellectual creations of individual nations become common
property. National one-sidedness and narrow-mindedness
become more and more impossible, and from the numerous
national and local literatures, there arises world literature."[5]

• "In place of the old local and national seclusion and self-
sufficiency, we have intercourse in every direction, universal
interdependence of nations."[6]

• "Independent but loosely connected provinces, with separate
interests, laws, governments, and systems of taxation, became lumped together into one nation, with one government,
one code of laws, one national class-interest, one frontier,
and one customs-tariff."[7]

The above quotes about world markets, global communication,
planetary interdependence, technological advances, world literature—
aspects of life all characterized by a head-spinning pace and depth of
change—come from the section of the *Manifesto* titled "Bourgeois
and Proletarians." For Marx, globalization isn't just about stunning
technological, economic, political, and cultural transformations. It is
also about the clash between these two social groups separated by
great disparities in wealth and power. Perhaps even more fundamentally, it is about transmuting all values so as to place them in service of
monetary worth, about the commodification of reality and the loss of

humanity. In all this—in what it tears down and what it builds, in the pain it inflicts and the ease it makes possible, in its expansion of horizons and the contradictions it creates—globalization is, for Marx, one massive preparation for the dawn of the new age of global communism.

Very few people today believe that in the bowels of the present capitalist globalization a new communist one is gestating, ready to be born when the present system, riddled with unsolvable contradictions, implodes. Marx's hope has proven false; he was a bad prophet. But we don't need to share his grand expectations and value judgments to agree that he was a great observer. A century and a half older than when Marx first wrote about it and now armed with accelerating improvements in technology, globalization today looks remarkably similar to the way he described it.

Globalization Now

In 2014 when this text was composed, the iPhone was one of the most recognizable gadgets on the planet. A global marketing and distribution network helped generate intense longing for the sleek device; some 500 million ended up in the hands of eager customers. But even more than its distribution, the iPhone's creation and use clearly display contemporary globalization at work. It was designed in the United States under the hawkish eye of a genius out to revolutionize the world, and it is assembled at a furious pace in China in a factory of a Taiwanese firm (with a whole world watching over its labor practices); an international workforce of some seven hundred thousand in Germany, South Korea, Taiwan, the United Kingdom, and the United States produces the parts of the device, the raw materials for which come from at least as many countries. It may take a village to raise a child; it takes the world, connected in a complex global network of specialized industries, to create a single iPhone.

The creation and distribution of the device have lifted many out of poverty and wildly enriched a few. But the path from the design of the iPhone to its use leads through the valley of oppression, exploitation, and destruction, a consequence of the hunt for the best result at the lowest price on the part of both many iPhone producers operating in a competitive environment and millions of its buyers. In the Democratic Republic of Congo, young and unprotected children extract coltan, an essential component of electronic devices, under harrowing conditions imposed on them by warlords, who export it at huge profits to finance a seemingly ceaseless string of civil wars.[8] The manufacturer of iPhones, Foxconn, seems to be the largest sweatshop of ill repute in China; critics charge it with widespread worker abuse and illegal overtime.[9] A masterpiece of design and function, each of 100 million iPhones stepped onto the world scene from a trail marked by blood and tears—at least until 2012 when, under the pressure of global public opinion, Apple started working with the Fair Labor Association to mend its ways.[10]

The first iPhone was introduced in 2007. Within five years it had become ubiquitous. There is an average turnover rate of less than a year as a new and improved version makes potential customers believe that the old one is obsolete. For a while now, Apple's main competitor, Samsung, has been working furiously to supplant all Apple products.[11] If and when the iPhone falls prey to the competition, people throughout the production and distribution networks will feel the consequences. So will Apple shareholders, also a global group. That's global economic interdependence at work, intertwining the fortunes and misfortunes of peoples in the entire world.

In early versions, an image of the globe taken from outer space was the default setting for the iPhone's lock screen—the world's physical oneness symbolizing the social unity across time, space, cultures, nations, and religions that the gadget itself was designed to mediate. From just about anywhere, you can connect with people everywhere. Sitting on your deck on a Croatian island (as I often do in summers), it will take you a minute to start reading a book published in Australia, watching a movie made in Mumbai or Nairobi, or listening to music performed in Rio; from your home in a suburb of Cairo you can organize and direct a revolution to topple a dictator, and from Tahrir Square you can send footage of police and military brutality to the world; riding on a train from St. Petersburg to Moscow, you can buy and sell stocks in London, New York, Shanghai, or Dubai; from wherever you are, you can talk with your friends and collaborators in whatever city of the world they happen to be at the time.

But your connectivity doesn't just pay dividends; it also exacts personal, social, and cultural costs. As you use the iPhone you will have partly pulled yourself out of the immediate physical and social space you occupy—from the dinner party, from the circle of friends, from the classroom, from your workplace—to connect to another person similarly disembedded, at least for the moment. If you are on Facebook or Twitter, for instance, the nature of your friendships and interactions—indeed, as shortening attention spans testify, your own personal habits and even character—will subtly change. So will your religion, if you are a person of faith. Instead of opening a holy book, you might read feeds from the Dalai Lama, Pope Francis, Joyce Meyer, or some other figure who, you have decided, speaks to your needs and sensitivities and whose authority resides less in the position he or she occupies than in the "charismatic" appeal and the useful-ness of the "product" each offers. For many, the iPhone (or a similar mobile device, of which there are around 1.4 billion in the world) is so much part of daily life that they don't feel fully dressed if they don't have it "on them"; for some—even more, perhaps, for ordinary teenagers than for cosmopolitan globe-trotters—life as they know it would grind to a halt if the iPhone were taken away from them.

As the "romance" between iPhones and humans illustrates, we may think of globalization as a planetary process leading to a world with these characteristics:

- a high level of interconnectivity, in which information, goods, and services flow increasingly freely;
- an interdependence that is planetary in scope, with few, quickly vanishing independent localities;
- a contraction of social space, such that the whole planet is becoming "a new locality" and individuals in it "disembedded cosmopolitans";[12]
- a speeding up of time, with technological and cultural innovations coming at us at an accelerating pace and pushing centuries-long traditions out of existence;[13]
- a widespread consciousness of the world as a single whole; we are keenly aware of our unity but take the plurality of cultures, religions, ethnic groups, races, and the like as a given.[14]

There is more to globalization than these seemingly innocuous five bullet points about interconnectivity and interdependence, the speeding up of time and shrinking of space, and our sense of unity. Under the conditions they describe, globalization is marked by deep tensions.

- Hierarchies and divisions are rendered less and less relevant ("flat world"), and global interconnectedness is structured in ways that give "some people a head start" and leave others "scrambling just to get to the starting line."[15]
- Unprecedented economic growth is shadowed by a growing disparity in wealth, with opulent and powerful elites living alongside an underclass made up of millions upon millions of hopelessly poor, overworked, and disenfranchised people.[16]
- The spread of the rule of law, stability, and peace clashes with the strengthening of global criminal networks and local outbursts of violence.[17]
- Cherished ways of living are lost in the wake of cultural

homogenization—the demise of a village or trade, or the disappearance of a language and a whole culture with it—as well as renaissances of local cultural forms.[18]

- The robust reappropriation of tradition is accompanied by the inability to pass it on in a fast-paced and increasingly individualistic world.[19]
- Simultaneous environmental degradation and environmental improvement occurs.[20]
- Individuals are absorbed in their own personal pleasures and pains as well as involved with the suffering of people half a world away.[21]
- Social networks foster ease of communication as they facilitate loss of privacy; businesses and states alike engage in massive information gathering about individuals.[22]
- Life-saving and life-enhancing technological innovations arise along with possible trajectories toward human technological self-destruction.[23]

I will return to these and other ambiguities of globalization later in the chapter. But first I need to note two critical junctures in the long process that led to the current form of globalization, one tied to religions and a revolution in cultural reproduction and the other connected with economics and a revolution in material production. Much of the dynamism of globalization as well as many of its ambiguities emerge out of the intersection of these two revolutions.

World Religions, Global Visions

In *Bound Together*, Nayan Chanda argues that globalization started around the year 6000 BC. Thousands of years earlier, humanity had spread from its original home in Africa in search of food. Then, after "the rise of agriculture and emergence of settled communities of farmers that supported specialist craftworkers, priests, and chiefs," the process of global reconnection started. Four human drives were at work: "the urge to profit by trading, the drive to spread religious belief, the desire to explore new lands, and the ambition to dominate others by armed might."[24] Acting on these desires, traders, preachers, adventurers, and warriors engaged in the millennia-long process of reconnecting people from all around the globe, intermingling and intertwining them with one another in networks of economic, political, and cultural interdependence, and creating a globalized world.

Not all scholars agree with Chanda that globalization is so old, predating the ancient empires and world religions. Some date the origin of globalization to the late nineteenth century, when the European powers completed the division of the earth among themselves and established a truly global market.[25] Others, like Marx and Engels in *The Communist Manifesto,* place its beginning with Spanish and Portuguese exploration of the Americas in the fifteenth century, coterminous with the onset of colonialism. But I don't need to enter the dispute about the beginning of globalization. More important for my purposes is to understand two key junctures in its history (or two main forks in the road toward a globalized world, if you take globalization to be a more recent phenomenon).

The first juncture is tied to the origins of today's world religions. Chanda notes the importance of the drive to spread faith for globalization.[26] After his enlightenment, the Buddha sent out sixty-one of his monks with the following injunction: "Go ye now, O Bhikkhus, and wander, for the gain of the many, for the welfare of the many, out of compassion for the world, for the good, for the gain, and for the welfare of gods and men. Let not two of you go the same way. Preach, O Bhikkhus, the doctrine which is glorious in the beginning, glorious in the middle, glorious at the end, in the spirit and in the letter."[27] Similarly, after his death and resurrection, Jesus Christ issued the "great commission" to the apostles: "Go therefore and make disciples of all nations, baptizing them in the name of the Father and of the Son and of the Holy Spirit, and teaching them to obey everything that I have commanded you" (Matthew 28:19–20).

Before the bhikkhus and the apostles could fan out into the world, however, they had to have a message to impart. Articulations of a message intended for the entire world was an indispensable critical juncture in the development of globalization. The founders of world religions—including but not limited to Buddhism and Christianity—were the main sources of such global messages (though other sources include philosophers, notably Socrates). They were the world's first universal "ideologies," the first accounts of the self, social relations, and the good meant for all human beings.

A universal religion is meant for everyone and should be proclaimed to everyone; hence the Buddha's injunction to the bhikkhus to go on their mission out of compassion for *the world* and Christ's great commission to the apostles to make disciples of *all nations*. Missionaries of world religions cross political and ethnic boundaries to call people everywhere to embrace the faith and to form transpolitical and transethnic religious ties. World religions establish networks that connect people on the basis of shared visions of the good life across the globe.

But world religions do something even more momentous for the history of globalization than inspire global mission and establish transcultural networks: all of them in their own way teach the fundamental unity of all humanity. Each person is to understand himself or herself primarily as a human being rather than as a member of this or that tribe, ethnic group, or kingdom; there is one right path, one truth and, for some religions, one God to be embraced by everyone; outsiders should be treated the same as insiders (because, in the final analysis and notwithstanding claims found in the holy books of some world religions, there are no moral outsiders for world religions, as the same moral code applies to all).[28] Universal symbolic systems addressed to individual persons, the world religions were the primary source of humanity's awareness of itself as one.[29] Without an awareness of the unity of humanity, we would have connections, economic interdependencies, and multiethnic imperial states, but no genuine globality. Globalization was first a reality in the religious imagination before it became an economic and political project. In sum, world religions are the original globalizers[30]—culture-shaping forces with distinctive accounts of what they deem to be universal human values—and are major roots of contemporary globalization.[31] That's the first key juncture in the history of globalization. The second one is the creation of world markets; it both builds on the first and pushes against it.

World Markets

Human beings spread throughout the world primarily in search of food. When they started reconnecting, the search for "food"—desire for the necessities and conveniences of life—and the promise of gain played key roles, supporting and supported by exploration, conquest, and the spread of faith. Two millennia later, after the creation of world markets following the exploration of the Americas in the fifteenth century, the importance of traders increased and, without ever supplanting preachers, adventurers, and warriors, they became the main drivers of globalization.

That the market drives globalization today is a conviction common to communist and capitalist traditions alike. We can trace it back to the progenitors of the two traditions, Adam Smith and Karl Marx. Both considered the market the most revolutionary force on the planet, the unique engine of connecting and intertwining people across the globe, creating unprecedented wealth and radically transforming human lives. Granted, they overrated the impact of the market on politics, law, and culture. They underrated the importance of the modern state for the emergence of the modern market.[32] They also underestimated the extent to which both the state and the market had a set of specific religious convictions as their condition.[33] Still, Smith and Marx were right about the singular importance of the market in shaping all dimensions of the modern world. Ever since the discovery of America, the intensified processes of globalization have been market driven.

A revolutionary force, the market was for both Smith and Marx a moral phenomenon rather than a morally neutral tool of exchange— for Marx a predominantly negative one, distorting even human beings into commodities and throwing most of them into abject poverty; for Smith a positive one, channeling the self-interested behaviors of individuals away from socially destructive ends and toward socially beneficial ones, such as cooperation and wealth creation.[34] Again, they were right. The market's operation, its limits, and its effects all both presuppose and promote a moral vision, an account of who human beings are and how they should live.[35] Let me elaborate on the moral character of the market, for along with the profound influence of the market on political and legal institutions and cultural production, its impact on the self-understanding of human beings and their vision of flourishing is central to the main thesis of this book.

First, the market's *operation* presupposes and produces a view of human nature: it puts a premium on people's free choice, equality, individual responsibility, and personal merit; it organizes human interaction through the calculus of costs and benefits; it treats human beings as acquisitive, insatiable in their thirst for both profit and consumer goods.[36] None of these are value-neutral "natural facts" about human beings; all of them are value-laden and culturally formed features of human beings, contestable and contested.[37]

Second, the *limits* of the market are shaped by beliefs about the fundamental character of human life and its moral values.[38] Think of the *scope* of the market. There are things money can and ought to be able to buy (Internet access, a meal, a trip to Qufu, the city of Confucius's birth), and there are things that money should not be able to buy (a human being, a vote, access to Confucius's teaching). Or consider the *import* of the market. How much time and energy should a human being or a society devote to market activities? These, too, are moral questions. The logic of the market is invasive; it seeks to colonize all times and all spaces of life, to turn all things into commodities, consumer goods to be bought and sold. The very expansiveness of the market is a moral rather than a merely "natural" or "technical" fact: it reinforces the view of human beings as basically traders. But there are important alternatives to that view. Religious people as well as secular humanists argue that something fundamental about human beings and how they ought to live gets lost when the market oversteps its limits.

Finally, the *effects* of the market require normative assessment. For instance, left on its own the market tends to create great disparities in wealth: the weak (physically, psychologically, intellectually) lose, and the strong win.[39] Is this simply the consequence of playing the "natural" game of life, or must the game be "humanized" to prevent such a result? In either case, the decision is a moral one. Similarly, given the high rate of the obsolescence of commodities, the market demands great flexibility and adaptability, generating insecurity and major dislocations of people. Is this effect acceptable or not? Again, the question is moral in character.

As I will argue in chapter 2, whatever else world religions may be, they are fundamentally accounts of human flourishing, of the self, social relations, and the good. They have therefore a stake in the kind of moral vision incarnate in the most revolutionary force on the planet: the market, the most dominant among the multiple drivers of globalization since the age of exploration. This is the main issue over which world religions and globalization will either clash or find a workable modus vivendi.

In the remainder of this text, "globalization" refers to the "primarily market-driven and market-values-embodying-and-promoting" form of planetary interconnectivity and interdependence and a growing sense of humanity's unity. As I see it, this is only one form of globalization, a form that has become dominant in today's world. The communist vision of Karl Marx and its dubious incarnations in Lenin's Soviet Union and Mao's China was another, now defeated. Some adherents of world religions promote their own visions of globalization (like Tariq Ramadan or Christian religious leaders gathered around the "Alternative Globalization" project).[40] But as things stand now, the world market is the primary driver and shaper of globalization. Of course, market-driven globalization takes different shapes in diverse locations. Depending on cultural habits, political institutions, and specifics of local economic systems, market-driven globalization will acquire distinct local flavor, looking different in Beijing, New Delhi, Kuala Lumpur, Bangkok, Moscow, São Paulo, and, for that matter, in Berlin, New York, and London. A single market-driven globalization is played out in multiple registers that are often partly religiously inflected—Confucian, Hindu, Islamic, Buddhist, Orthodox Christian, Latin Christian, Protestant Christian, and so on.[41]

Religions, Markets, and the Affirmation of Ordinary Life

The centrality of the market, whether in Smith's and Marx's theories or in the globalized world of today, is tied to the "affirmation of ordinary life," a stance Charles Taylor identified as one of "the most powerful ideas in modern civilization."[42] A life of work and family, a life of health, wealth, and longevity, a life of ease and absence of pain—that's what human striving should primarily be about, modernity urges upon us, not a higher life of religious contemplation, philosophical reflection, or public deliberation. Ordinary life isn't mere infrastructure for a higher life. It's the other way around. In Adam Smith's words, "All arts, sciences, law and government, wisdom and even virtue itself" should serve ordinary life.[43]

One might think that the world religions had nothing to do with the affirmation of ordinary life, that it was all the market's doing. After all, the central feature of world religions is a cosmological chasm between the "transcendent" and "mundane" spheres, along with the conviction that pursuits associated with the transcendental realm matter incomparably more than those associated with the mundane (see chapter 2). For instance, the Gospel of Luke tells the story of two sisters, Martha and Mary, who through much of Christian history have been symbols of the two basic orientations in life and their relation to one another. Martha, a provider, is concerned with the things of ordinary life, and Mary, a meditator, prefers to put those things aside and listen to and reflect on Jesus's teaching. In his mild rebuke of Martha, Jesus declares that "there is need of only one thing" and that Mary had recognized it and chosen rightly (Luke 10:38–42). The ordinary life seems to matter little for world religions, and we might expect them to vigorously oppose a market-driven globalization at whose heart is a robust affirmation of ordinary life.

Yet this is not the case. The world religions are not predominantly dualistic, setting the transcendent realm in opposition to the mundane as if the two were always competing with one another. World religions have a complex relation to ordinary life, affirming it and doing so somewhat counterintuitively by subordinating it to the higher life. This is the key to their stances toward globalization. To explain, let me compare, in a sketch, the accounts of the good life in local religions, in world religions, and in market-driven globalization. (I will discuss the distinction between local and world religions in greater detail in chapter 2.)

- Local religions understand reality as cosmotheistic unity; they are primarily concerned with ordinary human flourishing, with prosperity, health, long life, and fertility.
- World religions distinguish between the transcendent and mundane realms and give primacy to the former; they are concerned with the good that goes beyond ordinary flourishing and contend that attachment to the transcendent realm is in fact the key to ordinary flourishing.
- Implicit in market-driven globalization is a notion of human flourishing in which relation to the transcendent realm plays no role; its concern is exclusively with the goods of ordinary life.

A structural ambivalence is built into the relation between world religions and globalization. On the one hand, because the world religions *are* concerned with the availability and distribution of the goods of ordinary life, they can affirm, under certain conditions, globalization. In fact, Judaism and Christianity (the latter especially in the form that the great Protestant reformers Martin Luther and John Calvin gave it at the beginning of the sixteenth century)[44] are among the major roots of both the modern affirmation of ordinary life and the current phase of globalization. On the other hand, the main bone of contention between world religions and globalization in its present form concerns the affirmation of ordinary life, specifically, the precise place that goods of ordinary life play in accounts of the good life. That's because globalization keeps people's desires, energies, and creativity focused on the flat plane of ordinary life, whereas the world religions, for which the transcendent realm is superordinate to the mundane, insist that we can properly attend to and truly enjoy ordinary life only when our primary attachment is to the transcendent realm.

World religions press globalization in its current form on two main issues. The first directly concerns ordinary life. Does globalization contribute to life going well for all people, or does it favor some, allowing them to amass power and wealth while great multitudes bear the burdens of abject poverty and environmental degradation? The second relates to the transcendent realm. Does globalization contribute to the genuine flourishing of people, or does it seduce them with false promise of happiness while trapping them in an endless cycle of work-and-spend and sapping their lives of deeper meaning and more complex enjoyments? The answers to these questions are the key to religions' responses to globalization. Perhaps surprisingly, today the main line of religions' engagement with globalization concerns the first issue. This will be evident from my discussion below of the stances of two prominent religious leaders toward globalization. They keep the issue of transcendence in the background, from where it governs their thinking. As I have indicated in the introduction, toward the end of the chapter I will foreground the issue of transcendence—the importance of the "Word" for the multilayered enjoyment and just distribution of the "bread" of ordinary life.

In engaging globalization on these two issues, adherents of world religions can be both globalization's sharpest critics and, in lesser numbers, its ardent supporters. Globalization is a sinful instrument of war against God and humanity, cry out some of them (who either engage globalization aggressively or withdraw from it into alternative communities).[45] Globalization is a grace-filled incarnation of faith's moral vision, a path to the Promised Land, respond others (who devote their energies to defending and fine-tuning it).[46] But most sense that globalization is too complex a phenomenon for religions to simply either reject or celebrate. As I see it, from religious and moral standpoints, there is no single proper way of relating to globalization *as a whole,* nor even to its dominant thrust; there are only many ways of accepting or transforming, enhancing or curbing and, yes, rejecting or celebrating various *aspects* of globalization.[47] We ought neither to demonize nor sacralize the present form of globalization but assess it using a given religion's account of the good life as a measure and advocate for its transformation so that it can contribute to authentic human flourishing and the global common good. That's what I hope to do in this book, and that's what two immensely popular and globally influential religious figures do, the late Pope John Paul II, Karol Wojtyla, and the present Dalai Lama, Tenzin Gyatso, to whom I now turn.

Globalization, Human Flourishing, and Global Common Good

Simple but profound convictions about the human self, social relations, and the good underpin John Paul II's stance toward globalization:

- The self: Every human being has inalienable dignity, "the source of all human rights and every [legitimate] social order," and by virtue of sharing the same human nature, is a member of "one great family."[48]
- Social relations: Justice, which is "rooted in love" and "finds its most significant expression in mercy," should rule all our relations: we must therefore seek the global common good and show special "love for the poor, the weak, the suffering."[49]
- The good: God, the creator, is love, and human beings find fulfillment when they share in Christ's universal mission of love.[50]

All three of John Paul's foundational convictions are about *living* life well, not directly about life *going* well or about life feeling good (see chapter 2 for a discussion of these three categories). Of course, the pope isn't indifferent to whether the lives of billions are marked by joy. Still, he believes that, irrespective of how well off people are, their lives and the lives of their neighbors cannot truly go well and

46

feel good unless they live them well. Convictions about living life well (doing justice and caring for the weak) both trump and underpin considerations about life going well (economic progress and freedom).

With markets at its center, globalization contributes to life going well for billions, John Paul II believes, for a market economy responds better than other systems "to people's economic needs while respecting their free initiative."[51] But the pope doesn't see only the virtues of the market; he has a keen eye to its vices as well. The market is an "intrusive, even invasive" force. It squeezes generosity and mercy out of social relations, replacing them with a calculation of costs and benefits. Equally troubling, the market generates "new forms of exclusion and marginalization,"[52] powerlessness and poverty above all. We need to rescue globalization from these destructive propensities and place it at the service of humanity.

To reform globalization, John Paul II offers simple but radical guidelines. They don't aim at making the global order more *efficient,* a well-oiled and smoothly purring planetary machine for creating and delivering goods and services. They aim at making globalization more *humane,* ensuring that it works for the well-being of all the earth's inhabitants.

- Treat a human being "as an end and not a [mere] means, a subject and not an object, nor a commodity of trade."
- Respect the diversity of cultures, especially religious beliefs and practices, which are "the clearest manifestations of human freedom."
- Create conditions for all "to live out, in the actual circumstances of their economic and political lives, the creativity which is a distinguishing mark of the human person and the true source of the wealth of nations."
- Seek "globalization without marginalization."[53]

A Buddhist stance toward globalization can be surprisingly close to John Paul's Christian one. The Dalai Lama starts his lecture "The Global Community and the Need for Universal Solidarity" with a brief description of globalization: the world has grown smaller; the world's people, constituting almost a single community, are knit together by a global economy and worldwide communications, and are both united and divided by great political and military alliances.[54] Is globalization a source of deep worry or an occasion for hope? The Dalai Lama's bare-bones answer is: it's neither because it's both.

As a result of globalization, some things have changed for the better. Especially since the end of the Cold War, violence has declined and nations are more willing to cooperate; most people and governments affirm the need for a new ecological order; science has helped us better understand our world and technology has improved our lives; as evinced by nonviolent populist movements, people are increasingly unwilling to live under tyranny; and growing mutual interdependence is "a source of hope" because it makes manifest that "considering the interests of others is clearly the best form of self-interest." Other globalization-related developments are causes for concern: appalling and growing economic inequality, especially between developed and developing nations, "remains the greatest source of suffering on this planet"; science and technology, champing at the bit to cast off ethical restraints, threaten to inflict "terrible harm on the delicate matrix of life"; religion, founded "first and foremost on the precept that we must reduce our selfishness and serve others," still sometimes "causes more quarrels than it solves."

The Dalai Lama's suggestions for improving globalization rest on the following account of the self, social relations, and the good:

- The self: Every human being desires happiness and seeks to avoid suffering, and all human beings are "part of one great human family."

- Social relations: Every human being "has an equal right to pursue" happiness and be free of suffering, and "each individual's genuine practice of love and compassion" is the most secure foundation of the world order.
- The good: Love and compassion are the "ultimate source[s] of human happiness, and our need for them lies at the very core of our being."

In the globalized world of today, an "undue emphasis on material development alone" is suffocating love and compassion. Bereft of altruism, we aren't merely incapable of rescuing globalization from its own dangerous shadows; more troublingly, we are betraying our very humanity. "Once we have lost the essential humanity, what is the point in pursuing only material improvement?" asks the Dalai Lama rhetorically. In such a scenario, we are "like animals who are content just to satisfy their physical needs." Global redesign efforts shouldn't be mainly about tinkering with globalization's mechanisms so as to increase its output in global health, wealth, longevity, and aggregate creativity; they should be primarily concerned with curbing restless and competitive acquisitiveness and generating compassionate generosity in each person's heart.

For the Dalai Lama and John Paul II, market-driven globalization shouldn't be embraced as an unequivocal blessing and, consequently, buttressed with religious values. Neither should it be rejected as a curse and replaced by another globalization. Globalization needs to be shaped so it can help make the lives of all human beings go well, provide them with what is needed to lead healthy, creative, and long lives. More important, globalization needs to be tamed so it will be less likely to rob us of our humanity by making our moral lives subservient to our material wants, whether these are very basic (like three simple meals a day) or highly exclusive (like a space tourism excursion). For both John Paul II and the Dalai Lama, religions can contribute to these crucial transformations of globalization by nurturing altruism and fostering global solidarity. Would the two agree on exactly what altruism and solidarity mean? They would not. Would a partial disagreement deter them from taking a common stance? I don't see why. The issue is too important for religions not to collaborate on it.

At the edges of their public speeches John Paul II and the Dalai Lama gesture to the source of both global solidarity and altruism: connection to the mystery that transcends our ordinary existence—to God as revealed in Jesus Christ, in the case of John Paul II, or to the "realm" of the extinction of desire beyond the cycle of rebirth, in the case of the Dalai Lama. According to all world religions, the connection to genuine transcendence is the lifeblood of authentic humanity, of human solidarity across cultural and national boundaries, and therefore of the search for the global common good. In contrast, market-driven globalization pulls human concern exclusively to ordinary life. This tension is the most significant issue in the relation between religions and globalization.

Transcendence, Insatiability, and Mortality

As I will argue in chapter 2, globalization is not a predominantly secularizing force. It neither assumes nor effects explicit contestation of the realm beyond ordinary life. Today, under the conditions of globalization, religions are undergoing resurgence in both their private and public dimensions. But the cultural effects of market-driven globalization are such that the phenomenon does tend to stand on its head the legacy of the world religions concerning the primacy of the higher life over ordinary life. Both by its success in offering new and enhanced ways of experiencing ordinary life for some and by its failure to do so for many, globalization reinforces in the imaginations of people, poor and rich alike, the assumption under which it operates: that nothing is more important in life than healthy and energetic, young and beautiful bodies at whose disposal are abundant varieties of food, clothing, gadgets, and games.

The main challenge of religions to globalization is to call that unstated but foundational assumption into question, to issue an effective reminder that, as Jesus said, "life is more than food" (Luke 12:23)—and that only when that is so does the food itself acquire deeper meaning and thus can be more richly enjoyed.

In monotheist religions, for instance, life comes from God, gets meaning from God, and reaches fulfillment through God and in God. On its own, ordinary life is too fleeting, insignificant, and "unbearably light."[55] Market-driven globalization is one massive, complex, and highly intelligent global machine, huffing and puffing 24/7 to enhance ordinary life—or at least so its supporters claim. But globalization can be only as significant as the ordinary life it serves.

Qoheleth, a writer of the ancient Jewish book of wisdom (commonly known by Christians as Ecclesiastes) noted two human predicaments that envelop the ordinary lives of human beings in the mists of melancholy. The first is *insatiability*. "All streams run to the sea, but the sea is not full; to the place where the streams flow, there they continue to flow. . . . The eye is not satisfied with seeing, or the ear filled with hearing" (1:7–8). Like Plato around the same period and Immanuel Kant many centuries later, Qoheleth believed it isn't in human nature "to halt anywhere in possession and enjoyment and to be satisfied."[56] We are finite, but our desires are infinite. Our insatiability gives the ever-flowing river of our work and play not just an insuppressible dynamism but also an aura of futility.

The second predicament is our *mortality*, more precisely, our *awareness of mortality*. "There is no enduring remembrance of the wise or of fools, seeing that in the days to come all will have been long forgotten. How can the wise die just like fools?" (2:16). "I made great works," Qoheleth writes. "I built houses and planted vineyards for myself; I made myself gardens and parks, and planted in them all kinds of fruit trees. I made myself pools from which to water the forest of growing trees. I bought male and female slaves, and had slaves who were born in my house; I also had great possessions of herds and flocks, more than any who had been before me in Jerusalem. I also gathered for myself silver and gold and the treasure of kings and of the provinces; I got singers, both men and women, and delights of the flesh, and many concubines. So I became great and surpassed all who were before me in Jerusalem; also my wisdom remained with me" (2:4–9). Then comes a surprising realization: "Then I considered all that my hands had done and the toil I had spent in doing it, and . . . there was nothing to be gained under the sun" (2:11). After he gained everything, Qoheleth realized that he had gained nothing.[57]

The melancholy conclusion that "nothing is to be gained" is a consequence of human insatiability and mortality.[58] For world religions, these two dimensions of the human condition color globalization's promise and set its limits. We are in for a disappointment if we celebrate ordinary life while forgetting human insatiability and mortality.

A Squirrel Wheel and the Storm from Paradise

Consider, first, insatiability and its relation to market-driven globalization. In his classic *The Affluent Society* John Kenneth Galbraith compares the struggle of modern societies to satisfy their wants with "the efforts of the squirrel to keep abreast of the wheel that is propelled by his own efforts."[59] Why does the squirrel keep running? What are its hopes? In Galbraith's view, the modern market economy doesn't so much respond to existing needs by producing goods as it "creates the wants the goods are presumed to satisfy"; it "fills the void that it has itself created."[60] Insatiable thirst for profit on the part of producers meets insatiable thirst for goods on the part of consumers—and the squirrel keeps running. No matter how much we produce and how equitably we distribute these goods, by economic means alone we can never meet economic needs, let alone achieve "happiness."[61] Purely economic solutions to economic problems ignore our fundamental insatiability—not only the insatiability of our human senses, which seek "conveniences according to the nicety and delicacy of taste,"[62] but also the insatiability of our inner vision goaded on by the promise of progress. Our insatiability undermines the goodness of objects of desire and dampens the joy of possessing them.

"Among the many models of the good society no one has urged the squirrel wheel," noted Galbraith drily.[63] But the squirrel wheel is what you get if striving for the higher life doesn't tame the restless pursuit of the conveniences and pleasures of ordinary life. The proper object of human insatiability is the infinite God, who both generates and satisfies human insatiability.[64] Some critics of religion argue that God's infinity is a projection of human insatiability.[65] Astute adherents of religions counter that we are engaged in the reverse projection: we hopelessly infuse the works of our own hands with the ability to satisfy our hunger for infinity. The rushing stream of new goods and services has become for us a cornucopia of mystery and salvation. Our desire for them is in fact *prayer*. To make worldly goods objects of our insatiability isn't just futile, a Sisyphean effort.[66] It robs us also of feelings of contentment and joy with what we have,[67] subverts love and compassion for neighbors, and undermines global solidarity and environmental responsibility.

Now consider death, which ineluctably takes away everything that market-driven globalization helps bring: improved health, extended longevity, increased wealth, and magnified opportunities. Between the two world wars, Walter Benjamin reflected on the subject of progress in a short, dense text titled "Theses on the Philosophy of History." Inspired by Paul Klee's painting *Angelus Novus,* he wrote about "the angel of history": "His eyes are staring, his mouth is open, his wings are spread. . . . His face is turned toward the past. Where we perceive a chain of events, he sees one large catastrophe that keeps piling wreckage upon wreckage and hurls it in front of his feet. The angel would like to stay, awaken the dead, and make whole what has been smashed. But a storm is blowing from Paradise; it has got caught in his wings with such violence that the angel can no longer close them. This storm irresistibly propels him into the future to which his back is turned, while the pile of debris before him grows skyward. This storm is what we call progress."[68]

All the wing-flaps of longings for the lost paradise—both food and fuel for insatiability—get whipped up into a mighty storm that propels history forward. That storm of desire drives globalization as well. What does the storm leave in its trail? Wreckage piled upon wreckage, smashed pieces everywhere, the dead, wrote Benjamin, with some exaggeration. But as we observe the price that progress exacts in oppression and suffering as well as the ineluctable crumbling of so many human creations into dust and their disappearance into oblivion, we are hard put to say that he was entirely wrong. True, temples, cathedrals, great monuments, and glorious music remain, as do rich cultural memories, sophisticated technological know-how, the beauty and the wisdom of the ages. But only for a while. Without a transcendent goal, everything will eventually turn into a "pile of debris." Leaving that pile behind and rescuing only some of its riches, every one of us moves into the future. When pushing forward doesn't claim all our attention, as if it were an obsession, like Benjamin's angel often we turn back with a longing "to stay, awaken the dead, and make whole what has been smashed." Yet, whichever way we are turned, the storm propels us forward, and we must leave the past, our present past and any future past, unredeemed.

Burdened by the injustice of the centuries on which its successes feed and piling debris in its wake, history, and globalization as its major driving force today, is both unjust and inconsequential—unjust in that it reaps where it has not sown and sows in the fields not its own, and inconsequential in that it builds sandcastles that the breakers of time destroy. Globalization cries after redemption and abiding significance, neither of which it can deliver. But world religions claim that they can. The Christian faith, for instance, points to the One who awakens the dead, renders justice for the victims of times brutal and irretrievably lost, and preserves all that is good, true, and beautiful.

The Difference Religions Make

Globalization is an ambiguous phenomenon, a thing of promise and of peril, I have argued in this chapter. It helps people's lives go well, or at least on the whole better than in the past. People are better fed and less stuck in degrading and difficult jobs; they live longer and healthier lives and, as we shall see in chapter 5, are less likely to die violent deaths than ever before; they understand the world better and can explore it more; and so on. But globalization also brings severe hardships. Injustice, suffering, and abandonment on a massive scale mark its march through history; it creates new and unprecedented risks; with the market as its driving force, it tends to turn things and people into commodities, to lock their gaze to the flat plane of ordinary life; it undermines enjoyment of the very goods it helps create and erodes altruism and solidarity. Even at its very best, if it avoided creating all these hardships while delivering on its promises, globalization might leave people with a sense of melancholy—it drives them to run furiously, covering great distances while in important regards staying in the same place, with all their efforts ultimately sinking into the night of oblivion as they, along with all their works, are swallowed by death.

Globalization, I have argued, needs world religions to deliver it from its shadows. Religions can situate the pursuit of life that goes well into a more encompassing account of flourishing life in which life being led well has primacy over life going well and life feeling good; they can help generate both a healthy sense of contentment, even joy, and foster commitment to global solidarity, thereby helping achieve a greater measure of global justice. But can religions *actually* deliver on this promise? Part of the answer concerns situating all mundane realities into an overarching framework. If religions can place the history of the entire universe into a larger framework (for instance, the one of creation, redemption, and new creation), there is no reason why they couldn't do the same with market-driven globalization. The more difficult part of the answer requires them to actually shape the present form of globalization, influence the cultural, legal, and political conditions under which it operates. Can religions shape globalization, or must their adherents go into exile, living in enclaves that either peacefully exist alongside larger society (as monastic communities do) or seek to change the world violently (as some terrorist groups do)? I see two challenges—one concerning the ability of *anyone* to shape globalization and the other concerning *the world religions' qualifications* to do so.

Can globalization be shaped? Toward the end of Max Weber's *The Protestant Ethic and the Spirit of Capitalism* we read the following famous words: "In [Richard] Baxter's view the care for external good should only lie on the shoulders of the 'saint like a light cloak, which can be thrown aside at any moment.' But fate decreed that the cloak should become an iron cage."[69] The old Puritan sage thought that the faithful could use the market as an instrument, as a garment that warms and protects the body but could be thrown aside if God commanded so. Weber thought Baxter was mistaken. The "tremendous cosmos of modern economic order" has come to determine "the lives of all individuals who are born into [it] with irresistible force," Weber states.[70] What seemed a light cloak turned out to be an iron cage.

Weber's stark metaphor of the iron cage suggests that the prospects for shaping globalization are dim. For Karl Marx, they would be even dimmer. Global in scope, the modern free market economy runs following its own internal logic and is impervious to moral and religious appeals and pressures. Marx was sure that change was coming, but he grounded his hope not in the moral insight and agency of people, as utopian socialists whom he despised did, but in the conviction, nourished by an account of history he adopted from Georg W. F. Hegel, that the internal contradictions of capitalism would lead to the triumph of proletarians and to global communism. Though very few today share Marx's optimistic view of historical development, many embrace his pessimism regarding the effectiveness of moral appeals. Partly because of the sheer complexity of globalization's multiple interdependencies and partly because of the conflicting self-interests nourished by the very operation of the system these interests help drive, globalization seems unstoppable in its course and unalterable in its character.[71] We live in a "runaway world," they think.

At the turn of the century, Anthony Giddens wrote a book on how globalization is reshaping our lives, titling it *Runaway World*. The title notwithstanding, he was optimistic. To the extent that the world needs steering, we can "reimpose our will" on it, provided we have robust global institutions in place.[72] Imposing our will on globalization and making it an obedient servant rather than a stubborn collaborator might be too much to hope for, but Giddens is right, I think. We are not utterly powerless in the face of social structures we ourselves have created, whose existence depends in part on norms we embrace, and whose functioning our daily participation sustains.[73] To mention an example to which I referred earlier, public opinion pushed Apple to change labor practices in factories assembling its products. On a grander scale, mounting resistance to ecological mismanagement is finding its way into legislation and changing both human behavior and the functioning of the system. A comprehensive endeavor to tame and shape globalization will have to be a massive collaborative effort of many people, adherents of diverse "ideologies" with a wide variety of expertise. For this effort, world religions have indispensable resources. They are neither the only nor the most creative agents of change around, and their track record is in many ways spotty. But as vibrant, growing, and politically assertive global communities with memberships constituting three-quarters of the world population, world religions have the power, motivation, and infrastructure for effective global engagement.

Yet, apart from ignorance about globalization and too frequent unconcern, two tendencies tend to undermine their efforts. The first concerns the relation of religions to one another, their mutual competitiveness. A world religion has a single truth for the whole of humanity, but there are multiple such religions. The consequence is competing visions as to how all should live in a single world, a clash of universalisms. To shape globalization with a view toward the global common good, religions will have to learn how to advocate universalistic visions in a pluralistic world without fomenting violence. To some, this may seem a task as difficult as—or even more difficult than—taming globalization itself. I will try to show in part 2 that this is, in fact, an achievable goal.

The second tendency, somewhat contrary to the first, concerns religions' relation to globalization and consists in their too easy accommodation to circumstance. On many occasions throughout their history religions have betrayed their original vision by making themselves instruments of secular causes: they became primarily markers of ethnic, cultural, or national identities, supporters of political rulers and consecrators of their wars, or transcendent reflections of economic interests.[74] Religions can shape globalization only if they resist being made its mere instruments, remain true to their universal visions of flourishing, and learn how to promote their competing visions in a constructive way. I'll address the second tendency in chapter 2.

2

Religions and the
Challenge of Globalization

eligions are alive today—for good and for ill.

The Dalai Lama, the most prominent Buddhist religious leader, is a world celebrity. During the election of Pope Francis (2013), the anticipation of the white smoke from the chimney of the Sistine Chapel kept hundreds of millions glued to mobile phones and TV sets. In a completely different league, pastor Terry Jones, who swiveled the world's cameras toward himself by threatening to publicly burn the Qur'an, had a flash of world fame, his robustly mustached face suddenly familiar to many throughout the world. And then there is the infamous Osama bin Laden, a zealous but unlearned reader of the holy book Terry Jones was intent on burning, a man who struck terror into the hearts of many.

Global media networks and the Internet gave these four men planetary exposure. Their fame, momentary or enduring, came from the global resonances of their deeds and roles, however. Few would have heard of bin Laden had he not made the world's giant, the United States, tremble in fear and then march into a "boundless global war on terror,"[1] imposing safety measures around the globe and waging wars half a world away supported by a global coalition of nations. Terry Jones would have remained what he is, an obscure leader of a minuscule band of believers, were it not for the 1.6 billion Muslims who consider the physical Qur'an to be the inviolable Word of God and perhaps as many religionists and secularists who harbor anti-Muslim sentiments, partly because of bin Laden's dark global success. The election of a new pope would have been a global nonevent—at most a fascinating odd rite conducted by elderly gentlemen dressed in scarlet robes and locked up, utterly cut off from the world, in a beautiful ancient chapel—were it not that the pope, without commanding an army, leads over 1.2 billion people on all continents. Finally, without millions of his Buddhist followers and abiding tensions between him and the government of the most populous country in the world, an economic powerhouse, the Dalai Lama would likely be merely a marginal monk.

With the exception of a few religious celebrities, religions draw media attention and flare into public awareness mostly when they are glaringly at odds with prevalent cultural sensibilities, when they are embroiled in major scandals, or when they get involved in some spectacular wrongdoing. Less frequently, religions show up in the media when they do some extraordinary good, like promoting debt relief for impoverished nations, tending to the dying abandoned in the slums of impoverished cities, or supporting a legitimate revolution.

But even today, in a media-saturated world, religions are alive mainly off-line, away from cameras and sometimes literally underground—in prayers and religious instruction at home, in communal worship services, in reflection on sacred texts at work, in celebration of births and harvests, in transitions from childhood to adulthood, from singleness to marriage, from life to death—and in all this religions are at work energizing, consoling, healing, liberating, and directing people's lives, giving them meaning. That's as we should expect, for religion is more a matter of everyday practices than of spectacular feats, above all a promoter of ordinary goodness, which tends to be much less fascinating than the many faces of evil. Today, as through the centuries, religions thrive in the daily activities of their adherents, somewhat like the art of cooking thrives not mainly because celebrity chefs display their culinary fireworks on television shows but because mothers and fathers prepare ordinary meals every single day, often more than once, for families and friends.

Religions are alive today, but what difference do they make beyond feeding people's souls and structuring their private and communal practices? In the last chapter I examined the character of globalization, how the world religions have contributed to its emergence, and the multiple ways in which they endeavor to tame and shape globalization into an instrument of their visions of human flourishing and the global common good. There, I sought to understand the connection between religions and globalization by looking at the two from the vantage point of globalization. In this chapter, I invert the perspective. I examine the character of world religions and their global vibrancy and assertiveness; I inquire about how globalization both subverts and energizes religions, how it transforms them and, perhaps surprisingly, how it helps them in some regards to be truer to their own original visions.

Growth of Religions

Measuring global religious adherence is not an exact science; the figures in various surveys don't match. But the main trend is clear: the number of people describing themselves as religious, particularly as adherents of world religions, is growing in both absolute and relative terms.[2] Take, first, the *absolute* numbers, tracked between 1970 and 2005. All major world religions increased in adherents, most boasting of spectacular gains:

- Buddhists: from 233 to 379 million
- Christians: from 1,236 to 2,135 million

- Hindus: from 463 to 870 million
- Jews: from 14 to 15 million
- Muslims: from 554 to 1,314 million

The world religions have continued growing steadily since 2005, especially Buddhism, Christianity, Hinduism, and Islam.[3] By 2030, the Muslim population of the planet is expected to reach 2.2 billion, for instance.

During the same period (1970–2005), the number of adherents of those religions grew in *relative* terms as well: from 67.8 percent to 72.4 percent of the world population.[4] By some estimates, almost 80 percent of living human beings believe in God. That leaves, of course, many who think of themselves as "convinced atheists" or, somewhat more vaguely, as "nonreligious," a term that generally and problematically includes also those who describe themselves as "spiritual" rather than identifying with organized religion. According to one statistic—likely exaggerated as the poll excluded some of the most religious countries in the world—the combined number for atheists and nonreligious comes close to 16 percent of the world population. That would be about 1.1 billion nonreligious human beings, slightly less than all the Buddhists and Hindus combined.[5] Still, though the *number* of nonreligious people is significant and growing, for now their *percentage* of the world population is gradually diminishing.[6]

Some believe that world religions are thriving *despite* globalization, booming as the last furious shrieks of unreason dimly aware of its pending demise. This is the argument of the advocates of the secularization thesis, who continue to believe that religion will finally disappear from the world as a superfluous relic of a superstitious phase of human development. But in fact, religions are thriving *with the help* of the instruments and social transformations globalization processes supply. In 2007 *Time* magazine named Amr Khaled—an Egyptian television preacher whose message is broadcast over satellite TV, the

Internet, and on audio- and videocassette tapes—one of the world's top one hundred most influential people.[7] Pope Francis tweets to millions of followers in multiple languages. These are just two prominent examples of the massive use of modern communication to spread faith. Transnational migration, another key feature of a globalized world, contributes to the vibrancy of world religions as well. Some have argued that by increasing religious pluralism, migration leads to the weakening of religious allegiance and the decline of religions. It is the other way around. Migration "promotes institutional and theological transformations that energize and revitalize religions."[8] In pluralistic settings, religion may not be "in the air"—the muezzin's voice calling *adhan* may not be broadcast everywhere; steeples and temples may not be dominating entire landscapes; ethnic or national identity may not be keeping people within a religion or drawing them to it. Yet precisely because religion is no longer taken for granted, religious beliefs and practices become more clearly articulated; religion morphs into a set of beliefs and practices people embrace consciously and pass on actively (often with the help of sophisticated marketing techniques).

In noting the vibrancy of religions in a globalized world, I am not reporting the results of a race, showing religion winning over secularism, and Christianity continuing its lead among world religions, with Islam, perhaps, threatening to overtake it by the mid-twenty-first century.[9] The number of a religion's adherents doesn't say anything about the validity of its claims (though the fact that many reasonable people espouse a view that differs from one's own has a bearing on the certainty with which one embraces one's own beliefs).[10] But statistics do demonstrate the *abiding relevance* of world religions. Whatever their truth or falsity, whatever good they may effect or damage they may wreak, their continued growth in both absolute and relative terms is a testimony to their immense attractiveness and power. They shape the lives of more than two-thirds of the world population, providing people with what they believe to be ways to attain salvation, cope in crises, and stay in touch with transcendent forces; giving them a sense of who they are as individuals and communities; and guiding them in how they should relate to others and what good they should strive to achieve. World religions have rendered such service to human beings for millennia while empires have come and gone, political and economic systems have changed in succession, and ideologies, languages, and whole cultures have disappeared. Today, world religions are thriving, and nothing suggests that will change in the foreseeable future.

Public Assertiveness

Religions aren't a force only in people's private lives. As the presence of religious figures in the media suggests, religions are also assertive in the public sphere. Only a few decades ago, religion was much more private, more a presence in individual and communal lives than a force in the public sphere. The authors of *God's Century,* a 2011 book subtitled *Resurgent Religion and Global Politics,* note a shift in the role and ambitions of religions at the beginning of the twenty-first century: "Over the past four decades, religion's influence on politics has reversed its decline and become more powerful on every continent and across every major world religion. Earlier confined to the home, the family, the village, the mosque, synagogue, temple, and church, religion has come to exert its influence in parliaments, presidential palaces, lobbyists' offices, campaigns, militant training camps, negotiation rooms, protest rallies, city squares, and dissident jail cells. Workplaces increasingly are the sites of prayer rooms and small-group Scripture studies."[11] Why did religions step into the public arena after a period of relative private containment? Clearly, religions weren't *forced* out of homes and houses of worship. They went public on their own, though often with the help of shrewd politicians.

The character of religions provided the impetus, and globalization offered the opportunity.

For most world religions, a purely private religion is a truncated religion. The nerve center of a world religion may be the hearts of individuals, but the domain of its influence is the entire *world*. Religions structure relationships between people and craft cultures, rather than merely shaping the interior lives of individuals and their private practices. World religions aim at adjusting people's public lives as well as their private ones to the unseen order. That's true today even of Buddhism, a religion of personal enlightenment, which is often counted among "mystical" rather than "prophetic" religions.[12] As the popularity of the self-designation "engaged Buddhism" attests, many Buddhists see themselves as having a public responsibility.[13] So do Hindus, as the example of Mahatma Gandhi attests: traditional Hindu ethics and concepts that are primarily aimed at self-sufficiency and individual attainment of the truth can be translated into communal instruments used to mobilize social and political action.[14]

But religions' prophetic impulse alone would not have sufficed to make religions publicly assertive in today's world. Globalization helped as well, just as it helps in their numerical growth. As Anthony Giddens has argued in *Runaway World,* advances in global communication significantly influenced the spread of democracy, "the most powerful energizing idea of the twentieth century."[15] As the democratic ideal conquered the world,[16] the door opened for religions to enter the space in which they saw themselves properly belonging. As José Casanova has argued, the democratization of politics carried on the wings of globalization processes led to the political assertiveness of religions.[17] The reason is simple, though it took the astute observer Alexis de Tocqueville to articulate it: when ordinary people, most of them religious, enter the political arena, they take religion with them.[18]

Conjoining democracy and world religions seems counterintuitive to many. Democracy, their line of reasoning goes, is about the agency of ordinary people, about honoring their diverse perspectives and letting them shape public life; religions, in contrast, are about the immutable precepts gleaned from ancient texts, about the one truth for all people and all times. The claim that world religions and democracy are incompatible is mistaken, however. The rule of the one God, to use the monotheist religions as examples, has historically had both authoritarian and democratizing effects: the one God at times underwriting the rule of the one earthly sovereign, but at other times affirmed as the only ruler who delegates management of earthly affairs to the entire people.[19] Today, the great majority of monotheists throughout the world endorse the second option.

As a counterexample, many today point to Muslims, who are reputed to be prone to authoritarianism. Research suggests otherwise. According to a 2013 Pew poll, the majority of the world's Muslims prefer democracy to a strong leader (except in South Asia, where only 45 percent do so). An overwhelming majority of all Muslims embrace religious freedom (with percentages ranging from 85 percent in the Middle East and North Africa to 97 percent in South Asia), which includes for them the freedom to bring their own religious vision to bear on public life.[20] For Muslims, as for many religious and nonreligious people alike, the difficulty isn't to embrace democracy but to embrace a *pluralistic form* of democracy. In chapters 3 and 4, I will argue that the world religions—including Islam—are compatible with pluralistic forms of democracy appropriate for a globalized world.

Under the conditions of globalization, religions are alive, growing, and publicly assertive.[21] Religions are not disappearing, as the proponents of the secularization thesis expected. But religions *are* changing. I do not intend to analyze here the many transformations of religions taking place today. For my purpose it will suffice to indicate the increased significance of one key function of religions and to note two major transformations. But before I do so, I need to identify the segment of the vast and vibrant universe of religions on which I am concentrating here.

What Are World Religions?

When I discuss "religions" in this book, I have in mind the so-called world religions, and among them primarily Buddhism, Hinduism, Confucianism, Judaism, Christianity, and Islam.[22] In many respects *religions* is not the happiest term, but it is useful and necessary to employ it in the discussion of the relation between religions and globalization.[23] As I have noted in chapter 1, world religions (or secondary religions, as some prefer to call them) set themselves apart from local religions (or primary religions)[24] in the context of "axial transformations."[25] Their defining features are most clearly visible in their charismatic originators as received by their immediate followers—the Buddha, Confucius, the Hebrew prophets, Jesus, or Muhammad. Concretely, however, world religions are tension-filled cultural phenomena, marked by both novelty and compromise with religions in the old mold, that have undergone major transformations in a long historical process since their emergence.[26]

Though each world religion is an ancient religious tree of its own kind, with many branches, they all share some common features—and argue internally and among themselves about how best to understand them. Drawing on the work of scholars like Charles Taylor and Jan Assmann, I have identified six features I consider particularly relevant for the topic of religions and globalization. As I see it, these features together neither name the common "essence" of world religions nor offer their full descriptions. Instead, they constitute a set of shared formal structural affinities that marks these as world religions. The contours of each feature emerge most clearly in contrast with local religions.

- "Two worlds" account of reality. Local religions are cosmo-theistic; gods and spirits are aspects of the world itself. World religions have what Friedrich Nietzsche called, critically, a "two worlds" account of reality.[27] Without necessarily being dualistic, they posit two categorically distinct, though related, realms, the transcendent and the mundane, and give primacy to the transcendent.

- Human beings as individuals. In local religions devotion is tightly linked to the social life of a group; people relate to gods and spirits primarily as a community, as a given socio-linguistic or civic group.[28] World religions address human beings as individuals;[29] the transcendent call either takes persons out of their original community, inserting them into a locally articulated transcultural religious community, or leaves them within the community but demands personal appropriation.[30]

- Universal claims. Local religions are, well, local; the gods you worship are the gods of your people, marking your social boundaries and helping your group to flourish. World religions make claims as to what is true, just, and good for *all* human beings, irrespective of their local cultures. They offer a diagnosis of the human predicament (for example, captivity to suffering, the problem of sin, lack of guidance) and sketch the way out of it (such as enlightenment, God's unconditional love, submission to God).

- The good beyond ordinary flourishing. Local religions are concerned with ordinary human flourishing. People invoke or placate divinities and powers in order to achieve prosperity, health, long life, and fertility and to be preserved from disease, dearth, sterility, and premature death.[31] World religions are concerned with the good that goes beyond ordinary flourishing without necessarily negating it. Human beings can attain the good even if they fail to achieve health, wealth, and longevity; they can attain it even *through* "a failing (like dying young on the cross)" or while "leaving the field of flourishing altogether (ending the cycle of rebirth)."[32]

- Religion as a distinct cultural system.[33] Local religion is "ineradicably inscribed in the institutional, linguistic, and cultural conditions of a society." World religions are autonomous systems, distinct (*not* necessarily separate) from a given culture and political community. A world religion can therefore "transcend all political and ethnic borders, and transplant itself into other cultures."[34]

- Transformation of mundane realities. Local religions are marked by a "mood of assent" (an attitude toward life that, in a neo-pagan way, Nietzsche echoes in his feisty "affirmation of life").[35] In world religions, assent to life gives way to "a kind of quarrel with life."[36] This is the consequence of splitting reality into transcendent and mundane realms and giving precedence to the transcendent.[37] Asceticism and prophetism are two basic ways of aligning mundane realities with the transcendent order: ascetic practices serve to adjust human bodies and souls to the transcendent order while prophetic engagement serves to adjust the circumstances of the world to the transcendent order.

Note four things about these features. First, I don't claim that world religions other than Christianity *ought* to be interpreted as having these features. I am a Christian, and I don't presume to be entitled to give normative interpretations of other religions, to be entitled to tell Muslims or Hindus, for instance, what it would mean to be good Muslims and Hindus. Instead, all I claim is that these religions *can be plausibly interpreted* as having these features and that *some of their own prominent adherents have interpreted them in such a way.* My larger point is that to the extent that world religions can be responsibly interpreted as having these features, then from my own Christian standpoint, possibilities open up for each religion to be true to itself in coexistence with others and, by arguing and collaborating together, to contribute to the common good.

Second, each world religion understands these features and their relative importance in a distinct way. For instance, Buddhism and Confucianism have tended to view transcendence in less personal terms than do monotheistic religions, and even monotheistic religions disagree in their accounts of transcendence.[38] To take another example, historically, though not today, Islam has tended to stress the goods of ordinary human flourishing more than has Christianity or Hinduism; Judaism and Confucianism have tended to be tied much more closely to a particular ethnic group than have other universalistic religions. The six features are not six identical building blocks used ready-made in each religion, but six shared formal structural affinities.

Third, in its long history, each world religion has changed the way it understands each feature and its relative importance, and has quarreled internally about the matter. In the terminology of David Martin, to which I will return later in the book, these traits are key elements in a religion's "repertoire of motifs."[39] At any given time and place, a world religion may foreground, background, or articulate these features and the relation between them with greater or lesser distance from its original vision. For instance, within Christianity, debates have been fierce about the relation between believing individuals and the community, with the Catholics and the Orthodox stressing more hierarchically structured organic community and Protestants giving priority to believing individuals; within Islam, debates have been vigorous about the nature of transcendence and its relation to the mundane realm, with Sufis stressing more the unity of the two and non-Sufis stressing radical distinction. Significantly, the differences that world religions and their rival versions display with regard to the six features often concern the levels of proximity or distance from the corresponding traits characteristic of local religions. As I will discuss later on in the book, the religions debate how enmeshed or distinct religion should be from cultural and political order or how involved religion should be in the service of ordinary flourishing.

Fourth, all six features of world religions are convictions that concern the nature and purpose of human existence. World religions are *more* than moral anthropologies and cosmologies, of course; they are more than a set of convictions situating people in the world and providing orientation for their lives. Each contains narratives, symbols, rituals, sacred times, places, and objects; each generates pervasive moods, even passions, and motivations in its adherents;[40] each is alive in local communities; each offers ways to ward off individual and collective misfortune as well as to enhance ordinary flourishing; each marks group boundaries and generates solidarities, and so on.

World religions are often also *less* than a set of such situating and orienting convictions. In the actual lives of people, they can be reduced to markers of identity or magical tools for enhancing ordinary flourishing, for instance. These are, I contend, malfunctions of world religions, and I will return to them shortly. First I need to further elaborate the way world religions understand the relation between transcendent and mundane realities.

Ways of Living Ordinary Life

A consequence of the split of reality into two worlds, the transcendent and the mundane, is a shift in world religions from assent to life to a kind of quarrel with life. In the light of transcendence, something is perceived to be amiss in the world and in need of transformation. But what does the quarrel mean? Does it imply that world religions

71

are world-*denying*—placing the transcendent sphere in opposition to the mundane and robbing it of significance? Many critics think so, especially those who follow the trail of Nietzsche, who argued that a hidden nihilism with respect to the ordinary life attends the affirmation of transcendence.[41] As I argued in chapter 1, the present form of globalization—market-driven globalization—revolves around the affirmation of ordinary life. If world religions deny flourishing in ordinary life or are utterly unconcerned with it, they will clash with globalization. If they affirm it in their own way, a productive—though tension-filled—relation between the two may be possible.

The world religions give a complex account of human flourishing, stretched between the "two worlds." They differ significantly in how they relate to ordinary life, but none of them sees itself as a mere means of escaping ordinary life. As the prominence of compassion in Buddhism attests, that's true even of Buddhism, a religion in which the ultimate goal of life is the extinction of desire and escape from the cycle of rebirth.[42] Similarly, the emphasis on *artha* (wealth) and *kama* (pleasure) as two of the four goals of human life (*purusharthas*) illustrates the Hindu affirmation of ordinary life.[43] In different ways and to differing degrees, world religions see themselves *also* as ways of living ordinary life. Each in its own way—a way that is in tension, sometimes to the point of irreconcilable contradiction, with the claims of other religions—teaches that we live our ordinary lives well when we have a purpose that transcends the goods of ordinary life and when this purpose regulates care for the goods of ordinary life. In sum, world religions both affirm ordinary life and claim that ordinary life comes into its own when aligned with the transcendent order.

The life and teachings of Jesus Christ provide a good illustration. In the course of foretelling that he would be killed for disturbing the religious and political order out of allegiance to the One he called his "Father," Jesus challenged his disciples to emulate him: "If any want to become my followers, let them deny themselves and take up their cross and follow me. For those who want to save their life will lose it, and those who lose their life for my sake will find it. For what will it profit them if they gain the whole world but forfeit their life? Or what will they give in return for their life?" (Matthew 16:24–26). People can find the true good only if following Jesus matters to them more than life itself. That sounds world-denying, yet Jesus clearly affirmed ordinary life as well. The Gospels are filled with reports of how he healed the sick, fed the hungry, and raised people from the dead. He both affirmed ordinary life and insisted that those who pursue only the goods of ordinary life will squander their life. Was he contradicting himself?

The key to the polarity in Jesus's teaching and practice is the *order of priorities* between the "ordinary life" and the "higher life." Consider Jesus's teaching about acquisitiveness and worry. In the Sermon on the Mount, he said: "Therefore do not worry, saying, 'What will we eat?' or 'What will we drink?' or 'What will we wear?' For it is the Gentiles who strive for all these things; and indeed your heavenly Father knows that you need all these things. But strive *first* for the kingdom of God and his righteousness, *and all these things will be given to you as well*" (Matthew 6:31–33; emphasis added). Our lives—all our desires and our strivings, our worries and our joys—shouldn't revolve around the necessities and conveniences of life. Life is "more than food" (Matthew 6:25), more than health, wealth, fertility, and longevity. As Jesus, starved after a forty-day fast, tells the Tempter, human beings don't live by bread alone; they need words "that come from the mouth of God" more (Matthew 4:4). We should strive *first* after God and God's righteousness. Yet, in principle there is no opposition between striving after God and working for food or between enjoying God and enjoying food. For in striving after and in enjoying God, the source of all things—of ourselves, of things as they are "out there" as well as of the way they appear in our experience of them—all other striving and enjoyment is encompassed and ordered;

with God's righteousness, the things of ordinary life, necessities as well as conveniences, are given and genuinely enjoyed.[44]

Take another example: the story of Job, a Gentile sage from Tanakh, the Hebrew Bible.[45] The narrator sets up the story by noting that Job was "a man blameless and upright, one who feared God and turned from evil," and that God had "blessed the work of his hands" so that he was "the greatest of all the people of the east" (Job 1:1–12). The drama of the story begins with a dispute between Satan and God. Satan, an incarnation of destructive suspicion, claims that Job fears God because God had made him such a great man. In other words, Job is using God. Proud of Job and of the integrity of his devotion, God disagrees. The rest of the story is about Job's reaction to the test to which God and Satan put him, the only way to settle the dispute about whether Job fears God "for nothing" (Job 1:9) or because of the health, extraordinary wealth, fertility, and longevity that God had bestowed upon him.[46] Stripped of all belongings, bereft of children, and afflicted with painful disease, Job neither cursed God nor gave up insisting on his integrity. Instead, he contended with God on account of the blatant injustice of his fate, an agonizing exercise rooted in his unwavering adherence to the God of justice. In the end, Job proved both himself and God right and Satan wrong: Job served God "for nothing," for no other reason except that serving God simply *is* the authentically human way of living. And yet, in the story of Job no less than in the teaching of Jesus, attachment to God and the affirmation of ordinary life aren't opposed to one another. Though Job serves God "for nothing," he doesn't end up with nothing. After Job had proven the purity of his faith through the ordeal, "the Lord gave Job twice as much as he had before" (Job 42:10). Attachment to God and moral uprightness have primacy; but material well-being is a positive good that God gives and whose enjoyment is enhanced by attachment to God.[47]

Expanding on Nicholas Wolterstorff's suggestion in *Justice: Rights and Wrongs,* I have proposed that according to the Christian tradition the good life has three formal components: *life being led well* (in Jesus's teaching, loving God and neighbor; in Job's case, fearing God and being righteous), *life going well* (in Jesus's practice, healing the sick, feeding the hungry; in Job's case, health, abundant possessions, many children), and life feeling good (in Jesus's teaching, joy; in Job's case, feasting).[48] Something similar is true in other world religions as well, I believe; it cannot be otherwise if they see themselves not as ways of escaping the world but of living well in it. They differ in how they conceive the nature of life lived well ("love of God and neighbor," "submission to God," "extinction of desire," to name some), in how they imagine a life that is going well (for example, the difference in the importance of progeny in Judaism and Christianity), in what positive emotion they highlight in life that feels good ("fun" in contemporary Western cultures or "joy" in Buddhism, Confucianism, Christianity, and Judaism), and in how precisely they see the relation among the three. These differences are important, as they express the unique character of each religion and can lead to fierce mutual contestations as well as to reciprocal learning and collaboration. Notwithstanding these differences, all three components of flourishing are present in all world religions; we are meant to live our life well, in alignment with the transcendent realm, and life is meant to go well for us and be marked by positive emotions and moods. The basic relation between leading life well and the other two is structured similarly as well: in world religions, leading life well has primacy over life going well and feeling good; leading life well defines and sustains life going well and life feeling good—and, in cases of conflict between them, trumps life going well and feeling good. Whatever else world religions might be, they are, at their heart, accounts of life worth living, of life being lived well, life going well, and life feeling good under the primacy of transcendence. Accounts of the good life are the most important gift world religions can give to the world.

75

But critics may demur, isn't this gift poisoned? Some secular critics, such as Christopher Hitchens, even go so far as to argue that poison is the only "gift" religions have.[49] I disagree. Religions have a genuine and indispensable gift to give, but they often get corrupted; they malfunction, and the gift turns into poison. In an interconnected and interdependent world these malfunctions can have disastrous consequences.

Malfunctions and Contentions

The most common malfunctions of religion are failures of practice. Let's call them *practice malfunctions.* Though the adherents of a religion will generally consider it a force for good, most grant that in the course of its history great evils were perpetrated under its aegis, evils clearly opposed to the religion's teaching. External critics often zero in on religious hypocrisy, but internal critics are no less discerning in spotting discrepancies between teachings and practices. Ancient Jewish prophets are a good example—Nathan, for instance, who confronted the great king David about his crime of adultery and murder for his lust (1 Samuel 11:1–12:14), or Isaiah, who exposed the emptiness of the religious rituals of those who "oppress all your workers" and who "strike with a wicked fist" (Isaiah 58:3–4).[50] People embrace a religion's authentic teachings but find themselves unable to resist their own base impulses. Worse, to quiet the voice of conscience and escape outside judgment, they cover the tracks of their iniquity with profuse avowals of loyalty to the religion's noble principles and with sanitized accounts of their wrongdoings. Whether successfully papered over or not, a gap yawns wide between profession and practice.

Less visible but perhaps more insidious malfunctions than the failures of practice are the *distortions of convictions.* Let's call them *teaching malfunctions.* A religion's teachings are often complex, originally given in circumstances different than adherents' own. They are more like a loose repertoire of related motifs than a tight system of precise doctrinal and moral postulates—more like, well, the Bible than like Kant's *Critique of Practical Reason*. Without much reflection about how to center and integrate a religion's "unruly" teachings, adherents cherry-pick convictions or highlight one set at the expense of others, often guided by interests at odds with a given religion's basic visions of life worth living—as when they offer religious justification for suppression of women, the practice of slavery, or violence against the innocent. Sometimes the indeterminacy of a religion's divergent teachings feeds failures in believers' practices. It also happens the other way around: failures of practice generate twisted interpretations of sacred texts and formative traditions. A vicious spiral of failures of practice and distortions of convictions makes a religion legitimize and inspire evil rather than curb it. These are two important malfunctions of religion.

In a globalized world of vibrant and politically assertive religions, particularly significant are malfunctions of religions associated with relations between groups. Let's call them *belonging malfunctions.* Belonging often isn't merely exclusive—I define myself largely by not being the other—but aggressively so. Adherents of different religions or their rival versions insult and persecute each other. To give examples from my native land: some Catholics and Orthodox deride smaller Protestant churches as "sects," and some adherents of those derided churches return the favor by refusing to recognize the Orthodox and the Catholics as Christians; some Christians disparage Islam as "demonically" inspired, and some Muslims and Jews respond by mocking Christians as "idolaters";[51] no name-calling is currently taking place between Jews and Christians in the country of my origin, mainly because the Jews, adherents of the "yellow faith" and "Christ killers," have been either exterminated or driven out. In such cases, religions and their rival versions are, arguably, malfunctioning: they have morphed into markers of group identities, boosters of political loyalties, defenders of a community's economic benefits. I will return to belonging malfunctions throughout the book.

The three malfunctions of religions—often pulling together like some mad horse troika—should be distinguished from contentions among religions. World religions and their rival versions have genuine disagreements about the nature of the self, social relations, and the good—about visions of flourishing.[52] A Buddhist account of the self is different from a mainstream Muslim one (though it has some affinities with a Sufi one), as are their visions of the ultimate goal of human striving; in one case the self is erased as its desire is extinguished, and in the other the self is affirmed as its desire is abundantly satisfied.[53] And both differ from the Confucian account of the self, whose striving, in taking on "the Way of Heaven," is aimed at perfection, both one's own and society's.[54] What is judged as spiritually and ethically right from the perspective of one religion can be deemed wrong, misguided, or inadequate from the perspective of the other.[55]

Some see the very contentiousness of world religions as their malfunction and advise keeping religions and their visions of the good life quarantined in the private sphere. That would be a mistake, I think. The endeavor would be both futile and oppressive. Equally important, if religions were consigned to the private sphere, humanity would be robbed of alternative visions of human flourishing tested over the centuries. As I argued in chapter 1, market-driven globalization needs religion-formed alternative accounts of the good life. The challenge is to help people of diverse religions live in peace while engaged in vigorous debates about the nature of the good life and the global common good. In effect, the challenge is to keep the malfunctions of religions out of their contentions. I will take up this theme in part 2.

In the following I will examine the most important contribution of religions to globalization and then note two major transformations of religions under the influence of globalization, one nudging them to align more with their original vision and the other pulling them away from it.

The Axis of Our Lives

In *A Secular Age,* Charles Taylor identified three senses of "secularization." As I have shown earlier in the chapter, the first two—the retreat of religion from the public sphere and the decline of religious belief and practice—are not occurring globally today. On the contrary: the world is "de-secularizing."[56] The third sense of secularization concerns a change in what Taylor calls "conditions of belief." Over the last five centuries in the West, a gradual transformation has taken place "from a society where belief in God is unchallenged and indeed, unproblematic, to one in which it is understood to be one option among others, and frequently not the easiest to embrace."[57] In the West—and, as a result of galloping globalization, increasingly elsewhere—we live within a seemingly self-sufficient order with no reference to transcendence, within an "immanent frame": human rights and the calculation of costs and benefits define the moral order, pluralistic democracies and free market economies define the social order, and science defines the cosmic order.[58] The immanent frame is compatible with religion, Taylor argues; we can "spin" it in a way that is either open to transcendence or closed to it.[59] But the "naturalness" of religion has given way to the "naturalness" of a-religion, requiring a conscious endeavor for many even to imagine an alternative to the immanent frame. Courtesy of globalization, the immanent frame is spreading throughout the world; alternatives to religion are becoming live options for many and "natural" for some. Gradually, many people are finding themselves in an open space, on a cusp, on which religious and a-religious winds push and pull from different directions. They must choose.[60]

Why choose religion? What do world religions still have to offer that we cannot get elsewhere? What are we left hungry for, despite all the accelerating enhancements of ordinary life that market-driven globalization armed with accelerating technological advances is helping deliver to many (and would deliver to most were it designed and managed so that income gaps aren't scandalously wide and the environment isn't irreparably damaged)? Unless we seriously misunderstand both globalization and world religions, the achievements of well-run globalization and the offerings of world religions aren't in competition with one another. More precisely: market-driven globalization in alliance with science and technology and globalization shaped by world religions aren't exclusive alternatives and need not clash; religions have their own contribution to make without diminishing the importance of science and technology.

I grant that you might disagree given the history of the contest between religion and a-religion over the past two centuries. The contest concerns mainly two alleged functions of religions: their ability to explain the workings and development of the world, as a whole and in its various aspects, and their power to manipulate the world for human benefit. Do religious cosmologies and anthropologies explain anything, or are religious "explanations" primitive substitutes for true scientific ones? Do blessings and miracles enhance and repair life, or are they make-believe "technologies" to be replaced by those that actually work? But to put the contest between religion on the one side and science and technology on the other in these terms presumes that religions, like science and technology, primarily aim at explaining and manipulating the world. The dispute between a-religionists and religionists is then about whether religion or science does a better job at those tasks. Debates framed in these terms are as vigorous today as they were in the past, but they are partly misdirected.[61] They leave out of consideration the most important dimension of world religions.

Augustine's *Confessions,* one of the most influential secondary texts of any religion, opens with the following famous line, addressed to God: "You move us to delight in praising you; you have formed us for yourself, and our hearts are restless till they find rest in you." Whether the world religions speak of God (like Judaism, Christianity, and Islam) or not (like Buddhism and Confucianism), they hold a formal position more or less like Augustine's.[62] With their feet firmly planted in ordinary realities, human beings always extend their hand beyond the stars into the transcendent realm. Explicitly or implicitly, world religions insist that stretching out to the divine realm isn't something human beings do or don't do depending on whether they are religiously inclined or not. Reference to transcendence isn't an *add-on* to humanity; rather, it defines human beings. That's the structural restlessness of human hearts.[63] When we come to "rest" in the divine—when we come to love God and surrender to God in faith, to formulate the matter in Christian terms—the relation to the divine becomes the axis of our lives. It shapes how we perceive ourselves and the world, what desires we have and how they are satiated. For world religions, life lived only on the flat plane of this-worldliness is too caged, too hollow, and too "light";[64] to be free, full, and flourishing, life must be lived in relationship to the divine, which gives meaning, orientation, and unique pleasure to all our mundane experiences and endeavors. That's a disputed claim, of course. But that's also the claim on which debates between religions and a-religion should center as it is the main claim world religions make, their stated raison d'être.

From the perspective of world religions, their central challenge isn't to gain a competitive advantage over science and technology or at least maintain their share of the same "market." World religions don't stand or fall on their ability to deliver more and better worldly goods to more people than do science and technology in the context of globalization—goods like health and longevity, the necessities and conveniences of life, or explanations of how the world and things in it function. World religions stand or fall on their ability to connect people to the transcendent realm and thereby make it possible for them to truly flourish, to find genuine fulfillment in both their successes and failures, and to lead lives worthy of human beings, lives marked by joyous contentment and solidarity. As I see it, this is at the heart of what the Buddha, Confucius, the Hebrew prophets, Jesus, and Muhammad, each in a distinct way, were after; and this—the nature of transcendence, flourishing, and of their relation—is what world religions primarily debate among themselves. Seen from the angle of world religions, scientific explanations don't negate the existence of the transcendent realm as the goal of human life, and technological advances don't make religion itself redundant;[65] rather, the transcendent goal gives scientific exploration, technological innovation, and all the enhancements of ordinary life a truly *human* purpose.

For many reasons, world religions are alive and assertive in a globalized world characterized by rapid scientific and technological advances and astounding rates of wealth creation coupled with abysmal inequities in wealth distribution:

- Many—billions, in fact—have not benefited much from globalization but have suffered instead; religion consoles them and makes them resilient.
- The rapid pace of change pulls many into a bewildering swirling storm; religion gives them orientation and stability.
- Some are overwhelmed by the possibilities and seductions of consumerism and entertainment; religion directs and disciplines their desires so they can care well for themselves and others.
- Some are victims of egregious and systemic injustices; religion motivates them to struggle against injustice and assures them that justice will ultimately triumph.

- Some experience the erosion of local cultures; religion, associated with a culture, provides them with a sense of communal identity.

Religions do all these things and many more, and that's partly why people embrace them.[66] But in all these things and in addition to them, world religions, each in its own way and none reducible either to another or to some alleged common core, seek to attend to the structural restlessness of the human heart by offering connection to the transcendent realm and meaningful and joyous life in response to it. That's their crucial and abiding role in a globalized world.

Globalization isn't stilling the hunger world religions are designed to satisfy. It isn't making world religions disappear;[67] on the contrary, it is helping them spread and exert social and political influence. Globalization is also transforming world religions. A full account of these transformations would be coextensive with a sketch of the history of world religions over the last few centuries. In the following, I will focus on two major transformations, one that concerns religions' relation to the state and the other their relation to the economy. Globalization is inducing a third major transformation of world religions as well: their relation to the environment, as it generates a deep sense of ecosystemic interdependence and planetary endangerment. For the most part, this transformation doesn't involve a return to the cosmotheistic unity of indigenous religions; rather, it is a shift from a near-exclusive concentration on human beings to a sense that the transcendent realm is related positively to the entirety of the mundane realm seen as an ecosystem, a recognition that the good life in response to transcendence involves living in sync with the environment.[68] (Significant as it is, this crucial transformation of religion falls outside the scope of my interest here because I don't take up in this book the relation between globalization and environment.)

Religions and the State

Globalization is transforming the relationship of world religions to the state. When a religious community is coextensive with a society, religion can serve to integrate society and provide its government with a legitimizing ideology. Religion, moral self-understandings of individuals and society, and the state align, and a political entity is integrated.[69] That's why King David, according to the biblical story, brought the Ark of the Covenant from Kiryath-jearim to Jerusalem— to establish the city as a religious, cultural, and political center of his kingdom.[70] For millennia, religions served that purpose; they functioned as "political religions." But when multiple religions—or multiple varieties of the same religion—come to coexist within the boundaries of a society, no single religion can articulate and celebrate the link of political society with the transcendent order and thus integrate society. After the Protestant Reformation introduced a major fissure into Latin Christianity, for instance, belonging to the state was gradually decoupled from adhering to a specific religion or a version of it. Progressive globalization, marked as it is by an unprecedented flow of commerce, ideas, and people across national borders, is transforming monoreligious societies into societies with multiple forms of religion and a-religion existing side by side.[71] The connection between a given religion and political society is weakening everywhere, and in some nations it is altogether nonexistent.

In reaction partly to globalization and partly to secular nationalisms, movements are afoot in all world religions to strengthen their connection to political order.[72] Many Buddhists in Sri Lanka are fighting to keep together the religion of Buddha, Sinhalese language and culture, and the Sri Lankan state.[73] Religious Zionists believe that the Jewish religion and the state of Israel are inseparable.[74] Some representatives of the Christian Right in the United States seek to reestablish a close tie between the Christian faith and U.S. national identity.[75]

"Political Islam" is perhaps the best-known and most thoroughgoing recent example of a religion's attempt to exercise dominance over all spheres of life. In *Milestones,* Sayyid Qutb, a prominent intellectual representative of political Islam, sums up his program by explaining that the most basic Muslim conviction, "No god but God!" means "no sovereignty except God's, no law except from God, and no authority of one man over another, as the authority in all respects belongs to God."[76]

But the attempts of religions to assert dominance and exercise an integrative function in political societies are, arguably, mistaken. First, as history teaches, the aspired dominance ends in a religion's subservience; more often than not, religions become tools in the hands of the powers that be.[77] Second, world religions pay for their bad bargain with the loss of identity. As I interpret them, world religions are cultural systems distinct from governments, and they form transcultural and transnational communities. Marking ethnocultural boundaries, integrating political entities, and legitimizing governments is not what these religions are basically about, at least not as conceived by the Buddha, Confucius, Jesus, or Muhammad. They address human beings qua human beings and therefore transcend ethnocultural boundaries and introduce a fissure into political societies;[78] they apply the same moral code to insiders and outsiders and are therefore motivated to build bridges to outsiders; they seek to align mundane reality with transcendent norms and are therefore self-consciously "unreliable allies" to governments (as Karl Barth wrote of the Christian Church).[79] When they see themselves as expressing the moral unity of a nation and furnishing political order with a sacred aura, world religions distort themselves and betray one of their signature features: the alignment of individuals, universal values, and religion. They revert to being local religions but now with universal pretensions. Finally, when world religions align themselves with the state they often underwrite violence toward citizens and foreign nations alike. As I will argue in chapter 5, religions turn violent above all when they see themselves as coextensive with a society and are entangled in the dynamics of its power and cohesion. The result is a serious malfunction of world religions. Local religions with universal pretensions are the most violent of all religions. In sum, when world religions enter into a marriage with the state, they lose influence, identity, and reputation. In terms of my earlier discussion of religions' malfunctions, the following principle applies: the more a religion is identified with a given society and entangled with political power, the more likely it is for selective interpretations that legitimize violence to develop, for belonging to turn aggressively exclusivist, and for gaps between profession and practice to open up.

With regard to world religions' relation to society and the state, globalization is more their friend rather than their enemy. By generating multireligious societies, globalization offers world religions an opportunity to return to themselves: to be the means of embracing a "cosmopolitan" god, to use Nietzsche's terms, a god "for everybody" who is "at home everywhere," a god impartial to "friend and foe";[80] to be carriers of universal visions of human flourishing, distinct from any particular political society and relating to all people as human beings, whether they are political insiders or outsiders.

Strong tendencies to see themselves as distinct from the state are today evident in all world religions. If Olivier Roy's argument in *Globalized Islam* is correct, this is increasingly true of Islam as well. The majority of the world's Muslims live today in religiously pluralistic societies. In countries where Muslims are the majority, the Muslim population is often divided among rival versions of Islam, and in some places non-Muslims form significant and powerful minorities. Moreover, one-third of the world's Muslims live as minorities in non-Muslim nations.[81] Notwithstanding the recent establishment of the caliphate (Islamic State, which most influential Muslim leaders believe is neither a state nor Islamic) and the gradual Islamization of other states, Islam's link to specific territories is progressively being severed. Islam is deterritorializing. In this situation, political Islam, with its goal of establishing a state based on Islamic law, is gradually becoming implausible. Not surprisingly, many people today embrace Islam as a universal religion of a transnational community at whose center is each person's appropriation of the religion.[82]

Will a personally embraced religion appropriate to a globalized world remain private and marginal? For some, it will. For them, religion will be either a communal practice, a way of life characteristic of a particular religious community, or a personal spirituality orienting their lives and infusing them with meaning. Yet, decoupled from the state, religion need not be privatized; emancipation of the state from religion doesn't spell the end of the political influence of religion. Because globalization pluralizes states internally and democratizes their citizenship, today just such individually embraced and personally appropriated religions are becoming increasingly publicly assertive.

The great opportunity for world religions today is to give up the self-betraying, violence-inducing, and futile dream of each in association with the state controlling public life and instead embrace social and political pluralism and the public role available to them (see chapters 3 and 4). In seizing this opportunity, globalization is their ally (even if in other regards it may be their rival). It is helping religions free themselves from the false alternatives of either being personal but publicly inconsequential or publicly significant but politically authoritarian. It is strengthening the possibility for religions to be personally appropriated, publicly engaged, and politically pluralistic all at the same time.

Religions and the Economy

In regard to religions' relation to political society and rule, globalization is nudging world religions to return to their original visions.

But in regard to religions' relation to health, wealth, longevity, and fertility, globalization may, conversely, be luring them to betray these visions. The temptation to turn into "political religions" is decreasing, but the temptation to morph into "prosperity religions" is increasing. Market-driven globalization is transforming the relationship of world religions to the economy, such that instead of denying the world in the name of transcendence they are turning transcendence into a means of affirming the world.

Earlier in this chapter, I made the case that world religions affirm and seek to enhance ordinary flourishing but do so by subordinating it to transcendent goals. To return to the example I used earlier, God blessed Job's "business" dealings and protected him from harm, but Job's attachment to God and integrity mattered to Job more than wealth and progeny, more even than health and life itself. Centuries later, in the early stages of the current market-driven phase of globalization, a similar relation between religion and material goods was on the books. It is not entirely clear what role Christian faith played in the emergence of a capitalist economy. The Protestant ethic might have given early capitalism some of its "spirit," the "inner-worldly asceticism" that imposed discipline both in work and in consumption, as Max Weber has argued.[83] Or Christian convictions about God's relation to the world may have, somewhat against their own grain, provided ideological underpinnings for the idea that one can achieve public benefits by giving free rein to certain private vices, like self-love.[84] If the Christian faith did give a boost to the capitalist economy, that boost occurred in the framework of the primacy of transcendent goals. Seventeenth-century Protestants, who are said to have given the "spirit" to capitalism, insisted that the heart must be "taken up with better things" than the acquisition of wealth. Following the words of the apostle, they considered "godliness" their main "gain" and material wealth its consequence, a sign of God's favor[85]—or at least so they claimed, thus allowing their religious convictions to put pressure on their economic pursuits.

The relationship between godliness and wealth, between the transcendent God and the mundane deity called "Mammon," wasn't stable, though. "Godliness as gain / wealth as sign" was always in danger of flipping into "wealth as gain / godliness as means," a position the apostle explicitly rejected, insisting that the main material gain of godliness lies in generating contentment (1 Timothy 6:5–6). Because world religions don't set ordinary life in opposition to transcendence but, rather, in the name of transcendence affirm the goodness of ordinary life, the temptation to turn religion into a maidservant of the economy was ever present. Over the past four centuries or so in the West, the temptation became irresistible to many. Concern with enhancing ordinary life gradually triumphed over attachment to the transcendent good (see chapter 1). Today, much of the engagement of religions with the economy is less about situating economic concerns within a vision of the good life marked by the primacy of transcendence and more about the contribution religions can make to economic progress.

Academically inclined religious advocates of the free market are keen to show that religions have resources essential for the smooth and efficient functioning of the market economy. A market economy needs virtues—trust, disciplined work, hope—and religions provide them, supplying "spiritual capital" or "managerial wisdom" to complement the requisite material, financial, and other social capital.[86] Miracle-obsessed preachers of "the prosperity gospel" promise not merely that God will empower people so they can make themselves prosperous, but that God will, according to a "proven wealth transfer system," hand over the wealth of the wicked to them.[87] Even adherents of world religions who reject the market economy and embrace a more socialist vision often link religion tightly to ordinary flourishing: many object not to the primacy of material wealth but to the means of achieving it (competitiveness and commodification) and bemoan its inequitable distribution (*everyone* should have a swimming pool!).[88] In none of these three examples is religion simply *reduced* to a means of ordinary flourishing, but in all of them ordinary flourishing has primacy.

Globalization is helping world religions resist the temptation to turn into "political religions," I argued in the previous section. At the same time, globalization is luring world religions into becoming "prosperity religions," religions bred for and harnessed to plow in the fields of ordinary human flourishing. With immense vigor, imagination, and success (on the whole), globalization proceeds under the assumption that what truly matters are the things of ordinary life— health, longevity, good and abundant food, many conveniences— and the pleasures these give. Religions are pulled into the vortex of market-driven globalization, offering themselves as means of achieving globalization's ends but without situating these ends within a broader account of human flourishing. Market-driven globalization is tempting religions to give up on their own deepest and most salutary insight and concern—an account of the good life whose focal point transcends the flat plane of mundane existence and its concerns for ordinary flourishing. Succumbing to this temptation, world religions give up on the most important contribution they can make in a globalized world: to foreground and pursue the questions of the character of truly flourishing life and of the ultimate goal of all our desires and loves.[89]

Clashing Globalizations?

In the first two chapters I have sketched a tension-laden, transformative, and potentially mutually enriching relation between world religions and globalization. Is this realistic? Doesn't each religion embody and promote a universal vision, claiming truth for itself and, in one way or another, seeking to become global? Doesn't market-driven globalization, too, embody a universal set of practices and convictions with a near-irresistible push to encompass the whole globe and permeate all spheres of life? Isn't each world religion bound to clash with others—and all of them ultimately to collide with the processes of globalization? When it comes to world religions and market-driven globalization, aren't we in fact dealing with competing global projects, in fact, with multiple competing religious and a-religious visions of globalization?

It is well known that the Marxist-inspired global vision was inimical to religions, persecuting them ruthlessly. Religions have also been inimical both to a-religious versions of globalization and to the global visions of other religions. The idea of the rule of God as the alternative to global empires goes as far back as the second century BC. According to the book of Daniel, the advent of the reign of God was to end the succession of empires with global aspirations culminating in Alexander the Great (Daniel 2, 7). Today, influential Muslims, for instance, think of Islam as the alternative to present-day market-driven globalization.[90] Some Christians, too, set "world Christianity" in contrast both to market-driven globalization and to its Muslim alternative.[91] Clearly, we have here competing universal visions.[92] Must these religious and a-religious visions of globalizations, and the people who espouse them, clash?[93]

To mitigate clashes of competing religious global visions, Wilfred Cantwell Smith, an influential Harvard scholar of religion of the previous generation, argued that the world community with social pluralism as its hallmark needs "a world theology." But why wouldn't a world theology exacerbate the problem by being just one additional universalism competing with others? Smith envisaged world theology emerging through dialogue in which "all the religions of the world" would participate.[94] Once formed, world theology wouldn't replace religions but articulate in a binding way their common core.

The world community would then have a single universally recognized theology lived concretely in distinct religions. Motivating the suggestion of a single world theology is a conviction analogous to the one that has guided the relations among religion, social norms, and sovereignty through much of human history: the three have to be integrated so that the social body can be united. Since the entire world has become one, a single universal "theology"—a kind of meta-worldview or "critical corporate self-consciousness"—has to provide a "collective representation" of its unity.[95]

It seems highly unlikely that any such world theology will emerge, certainly not any time soon. Adherents of world religions may see the need to reform their religion or to adapt it to new circumstances (indeed, this is what they ineluctably, even if often unconsciously, do), but very few will want to adhere to visions of human flourishing and common good in any way superordinate to their religions. Each world religion sees itself as an expression of ultimate commitments. A distillation of key commitments from all religions, putatively a core of them all, is unlikely to be more basic to adherents of religions than the religion from which they were distilled. That's the problem we would encounter if the distillation succeeded. Many are convinced, I believe rightly, that religions do not have a common core that could be distilled. A world theology is impossible.

Fortunately, a world theology is unnecessary. Here is why: the expectation that universal religions will inevitably clash rests on a sense, often not explicitly articulated, that religions are mutually exclusive, nontransparent, nontranslatable, and nonoverlapping cultural systems, balls that bump into each other but cannot occupy any shared space. But that's as little the case as is the case that they have a common core. Even though world religions have distinct metaphysical frameworks, readily distinguishable accounts of life worth living, and differing notions of the human predicament and of salvation,[96] they have, as I argued earlier, structural affinities and, equally important, they share some basic principles that guide human interaction, such as the commitment to truthfulness, justice, and compassion as well as the conviction that ethical norms apply universally, to coreligionists and outsiders. The document *A Common Word* is a good example of the kinds of overlaps I have in mind between the two largest and most opposed religions today: Christianity and Islam. Without in any way eliding the differences between these two religions, the document, endorsed by many globally influential leaders of both religions, argues that what binds them together is common commitment to love God and neighbor.[97] According to the document, the two religions disagree in many respects but agree in many others, particularly on the significant attributes of God and especially on the principles that guide human interaction. Overlaps among world religions in convictions yield nothing like "the world theology" or "the global worldview," but these religions' common convictions can underpin a set of global rules and commitments necessary for global order, civility, and the pursuit of common good. Within such a global order, adherents of world religions can be assertive in promoting their visions of human flourishing and yet live in peace with one another and with a-religious people. Religions would then "compete with one another," not only in "good works," as the famous verse in the Qur'an puts it (5:48),[98] but also in visions of the good life. They would then be able both to enrich each other and to help shape globalization.

The remainder of this book is an exploration of how adherents of world religions can live in peace with one another and with nonreligious people while robustly advocating their own visions of flourishing. For world religions to settle for less—either to seek to impose visions of flourishing on others with violence or to retreat into privacy and not strive for the global common good—would be to betray themselves and malfunction in the world.[99]

Part Two

3
Mindsets of Respect,
Regimes of Respect

R eligious intolerance is on the march, with both state and non-
state actors involved on a massive scale. That's bad news—
and not just for those individuals and communities on the receiving end of antipathy, discrimination, and persecution. In today's
intermingled and interdependent world of vibrant and assertive religions, that's bad news for just about everyone. Religious intolerance
is a global security risk, not just a personal or communal tragedy.[1] To
address the problem, we need to change culture and rearrange political institutions.

Recent reports on the freedom of religion and respect for religious
differences consistently note "negative trends" that "cut across national and regional boundaries."[2] Here is a sampling of the findings:

- 46 percent of the world's population live in countries with
  high or very high levels of social hostility involving religion.
- Almost 75 percent of the world's roughly 7 billion people
  live in countries with high levels of government restriction
  of freedom of religion.
- "In nearly 33 percent of countries, individuals were assaulted
  or displaced from their homes in retaliation for specific re-

ligious activities considered offensive or threatening to the majority religion, including preaching and other forms of religious expression."

- "In 30 percent of countries, religion-related terrorist groups were active in recruitment or fundraising."[3]

It is well known that anti-Semitism, in the restricted sense of hatred of Jews, is widespread. It is perhaps less known that Christians are the leading target of persecution and discrimination globally, with Muslims a close second.[4] *Islamophobia,* a cumbersome and imprecise term, has now been joined by the even more cumbersome *Christianophobia*—and for good reason. In the British *Report of the All Party Parliamentary Group on International Religious Freedom* (2013), we read: "It is estimated that there are at least 250 million Christians suffering persecution today, from harassment, intimidation and imprisonment to torture and execution."[5] In terms of numbers, that's as if the entire population of Brazil and Argentina combined were under persecution; and that's one persecuted Christian out of every eight or nine. Perhaps to a lesser degree than Christians, adherents of all religions are "under attack"—from adherents of rival religions or of rival versions of the same religion, from antireligious exclusivist humanists, and from states that identify with any of these groups.

Religions are under attack in part because they themselves attack, because the intolerant attitudes and practices that each religion often inspires keep the spiral of animosity toward all religions turning. As I will argue shortly, world religions have internal resources to affirm and promote the freedom of other religions and a-religions and to embrace pluralism as a political project. But first we need to stay a bit longer with religious intolerance.

And the Intolerance Prize Goes to . . .

Imagine an international prize for the most intolerant religion. Which one would win? As a jury, imagine critics of religion, past and present. In the minds of most such critics, all religions would be good candidates because all are blindly irrational and, therefore, irredeemably intolerant. Among religions, the world religions, which affirm a single true vision of the good life for all humanity, would quickly rise to the top, as they seem to stand for what the sociologist Pierre Bourdieu has called the "imperialism of the universal."[6] The Abrahamic religions—Judaism, Christianity, and Islam—might end up leading the pack, since they ground the single truth about the good life in an affirmation of the unassailable rule of the one true God. Given their history and prevalence, Christianity and Islam might end up as the two chief contenders. Christianity could be pronounced the winner for having sought to impose itself relentlessly on everyone under the guise of general benevolence, especially after the discovery of the Americas and in the trail of colonization, which is to say since the beginning of the present form of globalization. Or the jury of religious critics might award the perverse prize to Islam, a religion that many of its current detractors envisage as a blindfolded man with a scimitar in hand, as one Danish cartoonist infamously depicted its founder in 2006.

Religious people, prone to disparage their rivals, often join religion's critics. Many Christians believe that whereas Christianity is a religion of love and freedom, Islam is a religion of obedience and violence, with a fierce and irrational deity at its center demanding unconditional submission. Pope Benedict XVI made a tamer version of this charge in his famous 2006 Regensburg address, contrasting the Christian God of reason and love with the Muslim God of will and coercion.[7] Some Muslims return the compliment. I was in the audience when the former prime minister of Malaysia, Mahathir Mohamad, delivered a lecture in Kuala Lumpur to some three thousand Christians in which he argued that, as the divinely commanded genocide of the ancient Canaanites and its echoes throughout history attest, both Judaism and Christianity are more violent than Islam.[8] For their part, Buddhists boast of espousing the most tolerant of world religions, yet in places like Sri Lanka and Burma, Buddhism has turned intolerant and violent, as Hindu, Christian, and Muslim citizens of these countries are quick to point out.[9]

It may seem that, in contrast to the world religions, globalization itself, in its present-day market-driven form, isn't even a contender for the intolerance prize. Doesn't it spread freedom and toleration throughout the planet? Doesn't it help create pluralistic societies wherein people of multiple religions and a-religions inhabit the same social and political spaces? Isn't it resonant with a culture of expressive individualism whose basic rule of social interaction is that preferences in ways of living are almost as unassailable as choices of consumer goods? According to this rule, the values of each person are of his or her own choosing, and each is entitled to do his or her own thing provided no harm is done to others. The idea isn't that *anything* goes. As Charles Taylor pointed out, the rule articulates a firm though simpleminded moral obligation: "One shouldn't criticize others' values, because they have a right to live their own life as you do. The sin that is not tolerated is intolerance."[10] That's tolerance pushed to the limit and embraced as a moral ideal—with seeds of intolerance beginning to sprout.

Many today—and not just people of religious faith—experience globalization as deeply intolerant and even coercive, though less in the way a person is considered intolerant and more in the way a powerful machine might be thought of as "intolerant": it does its own thing with disregard for its effects on people and their cherished ways of life. As I have noted in chapter 1, Karl Marx remarked, with approval, on this aspect of globalization in his own time: it causes "uninterrupted disturbance of all social conditions"; "all fixed, fast-frozen relations, with their train of ancient and venerable prejudices and opinions, are swept away, all new-formed ones become antiquated before they can ossify"; in its trail "all that is solid melts into air, all that is holy is profaned."[11] Marx exaggerated, but he didn't utterly distort. Though not closed to innovation, world religions nonetheless live in traditions, rituals, and habituated practices, and they depend on a sense of the sacred. With impersonal and systemically generated disregard, globalization eats away at all these features of world religions, pushing them into painful resistances and transformations—and, as we have seen in chapter 2, opening new possibilities for their self-articulation.

A soft relativism of doing one's own thing and letting others do theirs is an echo in cultural sensibilities and philosophical arguments of a world in which "solid things" have largely melted and "holy things" have been profaned. World religions stand in deep tension with important aspects of the "intolerance of intolerance," a moral stance reinforced by present globalization processes. Granted, versions of world religions—some modern forms of Buddhism and Christianity, for instance—embrace soft relativism and see themselves primarily as healing and energizing spiritualities rather than substantive articulations of the good life. These forms of religion, often intentionally bricolaged and marketed, are in part a result of globalization. Still, by and large world religions continue to make universal claims, valid for everyone (the "solid"), about a way of life rooted in the primacy of the transcendent realm (the "holy"). They can neither affirm others' alternative values as true "for them" nor be indifferent toward these values. To make universal claims about what is holy is to make assessments, positive and negative, and to call people, implicitly or explicitly, to the right path. A certain form of intolerance—the intolerance of naming wrongheadedness, whether with regard to individual moral decisions or with regard to comprehensive accounts of the good life—is a positive good, according to world religions. From their perspective, intolerance of all intolerance is both wrong and, well, intolerant. That was the main thrust of Pope Benedict XVI's critique of the "dictatorship of relativism,"[12] to give one influential contemporary example.

In sum, taut tension marks the relation between world religions and globalization in regard to toleration. Globalization pushes against religions' rootedness in tradition, embrace of the sacred, and affirmation of universal ethical norms that exceed the right to do one's own thing as long as others are not harmed. Religions, on the other hand, resist globalization's corroding of traditions, its undermining of a sense of the sacred, and its paving of the way for soft relativism.

We have, then, two key issues in regard to world religions and toleration in the context of globalization. One concerns toleration among religions and the other toleration between the culture of "soft relativism" and religions. We can break down these two related issues into three main questions. First, can adherents of a world religion learn to respect adherents of other religious and humanistic ways of life even while strenuously disagreeing with them? Second, can adherents of world religions embrace freedom of religion and a-religion and support pluralistic democracy? Finally, can democracies be "religion friendly"—set up such that they are equally fair to religious as to a-religious ways of life—and therefore genuinely pluralistic?

I will address each of these questions separately in the course of this chapter, but first I will take them up together by examining what is likely the most influential Western text about toleration, John Locke's *Letter Concerning Toleration* (1689). Though Locke was a famous philosopher and a progenitor of political liberalism, his arguments in the *Letter* are predominantly theological; he makes a religious rather than a secular case for religious toleration. Moreover, as the first sentence of the *Letter* states, his main concern is to promote "mutual toleration" among adherents of rival versions of Christianity;[13] limiting the power of the state is an important but secondary concern. More than three centuries later, we all, Christians and non-Christians, may still profit from revisiting his arguments.[14]

Toleration

Though the *Letter* came off the press in London in 1689, Locke had composed it four years earlier, at the end of 1685, in Holland. On October 18, 1685, the French king Louis XIV decreed, "We forbid our subjects of the P. R. R. [Reformed Church] to meet any more for the exercise of the said religion in any place or private house, under any pretext whatever."[15] With this decree, Protestants in predominantly Catholic France lost all religious and civic liberties that Henry IV, grandfather of Louis XIV, had granted them with the Edict of Nantes (1598). After the revocation of the edict, four hundred thousand Protestants fled France; many who stayed were imprisoned or killed. This bout of persecution in France wasn't an isolated incident; it came at the tail end of 150 years of wars of religion in Europe.[16]

Most Protestants in the sixteenth and seventeenth centuries shared with Catholics the dual conviction that "the membership of the church was coextensive with membership in the commonwealth and that it was the duty of a 'godly prince' to promote and support the true religion."[17] By extension, the unity of the state was thought to require religious unity. Those with erroneous religious beliefs (heretics) and those who separated from the main religious community (schismatics) could not be tolerated. If either persisted in wayward ways, a Christian magistrate, guided by bishops or ministers, had the duty to coerce them back into the fold. Thus, when Latin Christendom started dividing along sectarian lines after the Reformation, concerns for political unity catalyzed persecutions and wars of religion.

In contrast to the prevalent view, Locke expected the peace of the commonwealth to come not from a uniformity of religious beliefs and practices but from the people's confidence in the commonwealth to protect both their civil interests and their right to choose and abide by their religious convictions. He argued, moreover, that religious intolerance was predicated on a mistaken interpretation of the Christian faith polluted by a desire for political domination. Here is how he argued his case.

First, the key mark of the Christian faith is love of neighbor: "charity, meekness, and goodwill in general towards all mankind, even to those that are not Christians."[18] No matter what other virtues a Christian may possess, without love he or she is not a true Christian. Both Locke and his opponents agreed on this, in principle. They disagreed, though, as to whether love was compatible with coercion in matters of religion. Since Augustine, the argument for coercion rested in its correctional value[19] (and on the flimsy scriptural pillar of a master in one of Jesus's parables commanding his servants to compel street people to attend his great banquet because the original invitees had better things to do).[20] Locke disagreed, considering it implausible that the "infliction of torments and exercise of all manner of cruelties" could ever be an expression of love.[21] Religious intolerance is, therefore, incompatible with genuine love.

But had not Locke made the task too easy for himself, setting up a straw man only to knock him down? What if we were indeed to reject "torments" and "cruelties" as incompatible with love but instead practiced milder forms of coercion, like obliging people by law to attend church? If mild forms of coercion brought people to faith, would they not be compatible with love? That's where Locke's second argument for religious toleration comes in. It rests on the character of human beings' relation to God, on the nature of faith in God and love for God: "True and saving religion consists in the inward persuasion of the mind, without which nothing can be acceptable to God. And such is the nature of the understanding, that it cannot be

compelled to belief of anything by outward force."[22] Given that we
cannot change deep convictions at will, a coerced belief is necessarily
a "false" one and, therefore, unacceptable to God.

Locke's argument that it is epistemically impossible and religiously
hypocritical to be forced to believe what we don't gets him only half-
way to where he wants to go. Let's assume for a moment that with
mild pressure and over a period of time we could induce a person
to alter his or her actual persuasions, as Augustine had argued more
than a millennium earlier and as Locke's insightful critic Jonas Proast
has insisted as well.[23] For Locke, that would be unacceptable, and the
reason he gives is the key to his larger argument for toleration: one
must not abdicate responsibility for the basic course of one's life and
for one's eternal destiny to another human being. He writes: "No
man can so far abandon the care of his own salvation as blindly to
leave it to the choice of any other, whether prince or subject, to prescribe to him what faith or worship he shall embrace."[24] People are
God's "workmanship" and God's "property," as he puts it in the *Second Treatise,* and therefore responsible to God for the basic direction
of their lives.[25] It is "an injury" for a "force from a stronger hand
to bring a man to a religion which another thinks the true."[26] With
regard to faith and the way of life associated with it, Locke argued
that no human being has either the capacity or the authority to coerce
someone else either to stay in or adopt a religion.

Finally, Locke argued for the separation of church and state, a consequence of the nature of faith and the responsibility of each for the
course of his or her own life. As evident from the New Testament,
the church concerns itself with the worship of God and regulates
people's lives "according to the rules of virtues and piety"; its tools
are the persuasive word and "exemplary holiness."[27] The state, on the
other hand, concerns itself with "civil interests"; its tools are "the
sword" and "other instruments of force."[28] When church separates
from state, the state transforms from a religiously monolithic and

partisan entity to a religiously pluralistic and neutral entity. Moreover, on theological grounds Locke insisted that there is "absolutely
no such thing under the Gospel as a Christian commonwealth."[29]
The consequence? All citizens—pagans and Jews no less than Christians of different denominations, though not Catholics, Muslims, and
atheists—should have equal civic rights.[30]

Locke offers what is a classic Christian case for the mutual toleration of people of faith. In the remainder of this chapter I propose to
improve on it. I will endorse his account of toleration of religion and
expand it to include freedom of conscience, which is to say freedom
for nontheists and atheists as well; I will recast his account of the separation of church and state, doing away with his proscription against
using in public debates reasons derived from positive revelation. Like
Locke, I will address both the problem of intolerance as it inheres in
religion's attitudes and, secondarily, as it manifests itself in the *state's
use of power*. But unlike Locke, I will advocate not just for freedom
of religion but for *respect* for some aspects of religions other than
our own and as well as for *toleration* of the aspects of religions we
find ourselves unable to respect—neither of which stances precludes
moral rejection or even legal proscription of what is intolerable. Correspondingly, my concern will be the positive appreciation of other
religions rather than the mere absence of coercion. In a word, my
theme is respect—respect for persons of other religions and a measure of respect for the religions to which they adhere.

As in the rest of the book, and like Locke himself, I will write from
a Christian standpoint and give a Christian take on a matter on which
each world religion (even each of its rival versions) will have its own
perspective. But unlike Locke, I write not for Christians alone, explor-
ing only what it would mean for Christians to respect people of other
religions; rather, I propose a mindset of respect embedded in a regime
of freedom that, I suggest, has independent grounding in other world
religions and that, I hope, will find resonance among their adherents.

Freedom of Religion

Today, adherents of world religions and secularists alike mostly speak of the freedom of religion as a human right. The global spread of thinking about freedom of religion in terms of rights is largely the legacy of the Universal Declaration of Human Rights (1948). Its eighteenth article reads: "Everyone has the right to freedom of thought, conscience and religion; this right includes freedom to change his religion or belief, and freedom, either alone or in community with others and in public or private, to manifest his religion or belief in teaching, practice, worship and observance."[31] The article offers a classic articulation of the *right* of every person to retain or adopt, to stay away from or abandon, any religion. The language of rights here implies (1) that by virtue of their humanity, all persons have the capacity to give basic direction to their own lives, and (2) that we wrong them if we hinder them in exercising that capacity by forcing a religion upon them or preventing them from practicing the religion of their choice. This is the argument for freedom of religion based on human dignity, formulated under the influence of Immanuel Kant: each human being has equal dignity and we must respect the autonomy of each, especially as concerns the capacity of each to direct his or her own life.[32] Many adherents of world religions—those, for instance, who believe that human beings have inviolable dignity because God created them and loves them—will be able to embrace this argument for freedom of religion. But another way is open to them as well, based on the way religion requires to be embraced. Let me sketch it by returning briefly to Locke.

In the *Letter* Locke notes in passing that the "liberty of conscience is every man's natural right,"[33] but he doesn't do much with this claim. Writing the *Letter* as a religious man and to a religious audience, he prefers arguments more directly related to the character of the Christian faith. As we have seen, much of his case rests on the conviction that faith is an inward persuasion and personal responsibility and thus should not be externally foisted on a person. At this point, a critic may raise an eyebrow out of suspicion that Locke might be importing "inward persuasion" into the Christian faith from outside. Locke has in mind a lone individual, before God, heeding the voice of his or her conscience alone. But such a person, a critic might contend, is the product of the individualism emerging along with early market-driven globalization,[34] in which people and their relations are roughly modeled to fit market exchanges. Locke himself was dubbed one of the progenitors of some such individualism.[35] Is "faith" practiced as inward persuasion and personal responsibility a cultural innovation influenced by the incipient form of market-driven globalization?

The eyebrow can safely come down. From the very beginning, Christians have insisted on the need to embrace faith with free inner conviction (though they identified the character of the agent of freedom differently than do the cultures of the modern West). The Apostle Paul wrote that "one believes with the heart," which is to say not by mere outward conformity to ambient influences or in reaction to dictates backed by force but with the very core of one's being (Romans 10:10).[36] Arguing against the persecution of Christians in ancient Rome, Tertullian, an early church father (160–220), wrote, "It is unjust to compel freemen against their will" to engage in religious rituals, for the gods "can have no desire of offerings from the unwilling."[37] This perspective informed the Edict of Milan (313), which granted "to all men freedom to follow whatever religion each one wished" because the "supreme deity" is served only with "free minds."[38] By its very nature, faith is a free act; a coerced faith is no faith at all. Both early and contemporary Christians agree on this point. Just for that reason, many reject a centuries-long hiatus in Christian affirmations of religious freedom.[39]

Freedom of religion isn't a specifically Christian value, of course.[40]

Though Buddhists, like Christians, have not consistently embraced and practiced freedom of religion throughout history, the Buddha himself taught it explicitly. He, like the representatives of the Christian tradition later on, stressed that each person is to make a decision as to what "lead[s] to welfare and happiness" and to follow that course in life:

Do not go by oral tradition,

by lineage of teaching,

by hearsay,

by a collection of scriptures,

by logical reasoning,

by inferential reasoning,

by reflection on reasons,

by the acceptance of a view after pondering it,

by the seeming competence of a speaker,

or because you think, "the ascetic is our teacher."

But when you know for yourselves, "These things are unwholesome, these things are blamable; these things are censured by the wise; these things, if undertaken and practiced, lead to harm and suffering," then you should abandon them. . . .

But when you know for yourselves, "These things are wholesome, these things are blameless; these things are praised by the wise; these things, if undertaken and practiced, lead to welfare and happiness," then you should engage in them.[41]

Like historic Christianity, Hinduism, and Buddhism, Islam is ambivalent about religious freedom. Consider the famous affirmation of the freedom of religion in the Qur'an—as robust an affirmation as any in the Buddhist, Jewish, or Christian sacred texts: "There is no compulsion in religion: Truth stands out clear from Error: whoever rejects evil and believes in Allah hath grasped the most trustworthy hand-hold, that never breaks" (al-Baqarah, 2:256). Now, many great Muslim teachers have argued that the verse doesn't actually forbid forcing people to embrace Islam, it merely states that there is *no need* for compulsion because Islam's truth is self-evident.[42] Others, however, read the verse to mean that there *should be* no compulsion in religion. Building his case partly on this verse, the great Persian scholar Fakhr al-Din al-Razi (1149–1209) argued that compulsion in matters of religion is not only unnecessary but is actually contrary to the nature of religion itself: "God has not built faith upon compulsion and pressure but on acceptance and free choice."[43] Many contemporary Muslim leaders, like Fethullah Gülen, echo al-Razi's interpretation.[44]

As Christian, Buddhist, and Muslim stances toward freedom of religion illustrate, world religions are ambivalent regarding freedom of religion:[45] they affirm freedom of religion, yet they also seek—or have historically sought—to curtail it as well. But to the extent that world religions do share the formal features I have identified in chapter 2, their more basic stance is affirmation of the freedom of religion rather than its denial. Here's why.

World Religions and the Freedom of Religion

Consider the following "deduction" of religious freedom based on the primacy of the individual and the stress on truth and universality in world religions.

- A world religion addresses itself essentially to individual persons; all persons are summoned to respond to a transcendent call and either to leave a network of relations in which they are embedded, joining a transnational religious community, or to appropriate it for themselves if it comes from within the community of their origin.

- Each world religion asserts that the way of life to which it calls a person is true—not merely in the sense of being appropriate for that person or for some group of people, but true universally, for all human beings at all times and places, designed to guide every person to fulfillment as a human being (which doesn't imply either that there is only one way to express a given religion's truth about the way of life or that all other religions are utterly devoid of truth).

- In issuing the call to individuals to embrace the true way of life, a world religion tacitly assumes that each person has both a capacity to espouse a way of life and a basic responsibility for the kind of life he or she leads; just as nobody can be born or die in place of another person, so nobody can assume responsibility for the basic direction of another person's life between birth and death.

- To have responsibility for the basic direction of one's life, a person must in fact be free to make decisions about the way of life he or she ought to lead and to act on them; this isn't merely freedom to embrace a set of convictions but the freedom to lead a way of life, and it isn't merely freedom to adopt a way of life but the freedom to adhere or not to adhere to the adopted way of life at any point in the course of one's life. Anything less would conflict with the basic personal responsibility for the direction of one's life.

- For a world religion, all other freedoms pale in significance when compared to the freedom to embrace or not to embrace a religion. For freedom of religion isn't about being uncoerced in doing this or that individual thing in the course of a life but about being at liberty to set that course of life itself,

about determining for oneself what sort of life is worth living and embarking upon it in response to a transcendent call.

The deduction of religious freedom I have offered here is based
not on respect for human dignity and on "personal autonomy" but on
*the sovereignty of the transcendent call and the responsibility of human
beings to heed it.* The argument is not original. As I have explained,
Locke, too, employed it.[46] More, the argument isn't specifically Christian. It is genuinely Islamic as well, for instance. Dabusi (d. 1039), a
prominent Muslim jurist, argued that all human beings, without exception, have rights, including the right to the free exercise of religion, because they are "responsible to fulfill the 'rights of God,'"—
that is, to worship and obey God.[47]

If this argument is correct, a world religion that curtails the freedom of religion is in deep tension with itself, and it may even be self-
contradictory. A world religion affirms freedom to embrace the true
religion, which it considers itself to be, but not freedom to leave it
and embrace another. Most Christians have endorsed this position
for a millennium and a half, many of them all the way to the middle
of the twentieth century, and most Muslims do so even today. Or
a world religion follows the rule "freedom for me but not for thee"—
as when adherents of a religion protest against being persecuted in
states where they are a minority but persecute their rivals where they
are a majority. English Puritans are a good example: they protested the
intolerance in seventeenth-century England and eventually fled from
it, only to institute a regime of intolerance in New England where
they settled.[48]

What explains this inconsistency in the teachings and practices of
world religions? First, the *stance toward truth.* A world religion considers itself true, a way of life that gives fulfillment and, for some religions, secures everlasting life in heavenly bliss. To grant freedom to
all religions would seem irresponsible: how can we believe a religion

is true and its way of life is the best and then let people harm themselves by abandoning it?[49] We can remove this reason for the tension between freedom and compulsion if we affirm that adhering to
a religion consists both in an inner embrace of a truthful way of life
and in an outer alignment of behavior with the truth embraced. Now,
conviction is impossible to force, but if we force practice in hopes that
the conviction will follow, two things result: persons are compelled to
disregard the transcendent call in their lives as it concerns practices,
and their religion turns into playacting—in theistic terms, the God
of the intolerant, like the master in Hegel's master-slave dialectic, ob-
tains mere conformity but no genuine recognition.[50] It follows that
freedom to embrace religion as a way of life isn't an optional extra
added on to practicing that way of life; freedom to embrace and hold
onto religion *is a constitutive component of a religion's way of life* without which that very way of life is fundamentally compromised. For
world religions, freedom of religion is a key substantive good.

If so, why are world religions so willing to cut a leg off the very
stool on which they are sitting? Because of their *stance toward a political community and the dynamics of its power,* the second reason for
tension between freedom and compulsion. As I argued in chapter 2,
a distinction between "salvation" and "rule" and therefore between
a religious and a political community is a key feature of world religions.[51] Yet, because they emerged out of and for centuries lived in
settings in which religious community was nearly coextensive with
political community and in which people believed that no political
order was possible without a single religion giving it unity, world religions have tended to erase lines of demarcation between religious
and political communities.[52] This is true of Judaism in the preexilic
period,[53] of Buddhism at various stages in its history, of Christianity
after Constantine, and of Islam after the immigration to Medina and
the conquest of Mecca. Devout rulers took on the responsibility to
enforce religious conformity so as to assure internal political cohe-

sion; heresy and apostasy were deemed treasonous and were often punishable by death. Still, even under these conditions, the world religions could not simply discard the affirmation of the freedom of religion, a constitutive value for them. They felt compelled to make state coercion in matters of religion somehow compatible with freedom of religion. As in the case of Augustine, they often argued that outer compulsion helps generate inner conviction.[54]

Apostasy and Conversion

Today, some of the fiercest clashes among world religions concern abandoning one's religion (apostasy) and embracing another (conversion). In India, for instance, Hindus are incensed about losing adherents to Buddhism, Christianity, and Islam; in Burma and Sri Lanka, Buddhists fear losing adherents to Christianity and Islam; from Indonesia to Mauritania, Muslims are angry with, as they see it, Christians luring people into abandoning the true religion. In all these countries and many more, laws prohibiting apostasy and conversion to another religion are on the books. More insidiously, vigilantes, often with the approval of law enforcement agents, go after proselytizers, apostates, and converts alike.

Apostasy is a particularly critical issue in the relations between Christianity and Islam, the two most widespread religions, both characterized by a strong missionary impulse but, presently, holding opposing stances toward apostasy.[55] Prince Ghazi bin Muhammad, the chief advisor to King Abdullah II of Jordan for religious and cultural affairs, named "fear and resentment of the massive missionary movement launched from the West into the Islamic world" as one of the top three roots of tensions in Muslim-Christian relations—immediately after the conflict in Israel/Palestine and the then raging war in Iraq.[56] Christian mission is war by other means: soldiers attack Muslim bodies and territories with sophisticated weapons, and missionaries attack Muslim souls and ways of living with carefully designed evangelism techniques backed by material inducements.[57]

The stance makes sense if conversion is a causal act, with one person *making* another person switch allegiance. It is nearly inescapable if the relation between religion and rule is tight, in which case converting to another religion comes close to committing treason. As I argued in chapter 2, world religions, including Islam, can be interpreted (and have plausibly been interpreted) as being not "political religions," in the sense of merging with a political community, but instead as carriers of a universally true message addressed to all human beings, all of whom are deemed responsible for their ultimate allegiance and the basic orientation of their lives. If a world religion sees itself in those terms, it will reject any practice of conversion that involves *forcing* someone to embrace a religion or to make merely an outward appearance of doing so. An authentic shift in ultimate allegiance cannot be a mere effect of an external cause; it must be an inner response to a transcendent call. And what holds true for embracing a religion also applies to remaining within a religion.

Seen in such a way, a world religion that forcibly prevents a person from embracing another religion and compels a person to remain in a religion unwillingly is inconsistent. When Christians punished apostates and heretics, as they did for much of Christianity's history, the Christian faith itself was divided. When Muslims insist, as many still do, that "once a person accepts Islam out of his free will he is not allowed to leave it," Islam, too, at is at odds with itself.[58] If religion is to be embraced freely, that free choice must obtain throughout the religious life of a person, not just at its beginning.

As a rule, adherents of world religions celebrate conversions to their own religion. From their vantage point, the converts have left the darkness of error and stepped into the light of greater truth. For that same reason, most adherents of world religions will be displeased with defections to another religion. They will want to defend their claims to truth against challengers and persuade their coreligionists not to apostatize, effectively exchanging truth for error. It may seem that anticonversion laws backed by the coercive power of the state could serve the same purpose: to protect not so much a religion but those who adhere to it. Yet, when religions coerce members into remaining faithful, they act both against the conscience of individual members and against their own fundamental convictions—provided that I am correct in stating that freedom in embracing a religion is a substantive good for world religions.

Perhaps it is possible to make an even stronger argument. World religions don't just have a stake in neutralizing the lure of what they deem to be their rivals' errors and half truths; they also have a stake in hearing and reflecting on the rivals' witness. World religions are, of course, missionary religions, some more so, others less so. They have a message for the whole of humanity; it is a religious duty of Buddhists, Christians, and Muslims to bear witness to their religion (though less so of Jews, Hindus, and Confucians). But adherents of world religions are more than witnesses to truth; they are also seekers of truth, or at least they should be. Rare are those who claim that their religion is true because they happen to be its adherents; most believe that they embrace a religion because it is true. At least implicitly, then, they all have an interest in the truth claims of all religions and therefore in the freedom of the adherents of those religions to bear witness to these truths. For instance, as a Christian I want to hear Jews explain to me that by worshipping Christ I am committing idolatry and to call me to true worship of the God of Abraham and Sarah; they nudge me to reexamine whether what I think is true isn't in fact a kind of fundamental error I am strongly committed to avoiding (unconscious embrace of polytheism). I could deem the challenge to my worship of Christ as an act of aggression, against me and against what I consider holy. Some Christians do. But provided I am free to continue worshipping Christ if I am not persuaded by the arguments of others, I may equally well experience the challenge to faith in Christ as an act of care for me and part of the joint struggle for truthfulness in what matters the most. To be respected as a human being endowed with the responsibility for my own moral identity and for deciding for myself the meaning and direction of my life, I have to be both free to bear witness and willing to receive it.[59]

Securing freedom to witness to one's own religion and to accept the witness of another is only the first step in dealing with the problem of apostasy and conversion. The next is a common code of conduct while bearing witness.[60] Since in all world religions some version of the Golden Rule is central to their moral code, I have argued in *Allah: A Christian Response* that it should serve as the basis for an ethics of witness. In the version Jesus gave it, the Golden Rule is universal in application: "In *everything*, do to others as you would have them do to you" (Matthew 7:12). "Everything" includes witness. Two basic rules follow: (1) bear witness to your religion in the way you believe others should witness to you, and (2) as you bear witness to your own religion, be prepared to let others witness to you.[61] The two rules don't state everything we need to know about the shape of responsible witness, but they do invite us to discern what it means to relate appropriately to another person whose claim to respect equals ours.

So far I have argued that the world religions ought to affirm freedom of religion—freedom to embrace or abandon religion, freedom to live it out publicly, freedom to bear witness to it; such affirmation is, arguably, a key substantive good for world religions. To grant this freedom is to respect people. But when we bear witness to our own religion to an adherent of another, aren't we disrespecting the other's religion, especially if we consider it untrue and wrongheaded? And doesn't such disrespect of religion redound to the person who espouses it?

Respecting Persons, Respecting Convictions

Respect for freedom of religion is a form of respect for persons and for their sovereignty in determining their way of life, regardless of whether or not we respect that way of life itself. *Respect for a religion* is respect for that way of life itself and for a set of convictions that undergirds and expresses it.[62] These two kinds of respect presuppose a distinction between the persons engaging in a way of life and the character of that way of life. To determine whether it is possible to respect people without respecting their religions we need to decide whether it makes sense to distinguish clearly between persons and their convictions, practices, and the basic orientation of their lives— or, in short, between "persons" and "work." We can then turn to an exploration of whether it is possible to respect a religion we find mistaken and, if it is, what such respect might look like.

The distinction between "person" and "work" is common in the Western philosophical tradition. On the basis of his notion of human dignity, Immanuel Kant gave this distinction its paradigmatic expression. All human beings have equal dignity, he argued, and therefore they deserve equal respect. The reason? All are capable of directing their lives as guided by rational principles. He didn't mean that human beings have dignity and deserve respect because they actually *make* rational choices; instead, they have dignity because of their *capacity* to do so. With regard to the capacity for rational choice ("person"), all humans have equal dignity, the virtuous no less than the vicious, the devils no less than the deacons; by virtue of this capacity, all of them, along with their exercise of that capacity, *deserve* equal respect.[63] It is different, though, regarding the content of the choices they actually make ("work"). The content of their choices must *earn* our respect by its quality.

Critics argue that the distinction between person and work is artificial and strained. Persons are responsible for their work, they note.

Persons' works aren't separate from themselves; they "stick" to their doers and qualify their identities. People somehow *are* their work—and are especially so when the work concerned is decisions about the direction of their entire lives—indeed, about their moral identity. How could we then respect people without respecting the content of their choices? Bad fruit comes from a bad tree, and neither seems to deserve respect.

Though the distinction between person and work may sometimes sit uneasily with us, most of us in fact make it, especially in regard to those we love. In Shakespeare's *Measure for Measure* Isabella pleads before the judge for the life of Claudio, her brother, urging him to condemn Claudio's fault but not Claudio himself.[64] She wants clemency, and to grant it is to separate the doer from the deed, the person from the work. This basic insight about the nature of love lies at the heart of the distinction between person and work in the Christian tradition. Martin Luther (1483–1546), the fierce German Protestant reformer under whose indirect sway two and a half centuries later Immanuel Kant would formulate his notion of human dignity, believed that it would be unworthy of a loving God to love human beings on account of their noble deeds or fail to love them on account of their dastardly ones. God loves and therefore creates human beings; and God loves created human beings just because they exist. At the same time, because God loves each human being unconditionally, God cannot love that which harms human beings. Hence God condemns wrongdoing and does so because of his love for all human beings, saints and sinners alike.[65] In loving fallen and fallible human beings, we distinguish person from work.

The distinction between person and work may seem specifically Christian, at odds with religions that center less on redemption through God's undeserved grace than on excellence in human practices. Take Islam as an example. In the Qur'an God is frequently said not to love certain kinds of people: "the disbelievers" (al-Rum, 30:45), "the aggressors" (al-Baqarah, 2:190), "the treacherous" (al-Anfal, 8:58), and "the evildoers" (al-Shura, 42:40). Rather than God disapproving of wrongful deeds while still loving the persons who commit them, here persons who have committed evil deeds becomes evildoers undeserving of God's love. Yet in a magisterial work, *Love in the Holy Qur'an,* Ghazi bin Muhammad argues that "God does not say—and in fact never says—that He does not love them [such human beings] *as people,* but rather that He does not love them *in so far as they are identified with* (and identify themselves with) *certain unlovable traits.*"[66] Thus Islam, too, can distinguish between relating to people *as people* (person) and relating to people *as doers of certain deeds* (work). As in the Christian faith, the distinction is rooted in the affirmation of God's love, in the fact that God, as Ghazi bin Muhammad puts it, "created human beings *out of* His Mercy and *for* His Mercy."[67] He concludes that, like God, "people should . . . hate certain evil deeds, but not hate people as such, even when they commit these evil deeds."[68]

The general principle of respect is this: we respect persons by virtue of their humanity, but we respect their work—their actions, convictions, character, and basic orientation—by virtue of its excellence. Formulated in terms of recipients rather than givers of respect, the principle is this: we can *claim* respect for ourselves as persons, but we must *earn* respect for our work. Applied to the relation between world religions, the principle of respect states that we must respect adherents of a religion irrespective of whether we respect that religion itself; for the religion to be respected, it must first earn our respect by its excellence, at least in some regard. If not, we may end up merely tolerating it, provided we have reasons for doing so, or we may be obliged to reject it and insist that it cannot be tolerated without reforming some of its practices.[69] Mostly we will end up somewhere between respect and toleration—we will respect some aspects of a religion and tolerate others.

Respecting Other Religions

The need for a religion to earn the respect it receives creates a difficulty. Most people crave being respected not just in their bare humanity but also in the basic orientation of their lives. As I noted earlier, they feel that, in a significant way, they *are* this orientation and the set of convictions, practices, and rituals expressing it. Respect for their most significant "work"—for the exercise of their most significant freedom—is a condition of respect for them as persons. A Christian may feel disrespected when a Jew or a Muslim deems him or her an idolater for affirming Christ's divinity; a Muslim may feel disrespected when a Christian or a Jew asserts that the Muslim is following a false prophet; a Jew may feel disrespected when a Christian claims that Judaism rests on God's old covenant made obsolete in Jesus Christ; a Buddhist may feel disrespected when a monotheist insists that the nirvana is closer to the kingdom of the dead than to supreme bliss. Disrespect for a religion, the argument goes, easily morphs into disrespect of the people who embrace it, even into violence against them. In *The Dignity of Difference* Jonathan Sacks puts the matter starkly: "If truth—religious and scientific—is the same for everyone at all times, then if I am right, you are wrong. If I care about truth I must convert you to my point of view, and if you refuse to be converted, beware. From this flowed some of the great crimes of history and much human blood."[70]

In the previous section I have argued that it is possible for world religions to distinguish between person and work and therefore to respect adherents even of a religion they don't believe has earned their respect, a position Sacks endorses in the second edition of *The Dignity of Difference*.[71] But is it possible for adherents of world religions to do more—to respect other religions themselves even if they disagree with them? Such respect may be difficult because world religions make what they deem to be universally valid claims about things of ultimate or near-ultimate significance—about God and humanity, sources of authority, moral codes, or human final destiny. As these claims clash, each negation diminishes the worthiness of its object and reduces respect; outright error in matters of faith can earn for itself some mixture of pity and contempt. To claim that one's own religion is universally true and simultaneously to respect another religion seems incompatible. Throughout this book I have argued that the claim to be universally true is a signature feature of world religions. Moreover, many of their adherents interpret this claim in a highly exclusivist way, an issue I will discuss in chapter 4. We are thus faced with a critical question: can adherents of a world religion respect rival religions while making differing universal claims, or must their respect be limited to persons who embrace these religions?

The answer depends partly on the meaning of respect.[72] To respect something commonly means to recognize or appreciate it as having worth or importance.[73] Religions may have different kinds of worth or importance. For instance, religions have power, like the power of Islam to claim the deep loyalties of many. Respect for the power of a world religion could be a version of what some philosophers have called "obstacle respect," a sense that we must take something into account and work around it if we are to achieve our goals.[74] We might then respect other religions in the way we respect formidable enemies: we despise what they stand for but acknowledge their power so as to better protect ourselves or combat them. Most religious people are happy for their religions to receive recognition as something to be reckoned with, but they crave for more—for affirmation of the excellence of the religion they embrace, or what is called "appraisal respect." To respect a religion in this stronger sense is to esteem what is stands for, at least to a degree, to ascribe some significant worth to the way of life it seeks to foster and to the convictions about ultimate reality that it contains. But can adherents of a universal religion give appraisal respect to a religion other than their own?[75]

There are three major ways religious people making universal claims to truth can and should give appraisal respect to religions other than their own. All three require that we grant other religions *an initial presumption of worth*. In "The Politics of Recognition," Charles Taylor sums up this stance and the reasons for it: "It is reasonable to suppose that cultures [and religions] that have provided the horizon of meaning for large numbers of human beings, of diverse characters and temperaments, over a long period of time—that have, in other words, articulated their sense of the good, the holy, the admirable—are almost certain to have something that deserves our admiration and respect, even if it is accompanied by much that we have to abhor and reject."[76] This is only an initial presumption of worth, not of equal worth but of *some* worth. The appropriateness of this initial presumption will need to be confirmed through accurate understanding and critical engagement. But to approach a religion presuming its worth is already to show it a measure of appraisal respect; inversely, to approach it presuming an absence of worth is to disrespect it.

First, we respect a religion by *honoring its integrity*. Instead of denigrating another religion by destroying its holy sites, burning its holy books, or insulting its founder, we help preserve and protect those. Instead of distorting another religion by spreading false information about it, we endeavor to know it accurately—for instance, engaging it, we tarry in the posture of "nonunderstanding," open to learn from those who study and practice it—and speak truthfully about it. We don't rush either to simply contrast another religion with our own or to declare that its adherents are unknowingly our own coreligionists ("anonymous Christians," as Christians who advocate the so-called inclusivist position like to think of adherents of other world religions); instead we honor both the commonalities of another religion with our own and its differences. Finally, in evaluating a religion we judge fairly—for instance, we don't compare our own religion at its best with another religion at its worst; we compare the malfunctions of one with the malfunctions of another or a period of glory of one with a period of glory of another.[77]

Second, we respect a religion by *critically engaging its truth claims.* In the strongest sense, "appraisal respect" is identical with approval, even endorsement: a religion I consider true and whose way of life I believe to be most excellent has my full respect. But I can show a religion appraisal respect even when I disagree with it. I do so not only by noting in it things I find admirable but also by deeming it worthy of critical engagement. I don't dismiss it as, for instance, a demonically inspired mimicry of the true faith or as mere superstition, idiocy dressed up in pomp and parading as supreme value; nor do I humor it as some quaint local or personal "truth" valid for a person or a group—the way I may humor and even encourage a child's belief in Santa Claus. Instead, I treat it as what it claims to be, a contender to being a true interpretation of reality and a compelling way of life. Even denial of a religion's truth can be a mode of respect, though the line between critical judgment and contempt isn't easy to draw. To respect a religion in this sense means to treat it as an object worthy of responsible critical judgment rendered truthfully, whether that judgment turns out to be positive or negative.

Third, we respect a religion by our *willingness to recognize its positive moral effects.* In engaging other religions critically, it is important to evaluate not just truth claims but also the effects they have on the lives of their adherents. World religions aren't merely alternative metaphysical constructions of the world and visions of the life worth living. They allege to be seedbeds of virtue and holiness. Even when we disagree with some central claims a religion makes, we may still be able to appreciate the positive moral effects it has. Martin Luther was a fierce critic of Islam and yet he recognized that sixteenth-century Muslims lived lives of greater moral integrity than Christians.[78] To recognize in another religion signs of holiness as judged by the standards not only of that religion but also of our own is to show respect for it.

What if a person's considered judgment *doesn't* result in respect for the main claims, important practices, or moral effects of a religion? What if it leads to the conviction that a religion is an irrational and morally pernicious superstition? In societies riven by deep and, at least presently, irreducible religious differences and disagreements, we can expect that the adherents of one religion will withhold respect to another religion or one of its versions. If the refusal of respect is an informed and considered judgment rather than a mere prejudice, we would find ourselves back at respecting adherents of a religion as persons. As to their beliefs and practices, we would either merely tolerate them in order to avoid social strife and achieve our own ends or, in some cases, show why these beliefs and practices are contemptible and make sure that they are not tolerated. Respect for beliefs and practices must be earned, and therefore disrespect and, at times, intolerance are the appropriate wages of contemptible beliefs and practices.

Blasphemy

Respect for persons of different religions and respect for different religions themselves sometimes align happily: we respect a person as a human being, and we respect that person's religion as worthy of admiration. An observant Jew, for instance, might not just respect a Confucian but also genuinely admire some forms of Confucianism. Or an orthodox Christian might respect a Hindu, a Jew, and a Muslim as well as the versions of Hinduism, Judaism, and Islam they embrace—as I do in the case of my friends Anantanand Rambachan, Alon Goshen-Gottstein, and Prince Ghazi bin Muhammad. Occasionally, as in cases of religious bigotry and discrimination, the two kinds of *dis*respect align: we disrespect a religion and on account of that disrespect we disrespect also the person embracing the religion. Mostly, however, the two kinds of respect are in tension.

125

Some see a tension between respect for a person and respect for religion at work in disputes about apostasy: on the one hand, out of respect for persons, we would want to affirm their right to abandon a religion; on the other hand, out of respect for a religion, for its truth and goodness and therefore supreme value for a person and a society, we might want to prohibit people from abandoning it. Earlier I argued that, to the extent that a world religion believes the transcendent call is addressed to individuals rather than families or entire ethnic groups, to permit apostasy out of respect for a person isn't to disrespect a religion but to enact one of its basic values. Understood in this way, world religions presuppose that persons have an inalienable responsibility for the basic direction of their lives. Freedom to exercise that responsibility is then an important feature of religion. There is no tension between respect for person (freedom of religion) and respect for religion (affirmation of its supreme value).

It is different in the case of blasphemy, when persons insult or show contempt for what is sacred in another religion or in a rival version of their own religion. Blasphemy is like "burning your enemy's flag," an act of "belittling symbols which other human beings have loved and even died for."[79] In the act of abandoning a religion, I don't necessarily disrespect it. In the act of blaspheming, I arguably disrespect both the religion and the person who embraces it. The crucial question is how we should relate in moral and legal terms to the disrespect contained in blasphemy.

Each in its own way, world religions condemn blasphemy, though they argue within and among themselves as to what exactly constitutes blasphemy and what actions does condemnation entail. As I have argued throughout this book, for world religions, the transcendent realm is superordinate to the mundane realm: human beings live lives truly worth living to the extent that they conform themselves and their world to the transcendent realm. Just as for world religions the freedom of religion is "the first freedom," so for them an insult against what they hold sacred is the most egregious possible, for that kind of an insult touches what ultimately governs the meaning and direction of their entire lives. In Judaism, the prohibitions against idolatry and blasphemy are the foremost commandments both for the children of Israel (Exodus 20:2–6) and the children of Noah, the remainder of humanity.[80] Christians have tended to think similarly. Echoing the prohibitions of the Hebrew Scriptures—which are part of their own holy book as well—Christians have traditionally believed, as the Heidelberg Catechism (1563) puts it, that "no sin is greater or provokes [God's] wrath more than the profaning of His Name."[81] The Qur'an puts its strong rejection of blasphemy in the form of two rhetorical questions: "And who does more wrong than he who invents a lie against Allah or rejects the Truth when it reaches him? Is there not a home in Hell for those who reject Faith?" (al-'Ankabut 29:69). World religions are opposed to blasphemy, but what constitutes blasphemy and what form should that opposition take?

For centuries and in all world religions, respect for religion has tended to trump respect for persons: their freedom to embrace convictions and engage in practices consonant with their basic orientation in life. Merely rejecting and contesting a faith, let alone ridiculing it, was deemed blasphemous, as the above quote from the Qur'an illustrates. Moreover, blasphemy laws were promulgated and enforced brutally. Though the United States was born in part out of a longing for religious freedom, the Massachusetts Bay Colony imposed stiff penalties on those who had a religious thought or two of their own. The 1697 Act against Atheism and Blasphemy reads: "That if any person shall presume willfully to blaspheme the holy Name of God, Father, Son, or Holy Ghost, either by denying, cursing or reproaching the true God . . . or by denying, cursing, or reproaching the holy Word of God; that is, the canonical Scriptures . . . every one so offending shall be punished by Imprisonment, . . . by sitting in the Pillory; by

Whipping; boaring thorow the Tongue with a red hot iron; or sitting upon the gallows with a Rope about their Neck . . . *Provided,* That not more than two of the fore-mentioned Punishments shall be inflicted for one and the same Fact."[82] The act echoes the condemnation of blasphemy in the Hebrew Scriptures, though the punishments are milder: no death penalty, as in Leviticus (24:16), at most only piercing the tongue with "a red hot iron."

Although blasphemy laws are still on the books in many historically Christian countries as well as in the state of Israel, they are almost never enforced now. Some majority Muslim countries, on the other hand, enforce strict blasphemy laws even today. In Pakistan, a section added to the penal code as recently as 1986 states: "Whoever by words, either spoken or written, or by visible representation, or by any imputation, innuendo, or insinuation, directly or indirectly, defiles the sacred name of the Holy Prophet Muhammad (peace be upon him) shall be punished with death, or imprisonment for life, and shall also be liable to fine."[83] Since 1999 the Organization of Islamic Cooperation, a body with fifty-seven member states considered to be "the collective voice of the Muslim world," has pushed to make the "defamation of religion" part of the human rights agenda of the United Nations. The goal is to shift the international human rights regime from protecting merely individual freedoms to protecting religions from insults.[84] The situation is somewhat different with regard to Buddhism than with Abrahamic monotheisms. Legal codes of traditional Buddhist cultures did not include blasphemy as a criminal offense.[85] Still, in recent years attempts have been made to promulgate blasphemy laws. In Thailand, for example, "179 members of the 250-seat National Legislative Assembly have backed a bill to make offences to Buddhism a crime punishable by stiff penalties."[86]

Notwithstanding world religions' widespread support of blasphemy laws, much of the teaching of the world religions, especially in their early and formative stages, speaks against such laws. The

Buddha, for instance, famously urges his followers: "Should anyone speak disparagingly of me, the Dhamma or the Saṅgha you should not get angry, resentful or upset because of that. . . . If others speak disparagingly of me, the Dhamma or the Saṅgha you should explain whatever is incorrect saying: 'This is not correct, that is not true, we do not do this, that is not our way.'"[87] According to the New Testament, Jesus Christ was put to death as a blasphemer (Mark 14:64).[88] Significantly, when he was reviled and abused, he did not revile and abuse in return, leaving an example to his followers (1 Peter 2:21–23; see also 3:9). Unlike later Islamic law, the Qur'an itself does not prescribe temporal punishments for blasphemy.[89] Why the shift, then, from merely rejecting blasphemy, even showing forbearance for it, to criminalizing it?

As in the case of laws against apostasy, at play were close ties between religion and political rule. In Christianity and Islam blasphemy laws appeared along with the establishment of Christian or Islamic states and empires. Similarly, the push to promulgate blasphemy laws in Thailand came in the trail of the movement to declare Thailand a Buddhist state. It was not just that once close ties between religion and the state were established the state could assume protection of important goods as defined by religion. More important was a sense that contempt for religion undermined civic, legal, and political orders. When a religion expresses unity of political community and provides legitimacy for the state, insults to what that religion declares to be sacred become a danger to the state.[90] Hence in the Hebrew Bible we find a close association between cursing God and cursing the king (1 Kings 21:10; Isaiah 8:21).[91]

It is a mistake to criminalize blasphemy. First, blasphemy laws are not needed. In most places, the tie between the civic and political order and a particular religion has been loosened and in many places is nonexistent. Civic and political order can survive a blasphemer or two; Salman Rushdie's *Satanic Verses* or Kurt Westergaard's depiction of the Prophet Muhammad in a turban with a lit fuse do insult a religion and its adherents, but they don't undermine political order in any significant way. Second, blasphemy laws are dangerous. As Paul Marshall and Nina Shea have argued in *Silenced* (2011), when blasphemy laws are enforced today, they serve mostly as tools for the majorities or political elites to politically oppress and economically exploit minorities;[92] under the pretense of defending God, blasphemy laws end up legitimizing violence of the strong against the weak. Finally, blasphemy laws are easily construed to curtail the first freedom of every person—the freedom to determine, publicly articulate, and defend against competitors the convictions directing the basic course of a person's life.

Though it is a mistake to criminalize blasphemy, it is a moral obligation to condemn it. "In democracy, we do not recognize the right not to be insulted," said Danish deputy prime minister Wouter Bos, defending insulting depictions of Muhammad in a magazine. He was right—well, half right. For he forgot to add that the affirmation of freedom to insult doesn't transmute hurling insults at others into a virtue. To insult is to wrong another person. As Richard Webster noted, "In the real political world which we all perforce inhabit, words *do* wound, insults *do* hurt, and abuse, especially extreme and obscene abuse, *does* provoke both anger and violence."[93] We wrong people when we make fun of their disabilities or sexual orientation. Similarly, when we hold to public scorn what they consider sacred, what gives them a sense of identity and sets the trajectory of their life, we don't just demonstrate "lack of imagination about the experiences and self-perception of others";[94] we also wrong the individuals concerned. More, the kinds of disrespect contained in blasphemy erode social cohesion in pluralistic societies and undermine our ability to engage in meaningful public arguments about the common good. In sum: critical engagement with the religious convictions and practices of others, yes; defaming those convictions and practices and insulting those who hold them dear, no.

Without criminalizing either blasphemy or apostasy, we need to foster a mindset of respect—both respect for persons, including their most important freedom, and, in a more qualified regard, respect for religions themselves. To grow and thrive, the culture of such two-fold respect needs an appropriate institutional environment. In Michael Walzer's terms, the "mindset" of respect needs support from "regimes" of respect.[95] A particular kind of pluralistic liberalism is a good candidate for a regime of respect, I believe. I grant that this is neither the only option available nor even the best one for all settings; a concrete form of a regime of respect will always have to depend on a given setting, its culture and political history.

Regime of Respect

If we are after political institutions expressing and sustaining mutual respect, two options are largely closed in a globalized world, though they continue to inspire the imaginations of many. One is exclusion of religion from the public space, and the other is the saturation of the public space by a single religion or single secular ideology. The proponents of exclusion of religion insist that in debates about political matters citizens ought not appeal to their religious convictions, especially not convictions derived from positive revelation. Instead, they should appeal to principles yielded by some source "independent of any and all . . . religious perspectives to be found in society."[96] In private, they are free to believe what their holy books and religious traditions tell them to believe; in public, these convictions should be idle, and religious adherents should act on judgments informed by reasons accessible to all citizens. The state and religious communities must be utterly separate from one another—the famous "wall of separation" advocated by Thomas Jefferson.[97] The most prominent representatives of the position are John Locke in the seventeenth century and John Rawls in the twentieth.[98]

Some religious communities, especially when living under very adverse circumstances, withdraw into the private sphere and see themselves as islands of aliens, a stark alternative to the godless society and state. But even when they withdraw, adherents of a world religion will under no circumstances cede ultimate authority over any aspect of their lives to the state, or for that matter to anybody else; the transcendent realm has primacy over the mundane and, as we read in the New Testament, God is to be obeyed more than human beings, *any* human beings, including state or religious authorities (Acts 5:29). But just because the transcendent realm has primacy over the mundane, most adherents of world religions consider a merely private religion to be a truncated religion, a religion not doing all the work it should. The immense popularity of the democratic ideal throughout the world, which remains unabated even if the process of increasing democratization has presently stalled and even partly reversed itself, has heightened religions' sense of responsibility for public life. In the public no less than in the private sphere, adherents of world religions will ultimately base their convictions and practices on religious sources—on Torah, on the teachings of the Bible, on the Vedas, or the Four Books and Five Classics of Confucianism, for instance. They perceive exclusion of religion from the public sphere as denial of freedom of religion and therefore a mode not just of disrespect but of intolerance and oppression—and rightly so.

In response to exclusion, adherents of a world religion often aspire to use the instruments of the state to dominate the entire political society. But when adherents of one religion aspire to shape public life, adherents of another worry: the universal social visions of one religion will collide with those of another, and social chaos, violence, and oppression will follow. Citizens with no religious affiliation worry as

well, not just about colliding social visions but about the very idea
that anyone should seek to base laws on appeals to supposedly irrational convictions. If you let religions into the public space, each one,
blind and zealous, will want to shut out all competitors, both religious
and a-religious. We could dismiss these worries as irrational anxie-
ties, were it not the case that world religions have a long history of
imposing themselves forcefully on the unwilling. I write these words
not long after Muslim militants declared the establishment of the Islamic State and proclaimed Abu Bakr al-Baghdadi as the new caliph,
the "leader for Muslims everywhere," intent on ruthlessly suppressing all internal dissent, systematically cleansing the territory under
its control of its Christian population, and waging aggressive jihad.[99]
This is the most recent and most extreme case, condemned as un-
Islamic by the vast majority of Muslims, of the tight unity of religion
and rule, of practicing a world religion as a "political religion"—and
a barbarically brutal one at that. Even in much milder versions, such
close unity between religion and rule always entails a lack of equal
respect and often leads to discrimination and at times to outright oppression of adherents of all other religions and of people with no
religious affiliation. This is what I mean by saturation of public space
by a single religion.

When world religions are publicly engaged, they threaten to exclude
all competitors; when they are pushed into privacy, they themselves are
objects of exclusion. These are the two unacceptable options. We need
an alternative that fits both the character of world religions and avoids
the exclusion and marginalization either of some or of all adherents
of world religions. It must be a position that secures conditions for
political stability and social cooperation of persons and groups whose
disagreements about conceptions of the good are irreducible. This is
one of the great political challenges of a globalized world. We can
meet it only with a model of political society that is, in the words of
Jocelyn MacLure and Charles Taylor, "founded, on the one hand, on

133

an agreement about basic political principles and, on the other hand, on respect for the plurality of philosophical, religious, and moral perspectives adopted by citizens."[100] But can world religions support such a model of political society, a relatively recent one in human history?

The universal truth claims of world religions, along with the mandate to conform mundane realities to the transcendent realm, seem to stand in the way. And yet, they do not, at least not necessarily. In their repertoire of defining motifs, world religions have the key building blocks of a pluralistic political order. In the list of generally accepted features of such a political order, MacLure and Taylor have helpfully distinguished between constitutive moral principles or values and operative modes or means. Freedom of conscience and equality of respect are moral principles; separation of religion and state and impartiality of the state toward all religions and a-religions are the operative modes.[101] World religions can affirm both the moral principles and operative modes without betraying their own deep identity. If they in fact do, each will have its own distinct reasons for doing so and the result will be not full unanimity but an "overlapping consensus," to use the famous phrase John Rawls coined.

First, *freedom of religion.* I argued earlier that world religions can and ought to embrace freedom of religion, which includes freedom to adopt and change religion as well as freedom to propagate religion and bring it to bear on all dimensions of life. Constitutionally guaranteed freedom of religion and a-religion understood in such a way is the most important element of any regime of respect.

Second, *equal moral value of all citizens.* Precisely because world religions are universalistic, they affirm the equal value of all people; a distinction between moral "insiders" and moral "outsiders" is in principle unacceptable to them. Hence they all embrace some version of the Golden Rule with its underlying principle of reciprocity. Equal value of all citizens entails also equal voice for all citizens, whether religious or a-religious, in public matters. In arguments about enforceable public decisions we should neither give preference to appeals to religious or ideological authorities (as in political systems with an official religion or ideology) nor subordinate religious reasons to generic "public reasons" (as in political systems guided by "public reason liberalism"). Instead, every citizen and every community ought to be able to appeal to any reasons they find compelling—and do so in a form that they hope will be persuasive to their fellow citizens who don't share their overarching perspective on life.[102]

Third, *separation of religion and rule.* I argued earlier (chapter 2) that just because world religions give primacy to the transcendent realm, they construe "religion" and "politics" as two distinct, though intersecting, cultural territories. Drawing the distinction between the community called the "Body of Christ" and the political order of the empire, early Christians, for instance, embraced graded levels of loyalty: Christ gives substantive direction to Christians' lives, and they give him ultimate allegiance; the political order provides for the conditions of their living, and they give it conditional loyalty.[103] All world religions have internal resources and motivations to make a similar distinction.

Fourth, *impartiality of the state.* The state should neither give preference to a single religion or ideology nor relegate religions and ideologies to the private sphere. Instead, the state should be impartial toward all religious and a-religious interpretations of life. As Rowan Williams put it in *Faith in the Public Square,* its role should be that of an authoritative legal "mediator and broker whose job is to balance and manage real differences."[104] To the extent that world religions can embrace freedom of religion, equal respect for all citizens, and a distinction between religion and rule, they will, arguably, be able to embrace this fourth feature of a pluralistic political order as well.

Clearly, it is not only adherents of world religions who need to be persuaded to embrace this version of political pluralism. Many nonreligious people aren't convinced either. A major reason for skepticism is the observation that most adherents of world religions are religious exclusivists coupled with the conviction that the affirmation of religious exclusivism is deeply incongruous with endorsement of pluralism as a political project. In the following chapter I take up that critical issue.

4

Religious Exclusivism and
Political Pluralism

Can religious exclusivists embrace political pluralism? Is it possible
for them to be consistent in their convictions and espouse pluralism as a political project? And do they have genuinely religious
reasons, rather than merely pragmatic motivations, for doing so? My
topic here is not the relation of world religions to political pluralism.
In chapter 3 I argued that even though most adherents of world religions aren't political pluralists, world religions have important resources for strong support of political pluralism. Here my question is
narrower but in some ways more critical: whether *exclusivist versions*
of world religions are compatible with the affirmation of political
pluralism. In a globalized world of vibrant, assertive, and widely exclusivistic religions, the future of "regimes of respect" depends in
part on the answer to this question.

Departing from the practice throughout this book, I will explore
this issue primarily with regard to one world religion, Christianity. I
have two simple reasons for limiting the scope of my inquiry. First,
Christianity has been religiously exclusivist for most of its long history and its exclusivism is of a particularly strong kind, stronger than
that of Islam, for instance, let alone than that of Buddhism, Hinduism, and Confucianism. Second, Christianity gave birth to the most

influential form of political pluralism today, liberal democracy. If
religious exclusivism doesn't stand in the way of Christianity's support of political pluralism, exclusivism is unlikely to preclude any
world religion's acceptance of pluralism—provided, of course, that
the religion has other good reasons to embrace it, a topic I discussed
in chapter 3. Whether this hypothesis is in fact true, of course, would
require a deeper exploration than I can undertake here.

Two Kinds of Exclusivism and Pluralism

What exactly is a religious exclusivist, and how does one differ from
a religious pluralist? How are religious exclusivists and pluralists distinguished from political exclusivists and pluralists? To understand
religions' relation to society and state it is important to keep straight
the two "exclusivisms" and two "pluralisms." My sketch of exclusivisms and pluralisms is rough and deliberately simple, made with
a charcoal stick and avoiding complicated discussions of their many
varieties.

A classic expression of religious exclusivism is found in Jesus's famous statement as recorded in the Gospel of John: "I am the way, and
the truth, and the life. No one comes to the Father except through me"
(14:6). A piece of pompous religious arrogance to some but dearer
than bread to others, the verse implies that religious exclusivism has
three related aspects: the truth, the right way of life, and access to
both.

First, religious exclusivists believe that their faith is *the true* faith.
The claim is not necessarily that outside that faith's beam of light
is only the darkness of falsehood.[1] Exclusivist Christians would, for
instance, gladly accept the claim that Jewish, Muslim, or Sikh beliefs
about God's oneness are true. For exclusivists, other faiths may contain significant insights, but the claims of the exclusivist's faith trump
the claims of other faiths. The exclusivist's faith isn't the only truth

in the world, but it's the yardstick by which an exclusivist measures the truth in all other faiths.

Second, religious exclusivists believe that their faith alone is the right path to God for everyone, that it alone fosters authentic human flourishing, and that it alone assures the hoped-for everlasting life. Again, the claim isn't necessarily that outside the one true faith people are utterly severed from the true God or that other faiths contain no correct teachings about right living. A Christian religious exclusivist would, for instance, accept as right Socrates' or Confucius's injunction to do the right thing irrespective of the consequences. Religious exclusivists don't necessarily believe that other faiths are utterly misleading, but rather that in following them, you won't reach you proper goal as a human being.[2]

Finally, for Christian religious exclusivists the final source of authority is the positive revelation contained in the Holy Bible (and, for most, in the sacred Tradition) as the witness to Jesus Christ. As the great Protestant theologian Friedrich Schleiermacher noted almost two centuries ago, revelation differs both from what people may excogitate with the powers of their intellect and from what they can discover in the realm of experience; revelation requires divine communication.[3] That's true of any revelation. The so-called *positive* revelation on which Christian exclusivism rests requires *special* divine disclosure that is not accessible to people independently of the original revealer. "*I* am the way, and the truth, and the life. No one comes to the Father except through *me*," said Jesus. Christian exclusivists don't claim just that their religious convictions are the final truth and their way of life the correct one; they claim that the *access* to that truth and right way of life is not through the wide gate of generically human reason and experience but through the single narrow gate of revelation: it is found in the single source of a specific divine self-disclosure to specific persons and passed on in the Bible and the Tradition.

In contrast to religious exclusivism, religious pluralism is the conviction that all world religions are roughly equally true, provide equally valid access to the divine, foster human flourishing equally well, and are equally effective means for reaching the hoped-for everlasting life.[4] Religions differ in rituals, convictions, and practices because they emerged in different cultures. Each may also have its own unique emphasis—Buddhism on overcoming suffering, Christianity on God's love, Islam on submission to God, and so on—a specific contribution to the single religious quilt.[5] But, to change the metaphor, each is a line connecting the circumference of a circle, where human beings stand, with its center, where the divine reality resides, each an equally direct way to get to that center.

That many religions share the same geographic and political space is an obvious and undeniable reality. That's the situation of plurality, pluralism as a social fact. How to manage the situation of plurality within a given state is a matter partly of cultural sensibilities and partly of political arrangements. There are two major and contrasting ways of managing plurality politically: political exclusivism and political pluralism.

The extreme form of political exclusivism is *totalitarianism*. It was instantiated most explicitly and most destructively in the Nazi and Stalinist regimes of the last century. These were built on the ideological fiction of one official truth, one acceptable way of life; they were legitimized by the myth of an inescapable war between the "noble" and "degenerate" races or the "philosophy" of history's ineluctable march toward a classless society; and they were maintained by the terror of a single, uncontested rule.[6] Common to all forms of political exclusivism—from deeply malignant totalitarian regimes to more benign authoritarian ones—is that the government is highly partial to one ideology, one religion, or one ethnic group, and that it employs coercive mechanisms to exclude others from participating in public life.

In the twentieth century, political exclusivism was associated with antireligious totalitarianisms. But throughout history, political exclusivism was largely religiously inspired. A single, exclusivist religion would give legitimacy to an exclusivist state. The state in return would impose that religion on all its citizens and guard the purity of its observance. On the whole, religiously inspired forms of political exclusivism were and continue to be less oppressive than Nazism and Stalinism were. Still, they are unforgiving of all heretics and schismatics, of blasphemers and apostates, and of anyone who deviates from the convictions and practices that the single exclusivistic religion espouses and the state enforces.

By political pluralism—a position I defended toward the end of chapter 3—I refer to that political philosophy, embodied always only partially in a set of political institutions, according to which freedom of conscience is guaranteed to all people, irrespective of their faith or lack of it, and they all have equal voice in running the affairs of common public life. Consequently, the state is impartial with regard to major overarching interpretations of life rather than, as in political exclusivism, highly favoring one over all others. As I noted in chapter 3 and will elaborate later in this chapter, political pluralism as I describe it here was originally developed in the West as a project of Christians who, in the name of their version of faith, contested their coreligionists' tight connection between their own brand of faith and the government. According to some, political pluralism is a specifically Christian political philosophy. Yet, though its core convictions—freedom of religion, equal voice in the public sphere, and the impartiality of the state—were historically drawn from the Christian faith, these ideas are widely shared, even if partly differently understood or emphasized to varying degrees, among all world religions. Other world religions, not just Christianity, are compatible with and can support political pluralism, or so I argued in chapter 3.

Today many assume that political exclusivism inescapably follows from religious exclusivism; a religious exclusivist cannot be a political pluralist. But is this assumption correct or does it rest on a prejudice fed by the historical association between religious and political exclusivisms? The question is important because religious exclusivism is prevalent today and it isn't going away.

Vibrancy of Religious Exclusivism

Even in moderate Islamic-majority countries like Turkey and Indonesia, over 60 percent of Muslims are religious exclusivists; the percentage is much higher in conservative Muslim countries. Christians are even more exclusivistic. In Africa and China, where Christianity is vibrant and rapidly growing, 87 percent of Christians are religious exclusivists; the percentage of Christians who are exclusivists falls below 50 percent only in nominally Christian Western or Western-influenced nations. Hindus, often described as religiously tolerant, are preponderantly exclusivist when it comes to the truth claims of their faith.[7]

Most adherents of the world religions are religious exclusivists. That's what the figures above suggest and, given the character of world religions, that's what we would expect. As I noted in chapter 2, fundamental to the major world religions, especially to monotheisms, is the distinction between true and false religion, and therefore an explicit rejection of false religion.[8] For Jews and Christians, the first divine commandment is: "You shall have *no other gods* before me" (Exodus 20:3).[9] The first part of the first pillar of Islam is: "There is *no god* but God." The pillars of Judaism, Christianity, and Islam are exclusivistic. Moreover, in them the distinction between the true God and false gods and between true and false religion rests on specific, positive revelation. As a consequence, people fall into two basic categories: those who have the revelation and know the truth and those who don't. The revealed character of these religions strengthens their exclusivism.

If the figures above are correct, between 2.5 and 3.5 billion people are religious exclusivists and, as religions are growing in both absolute and relative terms, we can expect more religious exclusivists in the future. Significantly, people with a vibrant, numerically growing, and publicly assertive religion, the sort of religion that makes the most difference politically, are predominantly religious exclusivists.[10] If religious exclusivists cannot be political pluralists, these statistics are deeply worrisome. To the extent that they are religious exclusivists, people of diverse religions then won't be able to live peacefully under the same roof or collaborate constructively.

But perhaps the worry is misplaced, at least in the long run. True, religious exclusivists abound and sometimes wreak havoc in a religiously pluralistic world of interconnected and interdependent people. But aren't globalization processes turning all religious people into religious pluralists simply by pushing them to live in close proximity with people of other faiths? Once people become religious pluralists, a widespread belief goes, religion will no longer hinder them from becoming political pluralists as well. Some religious pluralists may still prefer political exclusivism to political pluralism, perhaps because they believe that authoritarian states are, on the whole, able to provide a better life for their citizens or because they prefer to live in monoethnic and monocultural states. But religion will then have nothing to do with it.

In *A Far Glory* Peter Berger advocates the gradual disappearance of religious exclusivism. He believes that social pluralism—"the coexistence with a measure of civic peace of different groups in one society"—erodes religious exclusivism and leads to the affirmation of religious pluralism. Processes of globalization put into high gear the psychological mechanism—"cognitive contamination"—through which this transformation occurs. Berger writes: "The thought obtrudes that one's traditional ways of looking at the world may not be the only plausible ones—that maybe those other people have a point or two. The worldview that until now was taken for granted is opened up, very slightly at first, to a glimmer of doubt. This opening has a way of expanding rapidly. The end point may then be a pervasive relativism."[11] When people of diverse religions live side by side, a robust, pure, and clearly bounded faith gradually morphs into a tenuously held, porous, and contaminated faith, which eventually slides into outright secularity.[12] I am interested here in the middle stage, the adoption of religious relativism or, in my terms, of religious pluralism.

Berger's is an argument from social psychology, from the way people are likely to respond to others in a pluralistic setting. Intuitively, it seems plausible: (1) you live with others and, over time, (2) learn to appreciate them as human beings; (3) then you realize that their beliefs are not utterly false and their ways of living not pernicious, and (4) you eventually conclude that their "truth" is as good as your "truth," that you are just different without one being right and the other wrong or one being better than the other. Yet, as neat as such a schema looks, what actually happens is much more complicated. Even when people go through the first three steps, they often don't take the last one—they don't turn into religious pluralists. On the contrary, cohabitation with adherents of other religions often strengthens, not weakens, one's own faith commitments. Most sociologists of religion today have come to hold almost the very opposite of Berger's thesis: there is often a *positive* rather than a negative correlation between a plurality of religions existing in the same space and the vitality of each religion. Religions, especially exclusivist ones, thrive when they compete, especially in the context of a religiously impartial state.[13] The best examples are the two largest and most religiously diverse democracies in the world today, the United States and India, both home to vibrant religions.

Significantly, Berger himself holds that people aren't traveling on a one-way street from religious exclusivism to religious pluralism. The traffic goes the other way as well. A plurality of religions in the same space relativizes religious commitments, but that relativism also inspires absolutism and therefore reestablishes religious exclusivism. Why this turn in the other direction? Berger explains, "Pluralism creates a condition of permanent uncertainty as to what one should believe and how one should live; but the human mind abhors uncertainty, especially when it comes to the really important concerns of life. When relativism has reached certain intensity, absolutism becomes very attractive again."[14] So even for Berger, globalization's pluralizing forces do not necessarily erode religious exclusivism and thereby mitigate its alleged politically pernicious effects. By pushing people of diverse religious persuasions to live in the same political society, the processes of globalization do not make religious exclusivists disappear; they nudge some to abandon religious exclusivism but lead others to embrace it. For still others, they strengthen their already existent commitment to religious exclusivism. If religious exclusivists had to be political exclusivists, then in a world of vibrant and assertive religions sharing common political spaces two major options to achieve political pluralism would be available to us. The first would be to persuade religious exclusivists to become religious pluralists so that they could embrace political pluralism without contradiction. The chances of this strategy succeeding are close to zero. Religious exclusivists are not likely to be open to such persuasion because, even apart from people's personal investments in their own faith and their need for boundaries in an uncertain world, the arguments against religious exclusivism are not as convincing theologically and philosophically as is often assumed.[15] The second option is to exclude religious exclusivists from public life, the strategy of the programmatically secular state.[16] If the first option is unworkable, the second is morally repugnant; it is unfair and oppressive. Both, however, depend on the premise that religious exclusivism is incompatible with political pluralism. Do we have good reasons to accept that premise?

Incompatible or Not?

The two main arguments maintaining that religious exclusivism sits uneasily with political pluralism build on two features of religious exclusivism: exclusivity of the access to truth and exclusivity of the right way of life. In the following I will take up these arguments as they have been articulated in two politically highly influential texts from two different periods of Western history, Karl Popper's *The Open Society and Its Enemies* (1945) and Jean-Jacques Rousseau's *The Social Contract* (1762).

Many have argued that the stress on a single, exclusive, and divinely revealed truth has not only created a distinction between believers and unbelievers but has led as well to hatred of others, conflict, violence, and bloodshed. Acceptance of truth on the authority of revelation, the argument goes, makes it hard for religious exclusivists to be egalitarians and embrace political pluralism. Casting a worried eye on the aggressive totalitarianisms of Stalin's Soviet Union and Hitler's Germany, Karl Popper articulated an influential form of this argument in *The Open Society and Its Enemies*. His primary targets are the philosophers of "the closed society"—Plato, Hegel, and Marx. But he fires shots at world religions as well, seeing a despot lurking inside all those who don't hold *all* their convictions open to rational criticism.

Popper's argument rests on a contrast between rational and irrational attitudes. As he, an influential early philosopher of science, understands it, rationalism is, roughly, "an attitude of readiness to listen to critical arguments and learn from experience," a conviction that "I may be wrong and you may be right, and by an effort, we may get nearer to the truth."[17] Essential to rationalism is not merely the use of reason but three related epistemic stances: a fundamental respect for the force of arguments and evidence, a sense of one's own fallibility, and an openness to revise any position held. In contrast, irrationalism relies on the power of passions and, in the case of religions, on the authority of revelation. As irrationalists, Popper contends, we think "with our blood," "with our class," "with our race," or "by God's grace," rather than judging "a thought on its own merits."[18] This account of rationalism and irrationalism, developed early in the last century, is not the final word in the theory of knowledge, but many intelligent people today accept its validity.

Reliance on the passions—even on love, our best emotion—and on revelation tends to "divide mankind into different categories," friends and foes, compatriots and aliens, believers and unbelievers. With such a stance, Popper maintains, political egalitarianism "becomes practically impossible." Irrationalism feeds "the attitude that different categories of people have different rights; that the master has the right to enslave the slave; that some men have the right to use others as their tools. Ultimately, it will be used . . . to justify murder."[19] If critical reason gives way to the passions and authority, our very humanity will be destroyed and we will turn into rapacious beasts, he warns at the end of the first volume of *The Open Society and Its Enemies*.[20]

Religious exclusivists might respond that they, too, use reason—all the time. But Popper grants that: all irrationalists employ arguments and appeal to experience. But they do so only to explain how things are on the surface and to support deeply held positions and achieve basic goals that reason neither sets nor is allowed to alter. The crucial aspect of irrationalism is that at some point critical reasoning stops. For religious exclusivists, who access the truth of faith through positive revelation, reasoning stops before the most fundamental decisions are made about the nature of ultimate reality, the character of the self, the shape of social relations, and the account of the good.[21] As reasoning gives way to obedience in decisions about human moral identity, the line is drawn between "us" and "them," between those for whom we care and those whom we despise. Love of reasoned argument goes hand in hand with the love of human beings, insists Popper; conversely, hatred of rational thought and reliance on obedience are consonant with the hatred of human beings.[22] The demand for obedience to the dictates of faith easily morphs into the imposition of faith on others, at which point religious exclusivism slides into political exclusivism.

Not all religious exclusivists recognize themselves in this portrait. At least for some of them the prohibition against imposing their views on others—especially against doing so through the power of the state—is part of the positive revelation that they embrace as God's command. Popper himself recognized this, though many contemporaries who follow his account of rationality don't. He described early Christianity, a religion unquestionably based on positive revelation, as "the new creed of the open society," a successor of sorts to his hero Socrates. Popper believed that Christianity had a "tremendous moral influence" in part because it was a faith for all on equal terms and because it insisted on the freedom of conscience against the power of imperial Rome.[23] Still, throughout most of its history it was totalitarian. The reason, Popper thinks, is that Christianity is irrational, and unlike rationalism, which is universal, irrationalism is exclusive, splitting people into insiders and outsiders.[24]

The second major argument for why religious exclusivists must be political exclusivists concerns their alleged inability to respect people's decisions about how they should live. Toward the end of *The Social Contract*, a classic text about the reconciliation of individual freedom and the power of the state, Rousseau writes: "Those who distinguish civil intolerance from theological intolerance are, in my opinion, mistaken. These two kinds of intolerance are inseparable."[25]

In other words, if you are a religious exclusivist, you will necessarily also be a political exclusivist. Rousseau supports this claim by zeroing in on the aspect of "theological intolerance" that concerns the right way of life and eternal destiny. "It is impossible to live in peace with people whom we believe to be damned; to love them would be to hate God who punishes them. It is absolutely necessary to reclaim them or to punish them. Wherever theological intolerance is allowed, it cannot but have some effect in civil life; and as soon as it has any, the sovereign is no longer sovereign even in secular affairs; from that time the priests are the real masters; the kings are their officers."[26]

The simplest way to show that Rousseau was wrong might be to point to the many religious exclusivists who in fact do live in peace with those they believe will be damned. They work with them in offices and on construction sites, they sit with them around kitchen tables, and, on occasion, they even raise kids with them. In other words, they are reasonably comfortable with pluralism as a social phenomenon even if they may wish for things to be otherwise; they embrace the "coexistence with a measure of civic peace of different groups in one society."[27]

But perhaps these are religious exclusivists going about their daily lives rather than discharging their political responsibilities. Perhaps they are also inconsistent exclusivists whose hearts are smarter than their heads and practices better than their convictions. A consistent exclusivist, Rousseau maintained, would know that to live in peace with the damned and to love them is "to hate God who punishes them"; if you were to love God and align your behavior with God's, you'd seek either to "reclaim them or to punish them." Had he wanted to support his point with examples, Rousseau could have made a long list of just such forced reclamations and merciless punishments from the history of all religions.

Are Popper's and Rousseau's arguments that religious exclusivism entails political exclusivism persuasive? Before I respond to them, consider religious exclusivists' prospects as citizens if Rousseau and Popper are right: these are grim. Rousseau was particularly severe toward religious exclusivists, more severe than all but the most vicious despots. Since religious exclusivism is socially destructive, it ought to be outright prohibited. He writes: "Now that there is, and there can be, no longer any exclusive national religion, we should tolerate all those which tolerate others, so far as their dogmas have nothing contrary to the duties of a citizen. But whosoever dares to say: 'Outside the Church no salvation,' ought to be driven from the State, unless the state be the Church and the Prince be the Pontiff. Such a dogma is proper only in a theocratic government; in any other it is pernicious."[28] Traditional Catholics, who hold to the principle that there is no salvation outside the church, along with all other religious exclusivists—Muslim, Jewish, Hindu, Buddhist—are free either to conform or to leave. In Rousseau's society, all religious exclusivists are excluded. Most others who also see a close tie between religious and political exclusivisms are content with a milder solution. Rather than banishing religious exclusivists from the political community, they propose consigning exclusivist religious convictions to citizens' private lives: religious exclusivists must keep visions of the good life derived from their particular religion out of the public square. Either way, though, the result is undesirable: state-sanctioned persecution or discrimination, both signs of political exclusivism.

Fortunately, Popper and Rousseau are mistaken. First, though it is true that Christian religious exclusivists make a clear distinction between the saved and the damned, the consistent among them also—and without contradiction—reject the distinction between moral insiders and moral outsiders. The Golden Rule, a succinct summary of all Christian moral obligations, commands: "In everything, do to others as you would have them do to you"—do to *all* others, not just to a select few (Matthew 7:12). As the story of the Good Samaritan powerfully illustrates, the command to love one's neighbors is universal (Luke 10:25–37); it applies to friend and foe, good and evil, saved and damned. To love the damned is not to hate God but to obey and emulate God, who makes the sun to shine on the good and the evil (Matthew 5:45) and who loves those who have made themselves God's enemies (Romans 5:6–7).

Second, nothing in religious exclusivism demands that the state impose a religious moral vision upon the society. True, many religious exclusivists have availed themselves of the instruments of the state in pursuit of their religious goals. But that was a function not of their exclusivism per se but of their affirmation of close ties between church and state. A religious exclusivist can without self-contradiction affirm a fundamental distinction between God's judgment and the state's justice, advocate a clear separation of church and state, and insist on respect for religious freedom; all these convictions are perfectly compatible with religious exclusivism. For religious exclusivists who embrace these convictions, political pluralism will be a positive good rather than a fate to endure until they can establish their own totalitarian rule.

This thesis is not popular today—not among politicians, not among public intellectuals, not among academics (including those in my own field of religious studies and theology), and least of all among critics of religion. Though some contend that to be a political pluralist you must abandon all religion, most believe that to be a genuine political pluralist you must abandon religious exclusivism. In contrast, I contend that though there may be some affinity between certain kinds of religious pluralism and political pluralism,[29] there is no incompatibility between religious exclusivism and political pluralism. A consistent religious exclusivist can be a political pluralist.

A person who believes that the proof of the pudding is in the eating might well ask: "Where are such religious exclusivists who embrace political pluralism, and why don't they speak up?" One of them, perhaps surprisingly, was Roger Williams, a sixteenth-century

Puritan. He could even be plausibly described as the father of political pluralism.

Religious Exclusivism and the Origins of Political Pluralism

At the origin of Western political pluralism lie firm convictions held by religious exclusivists about religious liberty and separation of church and state, convictions so powerful that the people who held them not only preached and wrote about them but worked to create political institutions that would embody and reinforce them. The most prominent among them was Roger Williams (1603–83), an intransigent defender of religious truth if ever there was one. After being banished from the Massachusetts Bay Colony for what were deemed to be heretical and seditious views about religious liberty and for defending the rights of Native Americans, he went on to found Rhode Island and create "the first government in the world which broke church and state apart."[30]

If proof were needed that religious exclusivists can be political exclusivists, even political exclusivists of a totalitarian kind, the religious and political leaders of the Massachusetts Bay Colony furnish it abundantly. In the famous sermon titled "A Model of Christian Charity," John Winthrop, its first governor, sketched a vision of the colony as a "city upon a hill." The city was an earthly "new Jerusalem," dedicated to God and to obeying God's laws. Chief among the government's roles was enforcing those laws, including watching over the purity of religious observance. Flogging, mutilations such as cutting off ears or cutting out tongues, and (in cases of adultery, idolatry, and blasphemy) execution were some of the punishments for disobedience. As the "nursing father" of the church, to use a phrase of Richard Hooker, a prominent sixteenth-century theologian, the state was expected to be severe.[31]

When Williams arrived in the colony in February 1631, its leaders received him as "a godly and zealous preacher." At the young age of twenty-eight, he was offered an important and highly influential position in deeply religious colonial America: he was to be the teacher in the Boston church and therefore an authoritative religious thinker for the entire colony. To the stunned surprise of the colony's leaders, Williams refused the honor. For him, the Boston Puritans were not separate enough from the Church of England. Five years later, just a few months before they founded Harvard College, the magistrates purged the colony of the man who would not be their teacher on account of their impurity. What was his unpardonable offense? He advocated the seditious doctrine that the magistrates had no right to enforce obedience to the First Table of the Law, the portion of the Ten Commandments that regulates human duties to God. On this, he collided also with Winthrop, a man he considered his friend.

In a four-hundred-page book titled *The Bloudy Tenent of Persecution for Cause of Conscience* (1644), he later explicated and defended his position. Its main thesis, placed at the very beginning of the book, he formulated as follows: "It is the will and command of God, that since the coming of his son the Lord Jesus, a permission of the most Paganish, Jewish, Turkish, or Antichristian consciences and worships, be granted in all nations and countries: and they are only to be fought with that Sword which is only in soul matters able to conquer, with the sword of God's Spirit, the Word of God."[32] Except for Thomas Helwys (1557–1616), one of the founders of the Baptists,[33] no one before Williams had ever argued for such radical freedom of conscience within the confines of a state. As I noted in chapter 3, even half a century later, John Locke, who gave political liberalism its most influential expression, would not be as tolerant. As Rainer Forst argued recently in his massive *Toleration in Conflict*, Williams's arguments were not only "more beholden to a religious argumentative framework than Locke's" but also clearly went "beyond Locke's restrictions on toleration."[34] Why should, according to Williams, the conscience of absolutely every person in the world be free? Because all human beings are equal before God, and forced worship "stinks in God's nostrils." The government, therefore, has no right to compel anyone to worship rightly. Similarly, the church has no right to avail itself of the state's instruments of compulsion; it is "a true mark and character of a false church to persecute," Williams noted.[35] Williams insisted that compulsion in matters of religion is utterly incompatible with the Christian faith. It is "directly contrary to the nature of Jesus Christ, his saints and truths, that throats of men . . . should be torn out for his sake, who most delighted to converse with greatest sinners."[36] In a polemic written to refute the views of John Cotton (1584–1652), a learned and esteemed New England Puritan clergyman, Williams also warned of the consequences. With an eye to the "Indians," whose language he had learned and whose rights he championed, he argued that Cotton's insistence on the necessity of compulsion leads to utterly unacceptable and indeed impossible practice: if one must enforce a religion that one considers true for all times and places, then "millions of millions of blasphemers, idolaters, seducers, throughout the wide world, ought corporally be put to death."[37]

In the conclusion of *Roger Williams and the Creation of the American Soul* (2012), John Barry sums up Williams's stance: "With absolute faith in the Bible, with absolute faith in his own interpretation of it, he nonetheless believed it 'monstrous' to compel another person to believe what he or anyone else believed, or to compel conformity to his or anyone else's beliefs."[38] Williams incorporated this deeply held religious conviction, formulated in a religiously exclusivist framework, into the state compact for Rhode Island, which he founded for the express purpose of building into the character of its political institutions his ideas about religious liberty and the separation of church and state. A strong religious exclusivist, he became one of the main progenitors of political pluralism.[39] As Williams's biographers agree, his faith was both the source of his convictions and the motivation for his actions, not a mere instrument for achieving what were only social and political ends.[40]

For Winthrop, God would not be honored and would not bless the fledgling colony unless it obeyed God's laws, and the colony could not obey God's laws unless the government enforced them. For Williams, God is insulted by forced worship, and brutal punishments to enforce religious conformity are contrary to the character of the merciful God revealed in Jesus Christ. Both men were devout Christians, and both were religious exclusivists. Yet Winthrop's religious exclusivism led to political exclusivism, and Williams's to political pluralism. The *content* of faith—what in the repertoire of the Christian faith each found important to emphasize and how each fitted what he emphasized into the whole—made the difference, not how exclusive their faith was and how firmly they subscribed to it. At issue between them was the substance of the interpretation, not the force and exclusivity of conviction. Many would judge Williams as the better interpreter of the two. Commenting about the seventeenth-century struggles for religious liberty, John Plamenatz, British intellectual historian, noted: "Liberty of conscience was born, not of indifference, not of skepticism, not of mere open-mindedness, but of faith."[41] The reasoning was not "Because faith is supremely important, we must impose it" but "Because faith is supremely important, all human beings must be allowed to live by the faith that they hold true." The strong exclusivist convictions that gave freedom of religion its birth can sustain it now as well.

The Christian Right and Political Pluralism

Williams's religious struggle for political pluralism took place in the seventeenth century. But where are the religious exclusivists who embrace pluralism as a political project today? Travel with me forward in time over some 350 years from the early colonial period to contemporary America. In the second half of the twentieth century, conservative Christians, mainly Protestant fundamentalists and traditional Catholics, stepped with fierce determination onto the public scene in the United States. America had fallen under the dominance of a secular culture, they believed. It was important to realign it with its original purpose to be "a city upon a hill," obeying divine laws rather than living by the permissive standards of secular morality. The movement, named the Christian Right, is made up predominantly of religious exclusivists.

Some have charged the Christian Right with compromising democratic values and wanting to turn the United States into a theocracy.[42] Critics as well as supporters have characterized its leaders as the contemporary heirs to the theocratic John Winthrop.[43] Yet on a closer inspection it turns out that the movement inherited much from Roger Williams as well. Christian Right leaders and activists are in fact an important contemporary example of religious exclusivists who embrace pluralism as a political project. My purpose here is not to evaluate the worth of the Christian Right's substantive positions (on military interventions, abortion, euthanasia, gay rights, and so on); it is rather to show that they, religious exclusivists, promote these positions as political pluralists.

Just how much of Roger Williams is there in the Christian Right? In 2009, Jon Shields published a book, based on his doctoral dissertation, with a surprising title: *The Democratic Virtues of the Christian Right*. Shields was able to detect virtues where critics saw unmitigated vice by closely examining Christian Right organizations and studying "how the Christian Right leaders shape the public behavior of ordinary Christians."[44] The outside perception of the Christian Right becomes distorted in two principal ways, Shields argues. Critics mistakenly identify it with the militant fundamentalism of Randall Terry (Operation Rescue) or Jerry Falwell (Moral Majority). These figures, darlings of the media, were the Christian Right's embarrassments, not its leaders. Moreover, critics evaluate the democratic character of the Christian Right by focusing on its policy ends. But policy issues are the matters of disagreement, the subject of political debates. The question here is how democratically virtuous is the Christian Right, and the primary way to determine this is to inquire about its "effects on participation and public debate."[45] So what are these effects?

First, many Christian Right organizations have helped "create more participatory democracy by successfully mobilizing conservative evangelicals, one of the most politically alienated constituencies in twentieth-century America."[46] More surprising and equally important as the Christian Right's success in mobilization is its effect on public debate. Drawing on organizational materials and interviews with leaders in thirty different Christian Right organizations, Shields concluded that these leaders have inculcated "deliberative norms in their rank-and-file activists—especially the practice of civility and respect; the cultivation of real dialogue by listening and asking questions; the rejection of appeals to theology; and the practice of careful moral reasoning."[47]

Critics may object that Christian Right leaders have strong pragmatic incentives to teach these values; if activists abide by them, they are more likely to achieve their political goals. That is, of course, true. Still, it is significant that the movement leaders ground these norms in sacred texts, the Word of God. "Activists are regularly instructed to practice civility because the Gospels command Christians to love their neighbors, and they are encouraged to be honest because God forbids believers from bearing false witness. Likewise, Christian apologetic organizations teach thousands of citizens every year to make philosophical arguments rather than scriptural ones because Peter instructs Christians to give reason for their beliefs."[48] Shields's conclusion: as the Christian Right leaders and activists see it, ignoring deliberative norms would not be merely impolitic; it would be also religiously unfaithful.

Ralph Reed, the director of Christian Coalition, a major Christian Right organization, instructed rank-and-file members to "avoid hostile and intemperate language," to "acknowledge the opinions of others and sincerity of their beliefs," and to remain "tolerant of diverse views and respectful of those who espouse them."[49] Without employing such values there is no effective communication and no political victory, of course. And yet for Reed, as for many other Christian Right political leaders, these values are also an expression of Christian convictions, not mere rhetorical strategies that can be abandoned when the situation changes. For Reed, as for Focus on the Family, to name another major Christian Right organization, it is crucial that the behavior of political activists "reflect the love and compassion of Christ."[50] Have Christian Right leaders and activists always behaved according to this principle? Of course not. But they have done no worse than most more liberal groups, whether religious or secular.[51]

Clearly, not all would agree with the goals the Christian Right seeks to achieve; many would in fact dislike these goals intensely. But that goes without saying—and the Christian Right's activists and sympathizers would return the compliment. The point of democratic participation is to effect change in accordance with one's own vision of the good life. Pluralistic democracy is all about negotiating such disagreements in a way that respects the dignity of all (one important subject of negotiation being what exactly constitutes "respect"). Important for my purposes here is that the religious exclusivism of the Christian Right does not prevent it from participating in the democratic process in a way that unquestionably displays the virtues of pluralistic democracy. On the contrary: its members have taken the values their exclusivist faith teaches and translated them into the deliberative norms of a pluralistic democracy. They are the most prominent contemporary example of religious exclusivists whose religious convictions align well with pluralism as a political project.

Why Religious Exclusivists Are Good for Globalization

The Christian Right doesn't exemplify one deliberative norm some advocates of democracy consider very important:[52] holding truths provisionally, quickly abandoning beliefs when these are challenged by counter-evidence.[53] In this, they are typical of other religious exclusivists: all of them hold onto what they believe to be the truth with a firm and enduring grip. But perhaps holding lightly truths about what kind of life is worth living is not a virtue at all, and therefore cannot be a democratic one either. And perhaps what a globalized world needs from world religions is not a loose grip on truth about the good life but a firm one—provided that this doesn't lead adherents of world religions to want to take others' convictions about the good life out of their hands, which is to say, provided that they espouse political pluralism.

Religious exclusivists who dictate to others what their decisions about the good life ought to be are political exclusivists; they use the power of the state to subordinate others to their vision of the life worth living.[54] Political exclusivists of all stripes—secular and religious—are on a collision course with one another and with the processes of globalization, because these processes pull and push people of diverse faiths and secularists to live in the same political society. Political exclusivists find the prospect of such a "mixed household" unacceptable, for they are committed to a single vision of the good life and to imposing it on all citizens (some even want to force their view on the inhabitants of the entire world). As a consequence, they assault people's dignity, perpetrate violence, and threaten the world's prosperity. Religious exclusivists who advocate political exclusivism are bad for today's world. But the argument of this chapter was that religious exclusivists need not be political exclusivists, that they can be—and in fact many of them are—political pluralists. I will end the chapter by suggesting that religious exclusivists who are political pluralists may in fact be good for a globalized world. How so?

What kind of religious convictions will be able to give meaning to human lives and help them seek the common good? It will have to be a faith of strong (though not in principle unalterable) convictions rather than provisionally held beliefs, for only such a faith will be able to inspire a social movement for cultural and political change. That's where the religious exclusivists—of a certain stripe!—come in. As much as any group in the world today, they nurture reflection about what makes life worth living and are capable of being agents of cultural transformation—by founding new religious communities (all of which are, in one way or another, committed to leading the good life), by financing educational institutions in which students engage in a conversation across the centuries about the life that is worth living, by advocating for needed legislative change, and so on.

Will religious exclusivists live up to that potential? That depends on whether they are willing to embrace political pluralism while retaining robust and reflective religious convictions. If they are, religious exclusivists will do more than just push for responsible visions of the good life and cultivate a sense of global solidarity. They will place themselves in a position to be agents of reconciliation rather than fomenters of violence.

5

Conflict, Violence,
and Reconciliation

onflicts between communities are a critical challenge in a highly
interconnected and interdependent world. Opinions are sharply
divided on whether religions cause conflict or are peaceable. Religious and a-religious critics of any given religion tend to deem it violent; its advocates as a rule argue that it is peaceable. Both are wrong
because their positions are too simplistic. World religions, as historically practiced, are neither simply violent nor simply peaceable but
ambivalent: to various degrees at different times and places, all major
world religions have been implicated in violence and all have contributed to peace. In the second half of this chapter I will (1) propose
that world religions, though often bitterly at odds with one another and
employed to ignite or fan the flames of conflict, nevertheless contain indispensable resources for reconciliation among people, and (2) identify
the factors that turn religions into instruments of conflict.

Opinions are no less sharply divided on whether globalization fosters violence or contributes to peace. Some critics, both secular and
religious, see globalization as violent to the core: cutthroat in competition, oppressive to people, and destructive to nature. Defenders,
perhaps a minority, praise its pacifying effects. In the first part of this
chapter, I will argue that globalization, too, is ambivalent when it

comes to violence and peace. More controversially, in the main body of the chapter I will contend that a globalized world needs religions' reconciling potential if its people are to live in peace. But let me start not with globalization's deficiencies but with its strength—that is, with its surprising contribution to a widespread decline in deadly violence.

The Decline of Violence

In *The Better Angels of Our Nature: Why Violence Has Declined* Steven Pinker writes: "Believe it or not—and I know that most people do not—violence has declined over long stretches of time." He continues: "Today we may be living in the most peaceable era in our species' existence."[1] His book is thick, full of graphs, statistics, and probability calculations marshaled to counter the sense of many that his thesis is wrong and the conviction of some that it is positively dangerous.

Resistance to Pinker's contention comes from two main sources. One is a prevalent view of human nature. Jean-Jacques Rousseau has articulated it influentially in *Discourse upon the Origin and Foundation of Inequality* (1755), one of the founding texts of modernity. He argued that humans are peaceable by nature, but civilization makes them violent.[2] Riding in part on the cultural memory of the serene Garden of Eden, Rousseau's account of original innocence spread widely. Notwithstanding the common belief in progress, many today tend to believe peace existed only in the distant past and expect the present to be drenched in violence. The other reason many resist the idea that we live in the most peaceable era of human history is the undeniable carnage of the last century: two world wars, Stalin's, Hirohito's, and Pol Pot's killings, and major genocides and ethnic cleansings, to name just the main examples of violence in the century with the highest body count in human history. A rosy view of original human nature and the blood-splattered accounts of twentieth-century violence suggest a conclusion exactly the opposite of Pinker's: the more developed we are, the greater potential for harm we build, and the more violent we in fact become.

But Pinker argues that we have gotten both human nature and world history wrong. As to the first, there is little scientific data in favor of primitive innocence and much that speaks against it—such as widespread evidence of prehistoric remains testifying to their owners' violent end. Even according to the sacred story of human primal history in Genesis, it didn't take long before violence spoiled the Edenic peace. As to the twentieth-century death toll, the carnage was unspeakable. But if we judge not on the basis of absolute numbers but of relative numbers—if we ask not how many people have been killed but what proportion of the population did the killing and what was the chance of any one person being killed—the picture changes drastically. In the bloody twentieth century, a *lower* proportion of the world population was killed through human violence (3 percent of all those who died) than in prehistoric nonstate societies (between 4 percent and 30 percent). Population growth makes the difference; it explains the inflated numbers of dead despite reduced death rates. Pinker concludes, "Modern Western countries, even in their most war-torn centuries, suffered no more than around a quarter of the average death rate of non-state societies, and less than a tenth of that for the most violent ones."[3]

Pinker's thesis aligns with his anthropological conviction, rooted in evolutionary biology, that human beings are "survival machines," a phrase he borrows from Richard Dawkins's *The Selfish Gene*.[4] As members of the species, our goal is always that the expected benefits to us and to our kin will outweigh the expected costs.[5] We are wired to survive and thrive; we are not wired to commit violent acts. We are violent *strategically* when we believe that it will benefit us more than it will cost, and we eschew violence and pursue peace out of the same motivations. The decline of violence over the course of human history is the consequence of changes in material conditions (above all, strong states and expanded commerce) and cultural sensibilities (above all, the so-called humanitarian revolution and escalator of reason),[6] such that increasingly people have a selfish stake in the well-being of others and therefore in desisting from violence against them. Create the needed conditions, and peace will follow. But is Pinker right?

Because he sees human beings primarily as rational survival machines, Pinker overestimates the extent to which they are motivated by cost-benefit calculus.[7] Correspondingly, he underestimates the importance of mutual respect and peoples' investment in their particular ways of living, whether religious or secular.[8] People may resort to violence not merely because, after cost-benefit analysis, they decide that the benefits of violence outweigh the costs; they may also choose violence because, as "moral believing animals,"[9] they consider that a perceived wrong committed needs to be redressed and their individual lives are less important to them than the honor or purity of the group. And they may work for peace not only because peace will benefit them but because it fits better with their deeply held moral convictions, such as the sense that they ought to practice strict nonviolence toward all living beings (as Jainism teaches), be compassionate to all (as the Buddha teaches), or love their enemies (as Jesus Christ teaches).[10]

Even if we grant a wider range of motivations than Pinker, still, whatever else people may be, they are *also* animals deeply interested in increasing benefits and reducing costs to themselves and their kin.[11] Consequently, humans are highly responsive to changes in their environment. That's why it is important to create the external conditions for peace. To identify such conditions, Pinker, in line with political scientists like Bruce Russet and John Oneal,[12] turns chiefly to Immanuel Kant's classic essay *Toward Perpetual Peace* (1795).[13] No other single text has been as influential on contemporary thinking about what it takes to live in peace than Kant's brief essay.

Conditions for Peace and Globalization

Kant thought that the natural state of people living in proximity with one another isn't peace but war, or if not war, then at least a "constant threat of an outbreak of hostilities."[14] It may then seem that "perpetual peace" could be found only among the dead, who "rest in peace," and not among the living, who always strive and struggle, a possibility to which Kant alludes by noting that the title of the essay comes from a satirical inscription on an innkeeper's signboard picturing a graveyard.[15] Kant's argument was that, though we cannot rely on the propensities of human nature to live in peace, it is nonetheless possible to establish conditions for peace. Peace is not a gift of unspoiled human nature, a paradisiacal state in a distant past, but a future goal, an achievement of civilization.

In *Toward Perpetual Peace* Kant named three conditions for peace. Contemporary scholars building on Kant have added a fourth, inspired by an observation Kant made.

- Democratic government dedicated to freedom, equality, and the rule of law. Since citizens decide whether there will be war or not and since they bear the brunt of war's costs, they will likely decide against it. Perhaps more important, since democracies wield power in order to safeguard "the rule of right," they are likely to extend that principle to dealing with other nations.[16]
- A league of nations governed by a law binding on them all. States, like individual persons, "give up their savage (lawless) freedom, accommodate themselves to public coercive laws, and so form an (always growing) state of nations . . . that would finally encompass all the nations of the earth."[17]
- Cosmopolitan rights, according to which people from one country have the right to visit and seek commerce in another

country, but no right to ensconce themselves permanently in it or to subjugate it.

- The spirit of commerce taking hold of every nation. As the spirit of commerce, which "cannot coexist with war," historically brought various peoples "into a *peaceable relation* to each other," it will continue to compel all states "to promote honorable peace."[18]

Two centuries and two decades after Kant's seminal text, compare his four conditions with four key features of the contemporary world:

- Most nations today have democratic governments, even if these democracies are all, in their own way and to varying degrees, imperfect.[19] More important, the great majority of the world population embraces the idea that the legitimacy of political power depends on its enforcing the "rule of right."
- A league of nations of sorts was established after World War II: the United Nations. Other more regional and tighter transnational political unions exist (the European Union, for instance), which come even closer than the United Nations to Kant's idea of states "entering a constitution similar to civil constitution, in which each can be assured of its right."[20]
- Cosmopolitan rights are now widely embraced. The world population is highly interconnected, interdependent, and intermingled and, though citizens of distinct nations, all human beings nonetheless live in what Marshall McLuhan has famously (and misleadingly) called the "global village." A violation of rights in one place is increasingly felt as a violation of rights everywhere.
- The commercial spirit, construed to include all economic exchanges, now encompasses nearly the entire globe and con-

tinues to expand. Information, money, goods, services, and labor flow with extraordinary ease across borders.

As we have seen in chapter 1, the four features of the contemporary world I just sketched are among *the most important effects of globalization:* political and economic integration, widening embrace of human rights, interconnectivity, interdependence, and intermingling of people, a sense that we are all, for good and ill, citizens of a single world. If Kant was right, a single word—globalization—can name all the most important external conditions for the decline of physical violence.

Globalization, Peace, and War

Perhaps we may sum up the conditions for peace and the features of globalization associated with them with three mythical images: *Leviathan,* the sea monster from the book of Job, symbolizing political power; *Iustitia,* the blindfolded Roman goddess of justice, holding scales in one hand and sword in the other, symbolizing the rule of law among individuals and states; and *Mammon,* according to the Gospels the god of economic gain, now made wiser by the insight that trade secures better takings than conquest. The three form the external conditions for the decline of violence over the centuries, and they do so when each works properly and when all three work in tandem.

In contemporary political philosophy the pacifying effects of this mundane "trinity" are termed "liberal democratic peace." The most powerful nations and major global institutions, such as the United Nations and the World Bank, insist that to achieve peace in war-torn regions and states we need to "hold and monitor elections, create constitutions that guarantee human rights and establish independent courts, reform military and police sectors, create the structures for

free markets, and place human rights violators on trial."[21] Globalization processes have been in part designed and are being steered with
these conditions in mind. Give them a chance to work, and civil wars
and violent conflicts between ethnic and religious groups still going
on in Africa and Asia will become a thing of the past.[22] So isn't globalization creating a world of perpetual peace? Isn't it likely to lead
the whole world to the condition of western Europe today? No wars
for almost seventy years, annual homicide rates in the neighborhood
of one per one hundred thousand.[23]

Not so fast. Let's look very briefly at the road the processes of globalization have traveled since the sixteenth century and then forward
into the future, at the carnage behind and the menacing clouds ahead.
Over the past four centuries, Leviathan, Iustitia, and Mammon have
proven to be not a particularly holy trinity; predictably, it was mainly
the bad company of the corrupt Leviathan and the greedy Mammon that warped Iustitia. It took a great deal of violence for states
to form; and it is often by violence, or at least a constant threat of
it, that states keep violence in check. Similarly, the global expansion
of the commercial spirit, especially in the long phase of colonialism,
was shadowed by a Grim Reaper with a busy scythe. Even today,
below the glitter of the undeniable successes of the global economy,
blood, sweat, and tears flow abundantly. The decline of violence
comes at a cost, which for many was and remains terrible, unfair, and
irreparable.[24] The march of the mundane trinity through history has
been marked by violence. A pacifying force that rests on horrendous
violence—that's part of the historical ambiguity of globalization
when it comes to violence and peace, as many contemporary critics
of globalization have noted.[25]

In addition to this tempestuous past, three dark clouds are on the
horizon of today's globalized world: the intermingling of culturally
and religiously diverse people with competing visions of the good life,
a widening gap between the rich and the poor and, perhaps most signifi-

cant, a likely ecological catastrophe. The present form of market-driven globalization itself is generating these three storm clouds, not merely individuals acting within its institutional framework. I will elaborate here briefly on the last two and in the remainder of the chapter engage more fully the first.

The gap between the rich and the poor is morally unconscionable: 1.5 billion people drowning in abject poverty while a fortunate few are surfing the waves of opulence; a world in which the richest 1 percent own more wealth than the remaining 99 percent[26] is an affront to the human dignity of both the rich and the poor. Such disparities in wealth aren't just morally unacceptable; they are also socially and politically unsustainable as they are bound to generate deep tensions and conflicts. The same is true of the damage currently inflicted on the environment. Resources are limited but appetites, stimulated by the seemingly limitless stream of new products and services, are not. The costs of environmental degradation are mindlessly and irresponsibly pushed onto future generations.

Add the two problems—the ecological limits of growth and the widening gap between the rich and the poor—together, and the problem is exacerbated. If the world's poor achieved the levels of consumption indulged in by economically developed nations, ecological catastrophe would ensue. At the level of present technological advances, the ecosystem cannot sustain, for instance, 863 motor vehicles per 1,000 people (as in Monaco) or use energy equivalent to 2.235 million kilotons of oil (as in the United States in 2010) in the world as a whole.[27]

Both great disparities in wealth and severe ecological degradation are bound to generate conflict, not just over gain and "ways of life," but above all over scarce resources and security.[28] Beyond a vague sense that all humanity is bound in a common destiny, the moral order embedded in globalization has limited resources to counter these pernicious effects of the system. Fueled as it is by self-interest and competitiveness on the part of the producers and by the insatiable desire for goods on the part of the consumers, globalization erodes a sense of solidarity and fans the flames of desire. To achieve peace, we need to redirect and limit consumption and strengthen global solidarity. That's where religions come in. They are the most significant repositories of the visions of human flourishing that don't foreground material goods and consumption and in which solidarity plays a key role.

As I argued in chapter 2, world religions share two important features. First, notions of human flourishing go beyond "natural" desires for health, prosperity, fertility, and longevity. Human beings find fulfillment and enjoyment when they align themselves with an unseen order transcending mundane realities. Prodded by the basic conviction that, though necessary and enjoyable, material goods can never bring about genuine human flourishing, each world religion seeks to school desires and enjoyments, curbing an unhealthy increase of the appetite for consumer goods that the growth hormones delivered through advertising and entertainment stimulate. True, world religions have been and still are often twisted into becoming "prosperity religions"—mere tools to achieve health, wealth, fertility, and prosperity (see chapter 2). But each has in its repertoire strong motifs calling people to place their desires and enjoyments into a larger spiritual frame and find true joy primarily in love of God and neighbor. Moreover, at least some world religions teach that the entirety of the cosmos and all things in it are God's gift. Experiencing the earth in its entirety and all individual things in it *as* gifts enhances their enjoyment. It therefore curbs acquisitiveness and consumerism and generates contentment.

Contentment with regard to material goods is an important feature of all great spiritual traditions.[29] Rather than being a dominant dimension of the good life, worldly goods are a subsidiary one; indeed, all of these traditions underscore that the pursuit of worldly goods is often harmful to genuine flourishing as it empties life of deeper purposes. When contentment is an essential part of flourishing, individual human beings find happiness, environmental degradation is slowed down, and a significant cause of social conflicts is removed.

In opening people to transcendence, world religions can also open them toward the whole of humanity. As I noted in chapter 2, world religions are universal; their parish is the entire world rather than a particular group of any kind. As a consequence, world religions affirm the equal worth of all human beings and teach that benevolence cannot stop at the boundary of one's own in-group but must extend to all. As we have seen, world religions have been and still are sometimes twisted into becoming ethnic and "political religions," resources for shoring up threatened group identities, legitimizing power, and motivating to violence. And yet, a central motif in the repertoire of each is the command to extend care to all human beings, outsiders as well as insiders.

All world religions teach that peace cannot triumph without an effective belief that human flourishing isn't primarily about health, wealth, fertility, and longevity but about the opening of the human spirit in love of God and all neighbors, those close by and those far away (as the three Abrahamic religions would put it), or in compassion toward all sentient beings (as Buddhists would put it). In Christian terms, we will both flourish and live in peace with ourselves and one another if our lives are, in Jesus's words, not primarily about "food" and "clothing" but about the search for God and God's universal righteousness. In the success of that search, all human desires are satisfied and all enjoyment fulfilled (Luke 12:22–31).

Why Reconciliation?

Let me sum up the argument so far. Globalization is helping create conditions for peace and contributing to the decline of violence—of interstate wars, civil wars, homicides, torture, and the like. That's in part the effect of Leviathan, Iustitia, and Mammon, as I noted earlier. When the rule of law is established and goods and services are exchanged fairly, people's incentives for violence lessen and their interest in peace intensifies. On the other hand, driven as they are by the "commercial spirit," in their present form globalization processes are undermining the health of the global ecosystem, widening the gap between the rich and the poor, and eroding global solidarity. Even as it is generating conditions for peace, market-driven globalization is simultaneously generating new conditions for violence.

There is a widespread consensus today that, in a globalized world, we should fight disruptive violence by pursuing "liberal democratic peace." In chapters 3 and 4 I discussed important elements of such peace—freedom of religion and a-religion, respect for persons and, to a degree, for their visions of the good life, and genuinely pluralistic political arrangements. Yet more is necessary in order to deal adequately with inescapable conflicts in a globalized world—to prevent them from flaring up or to bring about genuine peace after their fires have subsided.[30] As I have just suggested, to decrease motivation for conflicts, we need *alternative visions of human flourishing* that are not centered on "bread alone" and that place a premium on contentment and solidarity. Though necessary, all these conditions for peace are, however, not sufficient to address the problem of conflicts in a globalized world. We also need reconciliation.

Why do we need to reconcile? The short answer is that even when physical violence has subsided, conflict is inescapable when diverse people live in the same political society. Moreover, intermeshed and interdependent as such diverse people are in a globalized world, they often cannot exit relationships at will, or the exit is too costly. When we are in conflict with those from whom we cannot separate, we are pushed to reconcile.

It is hard to find a more pacified place than a Cistercian monastery, populated by monks or nuns dedicated to contemplation. Physical violence is virtually nonexistent within its walls. Strict adherence to the rule for communal living (in secular terms, Iustitia), enforced by an abbot or abbess with authority as the one who, according to the rule of St. Benedict, "holds the place of Christ" in the community (in secular terms, Leviathan), and a commitment to loving one's neighbors and enemies (in political terms, a pacifist ideology) keep physical violence at bay. Yet no Cistercian monastery is free of conflict. The main reason monks and nuns leave the order (or after a trial decide not to join) isn't the required ascetical practices—poverty, vigils, fasting, celibate chastity, obedience, manual labor—that make even the thought of monastic life forbidding to most of us. Rather, the frictions of communal living, sometimes resulting in deep wounds and resentments, drive people away[31]—unless, that is, they push them to keep reconciling.

Consider one more example of the need to reconcile even in the absence of physical violence, this time in society at large rather than in a circumscribed community, and among people of diverging visions of flourishing rather than among those with a shared ideology. Levels of animosity and prejudice between traditional Muslims and secularists in western Europe are soaring and conflicts are abounding. Yet despite some notorious cases—the murder of the Dutch filmmaker Theo van Gogh or death threats against the Danish cartoonist Kurt Westergaard—levels of physical violence between the groups are extremely low. Western Europe is more or less pacified, but reconciliation is still needed.

Common to the above examples is that the parties aren't easily able to exit the relationship: secular humanists in western Europe cannot sequester traditional Muslims or drive them out; and though monks can leave the order, such a step goes against the grain of their ideals and even their identity. If we are able to exit a relationship, the pressure to reconcile lessens: others have seriously wronged us, we possibly press charges to get justice but, whatever the outcome, we can walk away from them. But if we must live with those who have wronged us, we are pushed to reconcile. If we don't reconcile, we risk either being crippled by resentment or consumed by a cycle of revenge, and in either case being unable to cooperate with them.[32]

Globalization has taken down barriers between people and integrated all into a single large network. As individuals, communities, and whole nations we no longer live standing solely on our own two feet and moving within our own walls; we are thrown into a mesh of interdependence, forced to rely on one another, pushed and pulled to live under the same political regimes. We cannot exit relationships and must therefore learn to live together. When inevitable conflicts occur, we must seek to reconcile. This partly explains the popularity in recent decades of "forgiveness" among individuals and the proliferation of truth commissions, reconciliation commissions, and apologies among communities and governments.[33]

We can distinguish, roughly, three basic domains in which reconciliation takes place: political, cultural, and personal. *Political reconciliation* concerns situations in which state actors have committed wrong, primarily by violating human rights (both at interstate and intrastate levels).[34] *Cultural reconciliation* concerns situations in which communities and persons as members of particular ethnic, cultural, or religious groups are in conflict.[35] *Personal reconciliation* concerns situations in which individuals, often members of the same ethnic, religious, cultural, or subcultural community, are at odds with one another.[36] In the following, I will sketch a general account of reconciliation that cuts across these domains, while recognizing that each domain places distinct requirements onto the process of reconciliation. In the context of globalization, reconciliation in all three of these spheres is needed.

Remember and Forgive

To reconcile is to attend to the past—to deal with the past marked by violence in order to keep it from colonizing the future. It is part of the human condition that at any given time, our past, present, and future interpenetrate each another in our consciousness. The experienced past colors the occurring present and shapes the imagined future (just as, of course, the imagined future and occurring present color and shape the experienced past). As a consequence, a past marked by wrongdoing committed and suffered is never dead; as William Faulkner, a writer from the American South, famously put it, such a past is "not even past." With the help of individual and communal memory, it reaches through the present and into the future, infesting them with guilt, shame, resentment, and hatred and sowing the seeds of violence (or, when goodness and joy mark the past, memories often bathe the present and future in the soft light of happiness past). Reconciliation frees the past marked by wrongdoing from poisoning the present and spoiling the future.

Reconciliation has five basic elements. We can simplify them to five injunctions—remember, forgive, apologize, repair, and embrace—each easy to formulate but complicated to understand fully and difficult to practice.

Remember! More precisely, the injunction should read: *Remember rightly!*[37] Some ways of remembering keep resentments and hatreds alive and provide justification for further violence. But what does it mean to remember rightly? Above all, it means to remember wrongdoing suffered and committed *truthfully*. As the disputes about history in Germany, Ireland, Croatia and Serbia, or Rwanda illustrate,[38] what, precisely, the "truth" means here is contested, and the extent to which any given memory of a wrong committed and suffered is or even can be "truthful" is debatable. And yet, all the philosophical and historical contestations notwithstanding, we cannot imagine responsible social and political engagement without truthful remembering. Remembering truthfully is the first element of reconciliation, the one without which all others falter. Faced with wrongs committed or suffered, we need to look the "truth straight in the eye—without embellishment and without distortion," as German president Richard von Weizsäcker insisted in his famous speech in the Bundestag on May 8, 1985, the fortieth anniversary of the end of World War II.[39]

Why does truth matter so much? Every untruthful memory of a wrong committed and suffered is an unjust memory, unjust toward either victims or perpetrators, and usually toward both. When we remember wrongdoing untruthfully *we wrong others,* and we do so irrespective of whether we remember untruthfully as perpetrators, victims, or third parties. The inverse is often true as well: we are bent on wronging others and therefore remember untruthfully. We misremember so as to don a mantle of false innocence, to portray what is in fact excessive revenge as a legitimate struggle for justice, or in order to preemptively protect ourselves from imagined enemies, to name only the most common misuses of memory.

Perpetrators' memories are famously short. They flee into the future eager to "close the book of the past," as F. W. de Klerk urged after the end of apartheid in South Africa.[40] By forgetting the past they seek to erect a façade of innocence. But suppressed and hidden from light, wrongdoing committed gains in power and holds perpetrators captive. Painful as the truth may be, it alone will set them free. Whereas the perpetrators' temptation is quick and self-exculpating forgetting, victims' temptation is enduring and resentful remembering. Victims' memories are often long, and with the help of memory the past of their suffering and humiliation can usurp much of their identity, rob them of a future, and push them toward becoming perpetrators themselves. The light of truthful and public remembering can set victims free from the dead hand of the past, provided they are

able to forgive and so free themselves of resentment and the perpetrators of guilt, which brings us to the second injunction.

Forgive! Forgiveness is the central element of reconciliation. After
serious wrongdoing, victims' urge for revenge seems irrepressible.
But revenge is a self-defeating strategy, miring the victim and the
perpetrator alike in a cycle of violence and gradually erasing a distinction between them. Retributive justice would be more prudent
than revenge: not the "eye for a slight" or "life for an eye," which
revenge irrationally yearns for, but recompense proportionate to the
severity of the original wrongdoing. But can even retributive justice
deal adequately with the past marked by wrongdoing and suffering?
Desmond Tutu, Nobel Prize winner and one of the architects of the
peace in postapartheid South Africa, thought that it could not. He
famously insisted that there is "no future without forgiveness!"[41]

In *Exclusion and Embrace*, I noted two major flaws of retributive justice.[42] The first stems from the *predicament of partiality* or,
as Pinker has recently called it, the "moralization gap." "People
consider the harms they inflict to be justifiable and forgettable," he
writes, "and the harms they suffer to be unprovoked and grievous."[43]
The same applies when they seek to rectify wrongs suffered. With the
blindfold of partiality covering their eyes, victims see themselves as
seeking justice or even settling for less than justice while perpetrators
perceive victims as taking revenge. Under such conditions, the scales
of justice cannot be balanced. After "justice" has done its work, the
wound of wrongdoing remains and enmity sometimes deepens.

The second flaw of retributive justice stems from the *predicament
of irreversibility,* a phrase coined by Hannah Arendt in *The Human
Condition.* She used it to refer to the inability to "undo what one has
done though one did not, or could not, have known what he was
doing."[44] Even if revenge weren't enslaving and retributive justice
weren't always partly unjust, they still wouldn't undo the ravage of

the past for the simple reason that the past cannot be undone. The only way out of the predicament of irreversibility, Arendt believed, is through the power of *forgiveness*. Forgiveness is also the only workable way out of the predicament of partiality, I would add.

Put simply, to forgive means not to count the wrongful deed against the wrongdoer: we name the wrongdoing committed and condemn it and then, as I noted in *Free of Charge*, "give the wrong-doers the gift of not counting it against them."[45] Born out of free-dom, as Arendt rightly noted,[46] forgiveness liberates; it breaks the chain that links both the victim and the perpetrator to the past of wrongdoing. Revenge, in response to an urge, merely reacts to the wrongdoing; retributive justice, obedient to the proper measure, cal-culates the right degree of recompense; in both, the wronged, the wrongdoers, and their relationship are defined by the past. An act of free generosity, forgiveness names the wrongdoing in order to let go of it—releasing perpetrators from the rightful claims of justice and victims from understandable resentment. Freed from the burden of the past, both victims and perpetrators can embark upon a new fu-ture, each on their own and, possibly, together.

Though it releases the wrongdoer from the rightful claims of retrib-utive justice, forgiveness is not opposed to punishment; it is opposed only to retribution, one purpose of punishment.[47] Other purposes of punishment—such as deterrence, prevention, or rehabilitation—are all compatible with forgiveness. Perhaps it is better to call them dis-ciplinary measures, since punishment, strictly speaking, is backward looking while deterrence, prevention, and rehabilitation are forward looking, "focused exclusively on bringing about some future good."[48] There may be in fact good reasons to combine forgiveness with such disciplinary measures. We forgive so as to remove obstacles to peace from the past; we discipline so as to create conditions for peace in the present. In each case, we seek to make a better future possible.

Apologize, Repair, and Embrace

Forgiveness is a gift—somebody gives something to somebody else. But if the gift is to be successfully given, when one person gives, the other must receive. Generally, in the Christian traditions, especially in Protestantism, repentance is not a condition of forgiveness. Christians think of forgiveness among human beings in analogy to God's forgiveness of humanity: in Jesus Christ, the Lamb of God, who took away the sin of the world, God has forgiven before anyone has repented. Forgiveness is an unconditional gift. To repent is to receive that gift already given; not to repent is to not receive it or to reject it. The way wrongdoers receive forgiveness is through *apology* and *reparation.*[49]

The third injunction among the five components of reconciliation, then, is *Apologize!* To apologize means to *say* to the person we have wronged that we are sorry—sorry not that we have been caught, sorry not merely that the other person has been wronged, but sorry that we have committed the wrongdoing—and sorry not so much for our guilt and shame as for the suffering we have wrongfully caused. We pull down the veil of silence behind which we hide wrongdoing and bring the moral stain of our misdeed into the light of truth. For apology to be genuine, repentance must be sincere. In the Christian sacrament of confession, for instance, *contrition of the heart* must accompany confession of the mouth. To apologize, we must mean what we say. Finally, in saying and meaning that we are sorry, we *commit* ourselves to act otherwise in the future. We state to the victim and the wider public that the wrongdoing isn't a true expression of who we aspire to be and therefore how we intend to act in the future but a regrettable aberration in our moral history we are determined not to repeat.

It is hard to apologize genuinely. Having wronged others, we are often plagued by shame and guilt. We hesitate to admit the wrongdoing to ourselves, let alone acknowledge it publicly, in some instances because we fear disciplinary or legal consequences but in others because we mistakenly feel that an unacknowledged wrong is somehow an unreal wrong.[50] Yet the only path to freedom from the wrongdoing we have committed leads through contrition and confession, through apology. Refusal to apologize paradoxically highlights the stain on the moral image of wrongdoers; genuine apology makes the stain begin to fade.

Wrongdoers benefit from apology. So do victims. Apology elevates victims from the humiliation to which the wrongdoing has subjected them. As a wrongdoer, I don't apologize just *for* something, for the wrongdoing I have committed. I also apologize *to* someone, to the person I have wronged. I tell her that I am sorry and beg of her not to count against me the wrongdoing I have committed against her (or, if she has already forgiven me, I receive with gratitude her gift of not holding the wrongdoing against me). In wronging them, I disrespect victims. Through apology I acknowledge that the disrespect of having wronged another person is wrong and I return to a posture of respect.

Repair the damage! For reconciliation to take place, a wrongdoer must make a good-faith effort to remove as much as is reasonably possible of the damage his or her wrongdoing has caused. True, sincere apology already removes some of the damage: in disavowing the deed, the wrongdoer removes from the victim the harm of having been disrespected. As a rule, however, a wrongdoing involves more then mere disrespect; some further damage occurs—to the person, family, community, or possessions of the victim. That damage ought to be repaired as well, if possible.[51] Without willingness to repair that damage, the wrongdoer's apology remains hollow, mere words and empty sentiments, hovering over a damaged relationship rather than altering it, and inviting a suspicion that the purpose of the apology is to repair the wrongdoer's reputation on the cheap and to allow the person to continue benefiting from the wrongdoing.

Victims and perpetrators alike often dream of undoing the past,

the best of all reparations—if it were possible. But we cannot reverse the arrow of time. The ideal case of a *possible* reparation is
for me as a perpetrator to try to bring it about that you as a victim
"are roughly equally content with two states of the world: the first
contains the offence together with my repentance, apology, and reparation; the second contains neither." John Hare, a moral philosopher
and my colleague at Yale, whom I am quoting here, continues, "If
you, because of my actions, are indifferent between these two states
of the world, or have a preference for the first, then my tasks have
been accomplished on my side," and I have fully repaired the damage.[52] This is a *possible* return to the original state: a state at least as
good as that which the wrongdoing had disturbed. Though possible
in principle, in many instances—murder and destruction of cultural
heritage, for instance—such a return is unrealizable. Still, perpetrators owe a measure of reparations to victims to demonstrate the gen-
uineness of their repentance and to compensate them at least in part
for loss. Above all, perpetrators ought not to continue to benefit from
the wrongdoing they have committed.

Embrace! Perpetrators' apologies and reparations as well as victims' forgiveness are acts of liberation: they free perpetrators from
guilt and victims from resentment. The past, though unalterable, no
longer colonizes their present. Having escaped from captivity to the
past, they can now turn unburdened toward the future. But forgiveness, apology, and reparation do more than just liberate. They also
enact the commitment of both parties to the moral order essential
for life together. In removing the burden of past wrongdoing, each
reparation is, in Jürgen Moltmann's words, already "a beginning of
a new and just relationship between victims and perpetrators."[53] So
are each apology and each act of forgiveness. Some victims and perpetrators don't want a renewed relationship; they'd rather go their
own way, even after apology, reparation, and forgiveness. Globalization makes exiting relationships easier in some regards (for exam-

ple, ease of travel and flexibility of labor markets) but difficult and self-defeating in others (for example, intertwining people's lives by partly forcing and partly enticing them to cooperate). We are stuck with each other and therefore pushed to reconcile. Perhaps more important, as either victims or perpetrators, we are stuck with our own alienation from ourselves if we aren't willing or capable of returning to each other. But with the burden of the past lifted and conditions for peace in place, people whose history was marked by mutual violence and injury can turn toward each other with a measure of confidence.

Elsewhere, I have used the metaphor of "embrace" to describe the new common life of formerly estranged parties. The metaphor is too intimate for many settings (though even a handshake, which connects people while still keeping them at a safe distance, is a form of embrace). But it symbolizes well four essential requirements of reconciled living:

- a sense, perhaps a tenuous one, that even when we are in conflict and different in many regards, we nonetheless belong together on account of our shared humanity (signaled by holding the other and being held by the other);
- a willingness to keep boundaries porous in the journey through time with the other (signaled by the open arms that receive the other);
- a commitment to reciprocity (signaled by the arms of *both* parties opening and closing to hold the other and let the other go);
- an affirmation of each person's or group's discrete identity and rejection of attempts to erase the distinctiveness of each (signaled by letting go of the other, which is, of course, an essential condition of embrace).

Such "embrace" will never be perfect; it will inevitably always be partial, tension filled, and tenuous. Yet it will make a life of cooperation and mutual enrichment possible.

Religions, Worldly Goods, and Conflicts

But is reconciliation possible when *religions* are involved, especially universalistic world religions? Don't world religions show proclivity toward violence, a bitter fruit of unreason posturing as the life-giving truth about human existence? Aren't they therefore in the end bound to subvert all reconciling efforts?

For the record, the Christian faith inspired the account of reconciliation I have given above. As I have sketched it, reconciliation is rooted in that faith's core convictions, in beliefs about the character, actions, and commands of God as manifested in Jesus Christ. More important, the most successful large-scale reconciliation effort in the twentieth century—the South African Truth and Reconciliation Commission—was decisively shaped by the Christian faith along with traditional southern African *ubuntu* philosophy. Similarly, two major nonviolent political movements at whose heart was the idea of reconciliation—Mahatma Gandhi's struggle for Indian independence and Martin Luther King Jr.'s civil rights movement for the "beloved community"—were inspired by religions as well: Jainism, Hinduism, and Christianity. Are religion-inspired visions and movements of reconciliation anomalies, going against the grain of these religions themselves? To answer the question, we need to look into the relationship between religions and conflicts.

The main sources of conflict between people are well known. Almost four centuries ago, Thomas Hobbes might have said the last word on the matter. In the same chapter of *Leviathan* (1651) in which he famously described the life of humans in the "state of nature" as "solitary, poor, nasty, brutish, and short," he identified three principal sources of conflict: "First, Competition; Secondly, Diffidence; Thirdly, Glory. The first maketh men invade for Gain; the second, for Safety; and the third, for Reputation. The first use Violence, to make themselves Masters of other mens persons, wives, children, and cattell; the second, to defend them; the third, for trifles, as a word, a smile, a different opinion, and any other signe of undervalue, either direct in their Persons, or by reflexion in their Kindred, their Friends, their Nation, their Profession, or their Name."[54] This succinct summary of the causes of violence appears in Hobbes's chapter on the prestate condition of humanity. But Hobbes insisted that the three "principall causes of quarrell" are rooted not in a particular social arrangement but "in the nature of man."[55]

Some critics of religion think that religion is a major and independent cause of violence, a fourth source of conflict in addition to the three Hobbes outlined. And in many cases they are right. Historically, though, religions have contributed both to social discord and to social harmony, and they have inspired and legitimized both violence and peacemaking. Critics of religion recognize this ambivalence but have ready explanations for it: to temper their inherent violent proclivities, religions have tended to reach for the milk of human kindness or for the Enlightenment value of tolerance.[56] Many defenders of religions recognize the ambivalence as well, but they believe that the problem lies in a basic flaw of human nature; self-interested as we humans are when it suits our interests—our desire for gain, security, and reputation—we twist that which is best into the worst of all; in the hands of evil men and women, what is holy becomes demonic.[57]

As I noted in chapter 4, critics give two main reasons why major world religions have, as they see it, a strong proclivity toward violence. First, for most world religions the distinctions between true and false religion, justice and injustice, and good and evil are central. They affirm the goodness of the way of life they seek to follow and therefore reject others as imperfect, misguided, or even wicked. Second, in their own self-understanding, most world religions are based either on positive revelation (Moses, Jesus, or Muhammad) or on spiritual enlightenment (Buddha or Confucius) granted to foundational figures; reason stops at some point, critics object, and gives way to mere conviction. It follows, critics insist, that world religions are marked by irrational certainty. Moreover, unlike rationality, which all humans possess, revelation or enlightenment belongs only to a select few. World religions divide humanity into an in-group and an out-group. Insisting without sufficient reason on the truth of your own view of the ultimate reality and the way of life corresponding to it is bound to breed violence, many critics insist.[58]

But the distinction between true and false religion, which is tied with the concern of religion with justice, is a presupposition of responsible peace and not, as such, a cause of violence. As to the alleged irrationality of religion, the critical issue isn't that in religions reason stops at some point, giving way to conviction, for reason *never* goes all the way, not even in philosophy or science. The critical issue is the content of religious teachings, for instance, whether they urge you to be merciful and love your enemies or to kill the infidel, heretic, or transgressor.[59] But the defenders of religions aren't entirely correct either. It is too easy merely to blame corrupt human nature for religious violence. The connection between religion and violence is too tight not to examine the contribution of religions themselves to violence.

Both defenders and critics miss the actual way in which religions foment violence because they tend to see religions as monolithic and static wholes; defenders deem a particular religion or all of them to be peaceable, and critics deem them to be violent. Working with a more dynamic understanding of religion, David Martin has helpfully suggested that we think of religions as "repertoires of linked motifs internally articulated in a distinctive manner, and giving rise to characteristic extrapolations" about a way of life in the world, repertoires that are tied back to the original revelation, enlightenment, or wisdom but not identical with it.[60] Depending on a setting (for instance, features of the culture, other religions present, the needs of the political powers) and guiding interests, the character of a religion changes: some motifs from its repertoire are backgrounded, others are foregrounded, and most are "played" with various types and degrees of consonance or dissonance with the situation. Changing as they do depending on circumstances, religions are not infinitely malleable, however. Each religion's original articulation "creates a flexible but distinctive logic and a grammar of transformations."[61] Original articulations place normative constraints on religions as they change depending on circumstances. They are also the wellsprings of religions' internal reform.

Some forms world religions take foster violence whereas others don't. The critical question is what makes the difference. As I will argue shortly, the main culprit is the entanglement of religions with political power, either when the original articulation was made or as it was later transmitted, received, and its motifs rearranged. That's what both defenders and critics of religions fail to see when they trace religious violence back to the basic flaw of human nature or to exclusivism and irrationality. Why do world religions so easily get entangled with political power? Their adherents twist one constitutive feature of these religions: the claim that a particular religion is the true way of life. Instead of being content to bear witness to truth and thereby honor the responsibility of persons to embrace a way of life for themselves (which, as I argued in chapter 3, is also a constitutive feature of world religions), the adherents of world religions use instruments of the state's power to subdue and compel detractors. In the process, they reconfigure the religion, foregrounding its more bellicose motifs. Let me elaborate how the entanglement with political power and the corresponding reconfiguration of religion works.

Entanglement with Power

Two Western thinkers, Thomas Hobbes and Immanuel Kant, each the source of a dominant tradition in political philosophy, noted two major functions of religion in society. First, *religions are employed as tools of government.* Hobbes noted that rulers use religion to make it easier to govern their subjects. To that end, with the help of religious elites, they "nourish, dresse, and forme" native religious inclinations (which Hobbes thought stemmed from the fear of invisible powers), crafting religious convictions to dull people to suffering, legitimize oppressive rule, and justify unjust wars.[62] Second, religions function as *markers of communal identity.* Kant thought that in addition to diversity of languages the varieties of religions are the primary way nature separates people in groups. As markers of identity religions "bring with them the propensity to mutual hatred and pretexts for war," he believed.[63] These two functions of religion often merge into one. In the conflict between Christians and Muslims in Kosovo, the birthplace of Serbian Orthodox civilization now populated primarily by Muslim Albanians, as well as in conflicts between Hindus and Muslims in Ayodhya, at the birthplace of the god-king Rama and the site of Babri Mosque, religions functioned, arguably, primarily as such legitimacy-granting and aggression-motivating markers of identity.[64]

Giving Hobbes's and Kant's observations about religion in society a sociological twist (though without linking his proposal to either), David Martin identified special circumstances under which religions turn violent. "These special circumstances occur when religion becomes virtually coextensive with society and thus with the dynamics of power, violence, control, cohesion, and marking out of boundaries."[65] Religions are then not merely publicly and politically engaged; they have turned into "political religions." The temptation to blend religion, the moral and cultural self-understanding of a group, and political power is strong, as the three together can generate high levels of solidarity. Many think that the primary function of religion is to provide "collective representation" of social unity.[66] But, as I argued in chapter 2, in their basic formal structure, the world religions are not "political religions" but cultural systems distinct from politics; they must be *turned into* markers of political identity and legitimizers of a given government's power.

When religions become markers of group identity, they tend to exacerbate conflicts by providing groups with the aura of the sacred and thus energizing and legitimizing the struggles; inversely, conflicts between groups associated predominantly with a single religion push those religions to morph into markers of that group's identity. Similarly, entanglement with political power pushes toward the kind of configuration of a religion's motifs that will provide the political power with legitimacy. In situations of conflict, a religion thus configured ends up justifying the group's deployment of violence.[67] This dynamic can be observed in religions that were, in their original formulation, closely aligned to a specific group of people and its power (such as Judaism and Hinduism) and in religions that were not (such as Buddhism and Christianity) as well as in religions whose original formulation contains both a period of distance from and a period of closeness to political power (Islam).[68]

Perhaps the best recent example of such reconfiguration of a religion through tight association with a social group and its political rule is the paradox of a Sri Lankan Buddhist monk who has taken up the gun.[69] Buddhist monks are supposed to be deeply committed to nonviolence; they are required not only to refrain from killing but to keep at a distance from armies and traffic in arms. Not so in Sri Lanka in the second half of the twentieth century. According to Stanley Tambiah, many Sri Lankan monks came to believe that "the religion of the Buddha and the language and culture of the Sinhalese cannot flourish without a sovereign territory which is the motherland of Sri Lanka."[70] To give legs to this belief, they embraced "political Buddhism." Built on "certain canonical *suttas* dealing with ideal righteous rulers" and the Buddhist goal of "muting worldly desires," political Buddhism stood against "divisive party politics and . . . hankering after West-inspired materialist, consumerist, and capitalist self-seeking goals," proposing in their place "a simpler harmonious 'Buddhist way of life' in a 'Buddhist democracy.'" In the process "the substantively soteriological, ethical, and normative components of canonical doctrinal Buddhism qua religion were weakened, displaced, and even distorted"—not just its character "primarily as an ego-ideal and a mental discipline for personal salvation" but its characteristic stance toward violence as well.[71] As the sons of Buddha took on the identity of the "sons of soil," their religion was reconfigured and the affirmation of violence slithered into a religion whose central motifs establish a strong presumption of nonviolence.[72]

The single most significant factor determining whether a religion will be implicated in violence is this: the level of its identification with a political project and its entanglement with the agents striving to realize that project. The more identified a religion is with these, the more likely it will be for even the most peaceful religion to "take up the gun." In *A Public Faith*, I distinguished between "thick" and "thin" versions of religions. When they are "thick," religions map a way of life, foster a sense of connection with the ultimate reality, and sketch a moral vision embedded in an account of the self, social relations, and the good; part of such a religion is an extended argument about its nature as originally given and its relation to the changing world. As I suggested in chapter 2, all world religions were originally articulated, received, and practiced as just such "thick" religions. In contrast, religions are "thin" when they are emptied of their moral visions and reduced to "vague religiosity that serves primarily to energize, heal, and give meaning to the business of life whose course is shaped by factors other than religion (such as political or economic interests)."[73] For the most part, the "thinning" of religions, I propose, is created when they identify too closely with a given community and the dynamics of its power; and such "thin" religions are most susceptible to being used as merely a political and cultural resource, and occasionally even as a weapon in war.

To avoid inspiring and legitimizing violence, should religions be privatized and kept out of public life, barred from public engagement? In chapter 3 I argued against the privatization of religion. Here it suffices to note that public engagement is distinct from entanglement with political power. As the example of the great religious democratizers in Chile, Indonesia, the Philippines, or Poland attests, it is possible for religions to inspire and help guide public engagement without turning into mere markers of identity and instruments of political power. To avoid inspiring and legitimating violence, religions should (1) nurture a healthy sense of independence from either established or aspiring political authority, and (2) resist reconfiguring religion so as to reduce it primarily to a political and cultural resource.

Ways of Life

But religions aren't always reduced to mere tools crafted and used by combatants in conflicts, whether these are governments or communal leaders. Even thick religions can generate conflicts. Consider that whatever else such a thick religion may be, it is a *way of life*—or perhaps a quarreling family of diverse ways of life—both changing with times and circumstances and, on account of its abiding tie to its origins, remaining the same.[74] Put more abstractly, each religion articulates a vision of human flourishing, of the self, social relations, and the good, and provides ways to mobilize people's feelings and wills and to stabilize their character so as to live in accordance with that vision.[75] The alternative visions of flourishing often collide, and the people espousing them clash, especially when they live under the same roof. That's true even if religions have kept their independence from the levers of political power.

Arguably, the teaching of Jesus, with its stress on generosity, non-retaliation, and love of enemy, is among the most peaceable of all religious teachings. As such, it can illustrate well the conflict-generating character of religions practiced "thickly." Famously, and to some shockingly, Jesus said: "Do not think that I have come to bring peace to the earth; I have not come to bring peace, but a sword. For I have come to set a man against his father, and a daughter against her mother, and a daughter-in-law against her mother-in-law; and one's foes will be members of one's own household" (Matthew 10:34–36). How is it that Jesus brought the "sword"? Not because he provided religious legitimacy to quarrels around gain, security, and reputation or because he advocated either that religion make use of the state's sword or the state avail itself of religion's word. On the contrary, when Jesus's followers take up the sword over these issues, they betray his teaching. About gain he taught: "Do not store up for yourself treasures on earth" (Matthew 6:19); about safety he instructed: "Love your enemies and pray for those who persecute you" (Matthew 5:44); about reputation he commanded: "If anyone strikes you on the right cheek [a blow to the face as an insult], turn the other also" (Matthew 5:39).

The sword that Jesus came to bring doesn't stand for conflict about gain, safety, or reputation. Instead, it symbolizes conflict about a person's ultimate allegiance and the way of life entailed in it. Here is how he explains why it is that he sets a man against his father and a woman against her mother: "Whoever loves father or mother more than me is not worthy of me; and whoever loves son or daughter more than me is not worthy of me; and whoever does not take up the cross and follow me is not worthy of me. Those who find their life will lose it, and those who lose their life for my sake will find it" (Matthew 10:37–39). Ultimate allegiances often clash (here, family versus Jesus) and ways of life often clash (here, pleasure and self-preservation versus losing life in self-sacrificial love), and therefore people with alternative ultimate allegiances and ways of life often clash as well, especially when they live in a shared space. The critical question is whether religions have resources to "manage" conflicts that their differences generate, to prevent conflicts from turning violent, to treat "the sword" as a symbol for serious and respectful struggle between visions of the good life and their public implications rather than as an instrument for coercion and spilling blood.

The same processes of globalization helping to pacify the world are also pushing people of different religions to live in a single world under the shared roofs of discrete democratic states. The very proximity to others often heightens the investment of each in its own religious, ethnic, and other cultural differences.[76] And to the extent that religions are not like flags, empty markers of identity, but shape their adherents' respective accounts of the good life, religions also make their social visions diverge. When communities with strong identities and divergent social visions live together and have to arrange their common life, conflicts are inevitable.[77]

Globalization processes exacerbate conflicts around competing visions of social life—"our values and our way of life," as politicians in times of crisis often put it, but they don't create them. As Jesus's words about the sword illustrate, such conflicts are endemic to religious life in pluralistic settings, at least when world religions, to which truth and justice are central, are in play. But these conflicts need not be unproductive, and they certainly need not be violent. To make them productive, the parties involved need to meet two basic requirements. First, each world religion needs to grant the others freedom to take responsibility for their lives and to choose the way of life they deem best. In other words, religions need to affirm full freedom of religion to all individuals—freedom not just to believe in private or practice in a community but freedom to choose one's religion. Second, the parties involved must embrace the principle of reciprocity. Whatever rights and privileges they want to claim for themselves, they must grant the same to all others.

World religions, in fact, have internal resources to meet these two requirements. As I argued in chapter 3, in their repertoires of motifs, some version of the Golden Rule and therefore the affirmation of moral equality of all individuals has pride of place, and they all affirm freedom of religion in some form, an implication of their basic conviction that each individual has responsibility to follow a way of life in response to a transcendent call. Without loss to religion's integrity, these motifs can be highlighted and reshaped so as to make it possible for religions practiced thickly as ways of life to coexist peacefully under the same roof and negotiate their differences in a vigorous and yet productive way.

Let me sum up my argument about world religions, conflict, and reconciliation. First, *religions need not be breeding grounds of violence.* The likelihood of religions motivating and legitimizing violence is greatly reduced if people of diverse religions embrace the following four rules:

- Guard each religion's independence from political power and resist employing it as a marker of communal identity.
- Concentrate on the religion's vision of the good life, drawing on the full resources of original revelation and subsequent tradition.
- Embrace complete freedom of religion—freedom to practice it and to choose it.
- Don't compromise on the Golden Rule but affirm the moral equality of individuals.

Second, though often a source of conflict, *religions are also the primary drivers of reconciliation* among people. Historically, most reconciliation efforts have been religiously motivated, legitimized, and shaped. Religions have resources for constructing compelling accounts of reconciliation, and these resources are central, not marginal, to them. My own sketch of reconciliation above, and my writings that underpin it, have, I trust, demonstrated the reconciling potential of the

Christian faith. In *Just and Unjust Peace,* Daniel Philpott has shown the centrality of reconciliation in all three Abrahamic religions: Judaism, Christianity, and Islam.[78]

Combine the pacifying aspects of globalization (at its best), to which I referred with the images of Leviathan, Iustitia, and Mammon, with the reconciling efforts of the world religions (at their best), and the prospects for peace are good. By pursuing reconciliation, religions attend to the wrongdoing of the past, preventing it from colonizing the future; by establishing the external conditions for peace (among other things), Leviathan, Iustitia, and Mammon put in place significant obstacles to conflict and remove some of its major causes.

Epilogue

At 8:45 a.m., September 11, 2001, when the first hijacked passenger jet crashed into the north tower of the World Trade Center, I was concluding a speech on reconciliation. The venue was the United Nations, the occasion a prayer breakfast before the beginning of the Fifty-sixth General Assembly. My contention, wrapped into a meditation, was that religion has powerful resources for fostering peace. The inferno that engulfed the Twin Towers delivered an undeniable proof of religion's potential to bring about destruction and death. Devotion to God, the transcendent source of ultimate values, fused with resentment over Western economic, political, and cultural dominance and domination, fed the conflagration as much as did the thousands of gallons of jet fuel. It makes little difference that the hijackers weren't zealously religious; those who sent them on the suicidal mission were, and all involved believed they acted under God's guidance and with God's blessing against an oppressive and decadent enemy.[1]

Fast-forward from the beginning of the first decade of the new millennium to its end, to the year 2008, when the World Economic Forum established the Network of Global Agenda Councils. The founder and executive chairman of the organization, Klaus Schwab, described the network's yearly gatherings in Dubai with characteristic hyperbole: the "world's foremost intelligence network" in the "biggest brainstorming session ever to take place."[2] At the time, the world was in the throws of the Great Recession after the 2008 financial crisis—according to Ben Bernanke, former chairman of the Federal Reserve, "the worst financial crisis in global history, including the Great Depression."[3] Mr. Schwab charged the network with framing the Global Redesign Initiative. As a participant in these extraordinary gatherings, I heard much about financial regulation, economic growth, geopolitics, energy needs, sustainability, technology, innovation, proliferating security threats, and more; we also discussed values and religions, the topics of the two Global Agenda Councils to which I belonged, including the moral scandal of continuing widespread abject poverty and great inequality. All those issues were part of the crisis and had to figure in its solution.

Still, I came away from the gatherings convinced that we had failed to discuss what matters the most, perhaps because many of us believed that, with a commitment to fairness, we could allay our economic woes with technological, political, and economic tools alone. We hardly ever touched on the "dark horse of passion," which the great philosophers and founders of world religions believed pulled the chariot of the soul, often with the willing help of the "white horse of reason."[4] Arguably, what triggered the entire financial crisis was fired-up desire gone awry; it was the systemically stoked and rationally justified self-reproducing greed of lenders and the seemingly insuppressible craving of borrowers—the first longing to drive Bentleys rather than mere BMWs and the second eager to trade in rusty Corollas for sparkling Camrys. On the margins of the gatherings, we discussed happiness, including the insufficiency of the prevalent idea that proliferating and intensifying pleasure while avoiding pain will lead to happiness. But the relative importance in the ecology of the good life of things we design, create, and trade remained largely off the table. It could be that most of us at those big and brainy Dubai brainstorming powwows understood that global order should serve the good life. But we left unexamined what that good life might be and how Corollas and Bentleys along with all other goods and services fit into it.

Living through 9/11 in New York City and discussing the Great Recession at the meetings of the Global Agenda Councils in Dubai—these two experiences have shaped my concerns in this book. The one was an encounter with religion gone homicidal in reaction to the Western way of life and its geopolitical and geoeconomic infrastructure; the other experience was that of inattentiveness to distortions of human desire and of the visions of the good life in the face of the failure of both this very infrastructure and the individuals who make use of it.

A specter is haunting the world—not a specter of communism, as Karl Marx wrote at the beginning of the *Communist Manifesto*, but the specter of nihilism. In New York and Dubai I sensed nihilism at work in the world—not, for the most part, an explicit rejection of moral and religious principles or an avowal of the meaninglessness of life, but a stealthier kind of nihilism that either wears a clean, ironed, and buttoned-up uniform of moral order or romps around pushing against the parameters of a moral order designed to curb but not terminate it.

Our best insights about nihilism come from Friedrich Nietzsche, the son and grandson of Lutheran ministers, who lost faith after a semester of studying theology. In many of his writings, most notably in *On the Genealogy of Morality*, he argued that world religions, notably Judaism and Christianity, are culturally complex forms of resentment of the weak against the strong.[5] He didn't write much about religion and lethal violence, a problem at the forefront of our attention today. But it isn't hard to imagine that the resentful weak, after having acquired sufficient power, would want to destroy those

197

whom their religions, repositories of unacknowledged resentment turned into virtue, have declared to be evil. Nietzsche himself was more concerned with the pervasive, low-intensity violence he considered native to world religions. Their very moral order at its best is directed against life, suppressing its powers and joys in the name of transcendent ideals.

Building on Nietzsche, others have argued that true believers either reject ordinary life as mere refuse compared to the superabundance of celestial glories or bleach value and beauty out of ordinary life by making it a discardable ladder for the ascent to the divine. In Hubert Dreyfus and Sean Kelly's reading, mistaken, I believe, Dante's *The Divine Comedy,* one of the greatest epic poems ever composed, provides a good example. In the poem, Beatrice, the woman Dante had fallen in love with when he was only a boy and she a girl and who remained the abiding love of his life, leads Dante through paradise to achieve the beatific vision of God. But once Dante beholds God, all earthly joys, including the joy of that great and enduring love, become "irrelevant."[6] This is what Nietzsche called the "passive nihilism" of world religions. In its most zealous form it kills infidels and blasphemers; when it grows "weary," as in Buddhism, it gives up even on desiring; mostly it exists somewhere in the middle between these extremes, squelching life's energies and killing ordinary joys.[7]

The great philosophies and world religions were not, however, the only targets of Nietzsche's assault on nihilism. He also mocked, as bitingly as one can, the nihilism of what he called the "last men," a type of human beings he feared would be the end result of the development of Western civilization.

The earth has become small, and on it hops the last man, who makes everything small. . . .

"We have invented happiness," say the last men, and they

blink. . . . A little poison now and then: that makes for pleasant dreams. And much poison at the end for a pleasant death.

One still works, for work is a form of entertainment. But one is careful lest the entertainment be too harrowing. One no longer becomes poor or rich: both require too much exertion. Who still wants to rule? Who obey? Both require too much exertion.

No shepherd and one herd! Everybody wants the same, everybody is the same. . . .

"Formerly, all the world was mad," say the most refined, and they blink. . . .

One has one's little pleasure for the day and a little pleasure for the night, but one has regard for health.

"We have invented happiness"—say the last men, and they blink.[8]

Perhaps we in the West—perhaps all of us enjoying the blessings of market-driven globalization wherever we happen to live—are a bit like Nietzsche's "last men," weary of all great striving and obsessed with comfort and safety, dreaming petty dreams and enjoying unsubtle pleasures, entertaining ourselves to idiocy while imagining ourselves as the measure of humanity. Call this "weary nihilism light," a dumbed-down version of weary nihilism tailored for creatures who desire comfort, grazing lazily in the valleys between the "passive nihilisms" of great religions and the "active nihilisms" of "free spirits."

Most of us aren't entertainment-addicted flaccid consumerists out to maximize cheap pleasures, blinking away in sham happiness. Many of us want more, much more. True, you could argue that, notwithstanding the great difference in price, there is ultimately little difference in the substance of the experience between sipping Château Pétrus and downing a Miller Light or between wearing a designer dress with six thousand natural pearls and throwing on an old sweat suit. Even if so, the "wolves of Wall Street," to name just one category of today's high achievers, aren't the "last men." They work hard, they compete hard, and they walk over the bodies of the vanquished with smug indifference; when they aren't busy bending the shape of the world to align with their needs, they party hard as well. If you catch them at the right moment, they, too, say, "We have invented happiness"—but they do not blink.

Ruthless high achievers and connoisseurs of what are deemed to be the very best things in life, they are more like Nietzsche himself than the "last men" he so despised. And that takes us to the second type of nihilism, the one Nietzsche embodied rather than diagnosed. That's the "active nihilism" of "free spirits" who define their own values and live according to them. They are the people who believe, sometimes explicitly but more often tacitly, that human beings give value to things because, after the death of God or in the shadows behind God's back, no values are thought to be inscribed into the fabric of reality. But "when all meaning originates with us," we have no good reason to choose one thing over another or one way of life over another, except our own preference itself; "nothing has authority over us and power to move us" then, because what we freely give we can equally freely take back.[9] Whether we dwell in modern equivalents of grand chateaus or live crammed in dilapidated flats beyond the railroad tracks, after we have wiped the horizon clean of transcendence we find ourselves saddled with the crushing burden of an unbearably light existence.[10]

The two nihilisms, the passive one of religious world-deniers and world-destroyers and the active one of a-religious inventors of arbitrary values, are opposed to each other. The struggle between them isn't played out just in the hearts of individuals but on the world stage—among religious fundamentalists clutching transcendent meaning with desperate hands and between those fundamentalists and a-religious libertines, flanked by "last men" fighting for the pleasures and comforts of their way of life.[11]

As antagonists often do, the two nihilisms reinforce one another as well. The life of active nihilists, to whom nothing can matter and everything is unbearably light, is ultimately unsustainable. To escape it, people often call plague on the entirety of things that don't matter but powerfully attract, fleeing into a fundamentalism of transcendent values, some even joining the most brutal of fundamentalists, like the People's Vengeance in tsarist Russia, the Red Brigades a few decades ago in Europe, or the so-called Islamic State in the Middle East today. But though existence in the household of passive nihilists has meaning and weight, preset and unbendable order eventually squeezes out life and joy and the weight of significance becomes impossibly heavy. In *Thus Spoke Zarathustra,* in the section on the three metamorphoses of the spirit, Nietzsche describes what may happen next: the camel, who bears much in reverent obedience, morphs into a lion who kills the dragon of "Thou shalt," and the lion turns into a child, the spirit at one with itself, "willing its own will."[12] Throwing off the burden, fundamentalist camels resurrect as the childlike "free spirits," which is to say as active nihilists—the stance to life they found unbearable to begin with. Raised as he was among camels, Nietzsche himself did not anticipate that a child might long to morph into a camel.

The recursive struggle between these two nihilisms is one of the great antagonisms of our time.

In choosing between meaning and pleasure we *always* make the wrong choice. Pleasure without meaning is vapid; meaning without pleasure is crushing. In its own way, each is nihilistic without the other. But we don't need to choose between the two. The unity of meaning and pleasure, which we experience as joy, is given with the God who is Love. This conviction cradles this entire book; it is the main reason why I believe that we need religion in a globalized world.

But how are meaning and pleasure united? When I invoked God as Love, I signaled that I offer here a Christian answer. As in the introduction, so also here in the epilogue I give voice to my own tradition, rather than, as in the main body of the book, proposing a stance the entire family of world religions ought to take toward each other and toward globalization.[13] Let my Christian account of the unity of meaning and pleasure serve as an invitation to adherents of other religions and to a-religious humanists to articulate theirs.

Relationship to God, I argued in chapter 2, belongs to the very makeup of human beings. Whether we are aware of it or not, in all our longings, in one way or another, we also long for God. Our lives are oriented toward the infinite God and they find meaning in relation to the God who created the world and will bring it to consummation. Apart from God, with the earth of our existence unchained from its sun, the deeper meaning of our lives, the kind that doesn't subvert itself by its arbitrariness, eludes us. Parched for meaning, we then project the power to give meaning onto the finite goods that surround us—the muscle tone of our bodies, steamy sex, loads of money, success in work, fame, family, or nation. But looking for meaning in finite things is a bit—in one regard and to a degree only—like expecting sexual fulfillment from pornography: it isn't just addictively unfulfilling; as a crass simulacrum of a genuine good, it eats away at our ability to enjoy actual sex.[14]

When God gives meaning, doesn't God take away ordinary pleasure? When we embrace God, don't we drop from our hold the world and ourselves as beings whose senses are alive to the sounds and smells and textures and tastes of the world? But if God created the material world inhabited by sentient beings (Genesis 1:1), if God became flesh in the person of Jesus of Nazareth (John 1:14), if the bodies of those bound to God in faith and love are the temples of the Spirit (1 Corinthians 6:19), all central claims Christians make, the opposition between attachment to God and the enjoyment of the ordinary things of life must be false. More: not only is there no necessary opposition between them, but the two can be aligned: *attachment to God amplifies and deepens enjoyment of the world*. Let me explain, as the suggestion may be novel even to theologically trained readers.

Consider an ordinary object—a pen, for instance. You might think it's a mere material thing. It's not. In the *Phenomenology of Perception* Maurice Merleau-Ponty argues that all cultural objects are sediments of human activity and have around them an "atmosphere of humanity."[15] In feeling my gold-nibbed Pelikan fountain pen between my fingers, I don't just touch an object, I relate to my father, who gave it to me. To a lesser degree and in a more diffuse way, this is true also of any of my ultra-fine-point gel-ink pens. As I use them, I relate to myself and to others—for instance, by distinguishing myself, mostly subconsciously, from users of other kinds of pens: I am an "ultra-fine-point-gel-ink-pen guy" as distinct from my good friend Skip, who is a "blue-felt-pen guy"; or I feel a light additional bond to two friends who, like me, write with Pilot G-Tec-C4 pens. If you listen carefully, a simple pen will tell you that most things we encounter aren't just things; they are also social relations.

If things are social relations, then we also take pleasure in them as social relations. In *How Pleasure Works*, Paul Bloom argues convincingly against the commonsense view of pleasure: "People insist that the pleasure that they get from wine is due to its taste and smell, or that music is pleasurable because of its sound, or that a movie is worth watching because of what is on the screen. And of course this is all true . . . but only partially true."[16] The other part of pleasure, the bigger and more significant part, has to do with social relations inhering in things (or with "essences" of things, as Bloom names what I think is largely the same social dimension of things). We derive a great deal of pleasure when we think a painting is an original, which dissipates if we discover that it is a reproduction; we immensely enjoy an object that otherwise would leave us cold (for example, a tape measure) by virtue of its relation to a famous person (John F. Kennedy), and are willing to pay good money for the pleasure ($48,875).[17] What matters most for pleasure isn't the object "as it appears to our senses"[18] but an experience of the object as a thing that is also a particular relationship to other persons. To put it in theological language, we enjoy things the most when we experience them as sacraments—as carriers of the presence of another.

Now think of the world as a gift—the entirety of it and all individual things in it (though you may want to, and have good reason to, leave out torture chambers, children's cancer wards, and the like). To think of a gift, you must, of course, think of a giver. That would be God, the creator and sustainer of worlds (a statement in no way incompatible with the way the sciences describe the origin and evolution of the universe). And then there is you, the recipient. We have a giver (God), a recipient (you), and a gift (the world). A gift is not the object given as such. Little trinkets on the shelves of gift stores are not gifts; they *become* gifts when somebody gives them to somebody else. In other words, gifts are relations.[19] If the world is a gift, then all things to which you relate—and many to which you don't—are also God's relation to you.

Now imagine that you feel a bond to the giver of the gift that is the world, that you are a good Christian (or a Jew or a Muslim) and that you "love the Lord your God with all your heart, and with all your soul, and with all your strength, and with all your mind" (Deuteronomy 6:5; Luke 10:27). Imagine also that in response to the God you love, you also "love your neighbor as your self" (Leviticus 19:18; Luke 10:27). Spread wide and boldly the wings of your fancy, and imagine that all your neighbors do the same, which is, of course, exactly how Christians have for centuries imagined the world to come— as the world of love. Each thing in the world is now a relationship marked by love. Each distant star and every gentle touch, each face and every whiff of the freshly plowed earth, in sum, literally every good and beautiful thing shimmers with an aura both vibrantly real and undetectable to our five senses. Each thing in the world is more than itself and just so a source of deep and many-layered pleasure.[20] To return once more to the analogy between finite things and sex, from the vantage point of such "sacramental" experience of the world, looking for pleasure in finite goods, whether persons or things, as just themselves is a bit like expecting great sex in loveless relationships: pleasure may be there, even excitement, but the rich texture, depth, and the moment-surpassing quality of the enjoyment that love provides is missing. When we experience ordinary things as God's gifts and when we rejoice in experiencing them as such, the world, in a sense, reaches its completion, for the duration of the experience at least. The world then becomes to us what God created it to be. According to my take on one Hasidic interpretation, just this kind of experience of the world in relation to God and of God in relation to the world is the meaning of the Shabbat. On this one day of the week, a day toward which all days are aiming and from which they all gain meaning, human striving comes to an end, and the joy in the world as the gift and in God as the giver reigns supreme.[21] On the seventh day of creation—make it the eighth day, if you are a Christian—we don't go through the things of ordinary life to take delight in some deeper, eternal beauty and goodness in itself; we come to experience ordinary things as extraordinary—as the Lover's gifts—and therefore rejoice in them all the more.[22]

I have offered no argument that the convictions underlying my account of the unity of meaning and pleasure are true—the claims that God in fact *is* Love and that the creation *is* a gift. I couldn't have, not at the tail end of an epilogue, for these are some of the central pillars of the entire Christian faith, contestable, as any claims of such magnitude inevitably are, and repeatedly contested as well. My goal here was both more modest and more foundational than justifying these convictions. It was to show that the Christian faith, if true, makes possible a unity of meaning and ordinary pleasures. It is able to drive out the two nihilisms that egg each other on and chase each other around the globe, spreading desolation and melancholy, grinding this planet and our hopes into dust—and, like the water of life itself, it is able to make our lives, our communities, and our natural habitats blossom.

The argumentative thread of this book has been that globalization stands in need of the visions of flourishing that world religions offer, and that globalization and religions, as well as religions among themselves, need not clash violently but have internal resources to interact constructively and contribute to each other's betterment. In this epilogue, I have attempted to identify the unity of meaning and pleasure as a key wellspring of flourishing, a source of personal contentment, global solidarity, and common care for the planet that our globalized world needs and religions can foster, as I argued earlier. The idea can be expressed simply: the right kind of love for the right kind of God bathes our world in the light of transcendent glory and turns it into a theater of joy. To flesh out this claim and the vision of the good life it underpins will make up the bulk of my future work. I offer this sketch here in the hopes that others will join in the vital exploration.

Notes

Introduction

1. As I worked on this book, I had to choose between the terms *faiths* and *religions* as generic terms for phenomena like Buddhism, Judaism, or Christianity. Both have upsides and downsides, but in the end I decided in favor of the latter. Many Jews resist the description of Judaism as a "faith." Jacob Neusner, for instance, thinks that faith is a category imported from Protestant Christianity. Judaism, he insists, is a "way of life" at whose heart is a set of historical practices, not merely a "system of *belief*" or an act of faith ("From 'Judaism' to 'Torah': An Essay in Inductive Category-Formation," in *Religion and Theology,* vol. 3 of *Neusner on Judaism* [Burlington: Ashgate, 2005], 6–9; see also his "The Theological Enemies of Religious Studies," *Religion* 18.1 [1988]: 25–31). Talal Asad agrees, and with regard not just to Judaism but other religions as well. "Faith," he believes, suggests Protestant interiority, a privatized Christian conception of religion, which "emphasizes the priority of belief as a state of mind rather than as constituting activity in the world" (*Genealogies of Religion: Discipline and Reasons of Power in Christianity and Islam* [Baltimore: Johns Hopkins University Press, 1993], 47).

But "religion" is imprecise and contested as well. Some scholars consider forms of secular humanism, like Marxism, a religion. John Hick's theory of religion places Marxism in the "extended family" of religion, such that the twentieth-century Marxist societies do not count as exceptions to the "virtual universality of religion within human societies" (*An Interpretation of Religion: Human Responses to the Transcendent,* 2nd ed. [New Haven: Yale University Press, 2004]). Others, especially sociologists, look at sports as religion (see Joseph L. Price, ed., *From Season to Season: Sports as American Religion* [Macon: Mercer University Press, 2001]; Craig A. Forney, *The Holy Trinity of American Sports: Civil Religion in Football, Baseball, and Basketball* [Macon: Mercer University Press, 2007]; see also David Chidester, "The Church of Baseball, the Fetish of Coca-Cola, and the Potlatch of Rock 'n' Roll," in *Religion and Popular Culture in America,* ed. Bruce Forbes and Jeffrey Mahan [Berkeley: University of California Press, 2000], 219–37).

In this book, "religion" will primarily refer to "world religions," Buddhism, Judaism, Christianity, and the like. But the use of the term *religion* is contested even for world religions. Some claim that the term is a Western invention. They argue that none of the religions I engage in this book were "religions" until modernity, under Christian influence, separated religion from other spheres of life (see Asad, *Genealogies of Religion;* Daniel Dubuisson, *The Western Construction of Religion: Myths, Knowledge, and Ideology* [Baltimore: Johns Hopkins University Press, 2003]; William Cavanaugh, *The Myth of Religious Violence* [Oxford: Oxford University Press, 2009], 57–122). In contrast, I follow Martin Riesenbrodt, who has argued that "religious activity has always been distinguished from nonreligious activity, religious specialists from other specialists, sacred places from profane places, and holy times from profane times" (*The Promise of Salvation: A Theory of Religion*, trans. Steven Rendall [Chicago: University of Chicago Press, 2010], 1–2).

"Religion" isn't contested only among scholars. For many ordinary people "religion" has highly negative connotations, primarily because it evokes religious institutions bereft of authenticity. Take, for instance, pastor Dave Schmelzer's "six-word theory" to explain his faith in God but aversion to the "religious awfulness in the world": "God is good. Religion is bad" (*Not the Religious Type: Confessions of a Turncoat Atheist* [Carol Stream, Ill.: SaltRiver, 2008], 38). Many prefer the term *spirituality,* as when people say, "I am spiritual but not religious," meaning that their relationship to God or to the transcendent realm matters to them but that they don't care much for religious institutions, dogmas, and rituals (see Robert C. Fuller, *Spiritual, but Not Religious: Understanding Unchurched America* [Oxford: Oxford University Press, 2001]). But spirituality suggests more of a numinous feeling and inner centering than a moral vision, my primary concern in the book.

I predominantly use "religion" because this is the generic term most people employ to describe Buddhism, Hinduism, Confucianism, Judaism, Christianity, and Islam. This, too, is the term used by most national and international legal documents. I could have used "faith" as well because I am primarily interested in the one essential dimension of all world religions: their account of self, social relations, and the good, with a corresponding vision of human flourishing. Every world religion is more than "faith," Christianity—even Protestant Christianity—included; yet in all of them, faith, understood as a set of convictions expressing a commitment to a moral vision, is an essential component.

2. For the emergence of global networks of indigenous religions—"global indigeneity," giving planetary self-understanding to what were traditionally "local" religions—especially as evidenced in the campaign for Mother Earth rights, see La Donna Harris and Jacqueline Wasilewski, "Indigeneity, an Alternative Worldview: Four R's (Relationship, Responsibility, Reciprocity, Redistribution) vs. Two P's (Power and Profit); Sharing the Journey Towards Conscious Evolution," *Systems Research and Behavioral*

Science 21 (2004): 489–503; *The Universal Declaration of Rights of Mother Earth*, accessed January 26, 2014, http://therightsofnature.org/universal-declaration/.

3. Francis Fukuyama, *The End of History and the Last Man* (New York: Free Press, 1992). See also Francis Fukuyama, "The End of History," *National Interest* (Summer 1989): 3–18.

4. "The End of History," 3.

5. For an argument that in terms of world governance we need a "middle way" between West and East, see Nicolas Berggruen and Nathan Gardels, *Intelligent Governance for the 21st Century: A Middle Way Between West and East* (Cambridge: Polity, 2013).

6. There are nondemocratic, authoritarian forms of capitalism, of course, and antidemocratic military dictatorships have been established to protect capitalist economic policies, notably in Latin America. Since the end of the Cold War, though, capitalist economy and democracy have tended to go hand in hand. See Stephen Schlesinger and Stephen Kinzer, *Bitter Fruit: The Story of the American Coup in Guatemala*, rev. ed. (Cambridge, Mass.: Harvard University Press, 2005); Gerardo L. Munck, "The Origins and Durability of Democracy," in *Routledge Handbook of Latin American Politics*, ed. Peter Kingstone and Deborah J. Yashar (New York: Routledge, 2012), 3–20; and Michael Mandelbaum, "Democracy Without America," *Foreign Affairs* 1 (September 2007), accessed January 26, 2014, http://www.foreignaffairs.com/articles/62833/michael-mandelbaum/democracy-without-america.

7. See David Turton, "War and Ethnicity: Global Connections and Local Violence in North East Africa and Former Yugoslavia," *Oxford Development Studies* 25 (1997): 77–94. On the economic motivations for war in the Balkans, including excessive international borrowing and austerity measures of the IMF, see Susan L. Woodward, *Balkan Tragedy: Chaos and Dissolution After the Cold War* (Washington, D.C.: Brookings Institution, 1995).

8. In the last decades of the existence of Yugoslavia, the unitary state was weakened under the pressure of the self-assertion of ethnic identities. Both the reality of the unitary state and its gradual weakening contributed to the breakup of the former Yugoslavia. See W. Harriet Critchley, "The Failure of Federalism in Yugoslavia," *International Journal* 48 (1993): 434–47.

9. On the relation of globalization and organized violence, see Mary Kaldor, *New and Old Wars: Organized Violence in a Global Era*, 2nd ed. (Stanford: Stanford University Press, 2007).

10. For the "twice born" type of religion, see William James, *The Varieties of Religious Experience*, vol. 13 of *The Works of William James* (Cambridge, Mass.: Harvard University Press, 1985), 73, 121–22, 139–40; for the contrast between the "sect," which you join, and the "church," into which you are born, see *The Max Weber Dictionary*, ed. Richard Swedberg (Stanford: Stanford University Press, 2005), s.v. "church" and "sect."

11. Some trace the origins of Pentecostalism to Charles Parham of Topeka, Kansas,

with whom Seymour studied. But Seymour has a better claim to be its founder than anybody else. See Cecil M. Robeck Jr., "The Origins of Modern Pentecostalism: Some Historiographical Issues," in *The Cambridge Companion to Pentecostalism*, ed. Amos Yong and Cecil M. Robeck Jr. (Cambridge: Cambridge University Press, 2014), 13–30; Cecil M. Robeck Jr., "What I Have Learned about 'Azusa Street': An Interim Report" (opening plenary address at the Society of Pentecostal Studies meeting, Fuller Theological Seminary, March 23, 2006); Gastón Espinosa, ed., *William J. Seymour and the Origins of Global Pentecostalism* (Durham: Duke University Press, 2014).

12. Pew Forum on Religion and Public Life, *Global Christianity: A Report on the Size and Distribution of the World's Christian Population*, December 2011, 17, 69, accessed May 7, 2015, http://www.pewforum.org/files/2011/12/Christianity-fullreport-web .pdf. See Stephen Hunt, *A History of the Charismatic Movement in Britain and the United States of America: The Pentecostal Transformation of Christianity* (Lewiston, Idaho: Edwin Mellen, 2009).

13. See Harvey Cox, *Fire from Heaven: The Rise of Pentecostal Spirituality and the Reshaping of Religion in the 21st Century* (Reading, Mass.: Addison-Wesley, 1995). On Pope Francis and charismatic renewal, see his comments at the press conference during his return flight from Rio de Janeiro, July 28, 2013, accessed May 7, 2015, http://w2.vatican.va/ content/francesco/en/speeches/2013/july/documents/papa-francesco_20130728_ gmg-conferenza-stampa.html. See also the pope's message to the Kenneth Copland Ministries conference, January 21, 2014, accessed May 7, 2015, https://www.youtube .com/watch?v=eulTwytMWlQ.

14. For a very brief analysis of such links—of what sociologists call a Durkheimian modality of the relation between religion and society—see Charles Taylor, *Varieties of Religion Today: William James Revisited* (Cambridge, Mass.: Harvard University Press, 2002), 75.

15. For Catholics, that tie had loosened after Vatican II. *Dignitatis Humanae*, perhaps the most revolutionary of the documents of that reformist council, affirmed religious freedom (promulgated by Pope Paul VI, December 7, 1965, accessed July 14, 2014, http://www.vatican.va/archive/hist_councils/ii_vatican_council/documents/ vat-ii_decl_19651207_dignitatis-humanae_en.html.

16. See Thomas Helwys, *Book Two*, in *A Short Declaration of the Mystery of Iniquity*, ed. Richard Groves (Macon: Mercer University Press, 1998), 53–62. See also John Locke, *Two Treatises of Government*, in *Two Treatises of Government and a Letter Concerning Toleration*, ed. Ian Shapiro (New Haven: Yale University Press, 2003), 141–54.

17. See Miroslav Volf, "Materiality of Salvation: An Investigation in the Soteriologies of Liberation and Pentecostal Theologies," *Journal of Ecumenical Studies* 26 (1989): 437–67.

18. See Karl Löwith, *Meaning in History: The Theological Implications of the Philosophy of History* (Chicago: University of Chicago Press, 1949).

19. See Jürgen Moltmann, *Theology of Hope: On the Ground and the Implications of a Christian Eschatology,* trans. Margaret Kohl (Minneapolis: Fortress, 1993); Jürgen Moltmann, *The Coming of God: Christian Eschatology,* trans. Margaret Kohl (Minneapolis: Fortress, 1996), 25–26.

20. For the distinction between creation ex nihilo and creation ex vetere, see John Polkinghorne, *The Faith of a Physicist* (Princeton: Princeton University Press, 1994), 167–69.

21. See Moltmann, *The Coming of God,* 159–84. Moltmann rightly notes that, historically, Christians have tried to hasten the coming of God in the project of political and ecclesiastical millenialism.

22. See Hannah Arendt, *The Human Condition* (Chicago: University of Chicago Press, 1958), 8–9.

23. For the significance of "conversion" in response to the call of promise, see Moltmann, *The Coming of God,* 22–29, 44–46.

24. See Dietrich Bonhoeffer, *Letters and Papers from Prison,* rev. ed., ed. Eberhard Bethge, trans. Reginald Fuller et al. (New York: Touchstone, 1997), 297.

25. On such a stance, see Miroslav Volf, *A Public Faith: How Followers of Christ Should Serve the Common Good* (Grand Rapids, Mich.: Brazos, 2011). I originally developed it in my 1993 habilitation lecture at the University of Tübingen (Miroslav Volf, "Christliche Identität und Differenz: Zur Eigenart der christlichen Präsenz in den modernen Gesellschaften," *Zeitschrift zur Theologie und Kirche* 92 [1995]: 357–75). See also Kathryn Tanner, *Theories of Culture: A New Agenda for Theology* (Minneapolis: Fortress, 1997). For more recent takes on Christian engagement roughly aligned with my own—advocating neither wholesale revolutionary transformation (a position instantiated radically in some documents of the World Council of Churches [*Alternative Globalization Addressing Peoples and Earth: A Background Document* (Geneva: World Council of Churches, 2005)]) nor exit into an alternative *polis* called the church (a position associated with Stanley Hauerwas [e.g., *In Good Company: The Church as Polis* (Notre Dame: University of Notre Dame Press, 2010)])—see Luke Bretherton, *Christianity and Contemporary Politics: The Conditions of Faithful Witness* (Oxford: Wiley-Blackwell, 2010). In his own way, though less specifically Christianly inflected, Willis Jenkins takes a similar stance in *The Future of Ethics: Sustainability, Social Justice, and Religious Creativity* (Washington, D.C.: Georgetown University Press, 2013).

26. For Marx's humanism, see his foundational text, unpublished during his lifetime, *Economic and Philosophical Manuscripts,* in *Selected Writings,* ed. David McLellan (Oxford: Oxford University Press, 1977), 75–112; for Huxley's humanism, see Julian Huxley, *Evolutionary Humanism* (Buffalo: Prometheus, 1992).

27. Augustine, *Confessions,* 1.1.1.

28. Peter Sloterdijk, *Weltfremdheit* (Frankfurt: Suhrkamp, 1993), 106.

29. For the argument that the dual command to love God and neighbor binds Christians not only with the Jews but also with Muslims, see Miroslav Volf, Prince Ghazi bin Muhammad, and Melissa Yarrington, eds., *A Common Word: Muslims and Christians on Loving God and Neighbor*, 1 (Grand Rapids, Mich.: Eerdmans, 2009).

30. Circumstances, such as social arrangements, do affect our love for God and neighbor (and in conjunction with these two loves also love for ourselves), not only the mental energy we have to love God and the effectiveness with which we can love neighbors and ourselves but also the very existence of that love. But the effects of circumstances on our proper love for God, neighbors, and ourselves are not predictable; they are not causes that create certain effects. The experiences of the children of Israel as recorded in the Bible are instructive: both lives of oppression and want (as during slavery in Egypt) and lives of independence and abundance (as in the Promised Land) can pull people away from love of God and neighbor as well as nudge people to love God and neighbor more effectively. Social arrangements can both help and hinder people striving to lead their lives well.

31. See Volf, *A Public Faith*. See also, for example, Graham Ward, *The Politics of Discipleship: Becoming Postmaterial Citizens* (Grand Rapids, Mich.: Baker Academic, 2009).

32. Some may worry that my proposal is too indebted to the Christian faith, subsuming all other religions under that faith and offering it as the "sacred canopy" of the globalized world, a kind of contemporary appropriation of something like Hegel's account of world history (see Georg W. F. Hegel, *Lectures on the Philosophy of World History*, trans. H. B. Nisbet [Cambridge: Cambridge University Press, 1975]; Löwith, *Meaning in History*, 52–59), as if some marriage of the Christian faith and a certain form of globality were the goal of history. As will become clear in chapter 2, I think that such a "sacred canopy" for the entire globe is neither possible nor desirable.

33. On "dying by bread alone," see Dorothee Soelle, *Death by Bread Alone: Texts and Reflections on Religious Experience*, trans. David L. Scheidt (Philadelphia: Fortress, 1978).

34. Peter Berger and Thomas Luckmann, *The Social Construction of Reality: A Treatise in the Sociology of Knowledge* (Garden City, N.Y.: Doubleday, 1966), 57–58. For a discussion of both/and accounts of social causation and feedback loops between individual and social causation, see Matthew Croasmun, "The Body of Sin: An Emergent Account of Sin as a Cosmic Power in Romans 5–8" (Ph.D. diss., Yale University, 2014).

1.
Globalization and the Challenge of Religions

1. Nayan Chanda notes that the word entered Webster's dictionary for the first time in 1961, three years after the first artificial satellite, Sputnik, circled the earth, allowing

humans to see the entire globe (see *Bound Together: How Traders, Preachers, Adventurers, and Warriors Shaped Globalization* [New Haven: Yale University Press, 2008], 248–50).

2. Karl Marx and Friedrich Engels, "The Communist Manifesto," in *Karl Marx: Selected Writings*, ed. David McLellan (Oxford: Oxford University Press, 1977), 224.

3. Ibid., 223–24.

4. Ibid., 224.

5. Ibid., 224–25.

6. Ibid., 224.

7. Ibid., 225.

8. See Iain Marlow and Omar El Akkad, "Smartphones: Blood Stains at Our Fingertips," *Globe and Mail*, December 3, 2010, accessed September 28, 2013, http://www.theglobeandmail.com/technology/smartphones-blood-stains-at-our-fingertips/article1318713/; and Adriana Stuijt, "Dutch Labour Party Wants Coltan Ban to Stop Child-Slavery in Congo," *Digital Journal*, December 4, 2008, accessed September 28, 2013, http://www.digitaljournal.com/article/263036. Also see United Nations, "Security Council Condemns Illegal Exploitation of Democratic Republic of Congo's Natural Resources," March 5, 2001, accessed September 28, 2013, http://www.un.org/News/Press/docs/2001/sc7057.doc.htm.

9. See Charles Duhig and David Barboza, "Apple's iPad and the Human Costs for Workers in China," *New York Times*, January 25, 2012, accessed September 28, 2013, http://www.nytimes.com/2012/01/26/business/ieconomy-apples-ipad-and-the-human-costs-for-workers-in-china.html. Some of Apple's contracts are now being fulfilled by the Taiwanese manufacturer Pegatron, but according to China Labor Watch, conditions faced by Pegatron employees "are 'even worse' than Foxconn's." See Sharif Sakr, "Apple's New Suppliers," *Engadget*, July 29, 2013, accessed September 28, 2013, http://www.engadget.com/2013/07/29/apples-pegatron-china-labor-watch/.

10. "Independent Investigation of Apple Supplier, Foxconn," *Fair Labor Association*, accessed July 14, 2014, http://www.fairlabor.org/sites/default/files/documents/reports/foxconn_investigation_report.pdf.

11. See Mark Mayne, "Apple iWatch: Price, Rumours, Release Date and Leaks," *T3*, September 9, 2013, accessed September 28, 2013, http://www.t3.com/news/apple-iwatch-rumours-features-release-date.

12. Marshall McLuhan has famously described the world created by globalization processes as "a global village" (*Understanding Media: The Extensions of Man* [New York: McGraw-Hill, 1964], 93; see also Marshall McLuhan and Bruce R. Powers, *The Global Village: Transformations in World Life and Media in the 21st Century* [New York: Oxford University Press, 1989]). What's true about this description is that modern means of communication have made the world smaller. But a village is a place where

a person is embedded in a network of relations and tied to a particular territory. Conversely, a key feature of globalization is the increasing loss of "a sense of place" (Arjun Appadurai, *Modernity at Large: Cultural Dimensions of Globalization* [Minneapolis: University of Minnesota Press, 1996], 29). On time-space compression, see also David Harvey, *The Condition of Postmodernity* (Malden, Mass.: Blackwell, 1990), 260–307.

13. See Hartmut Rosa, *Social Acceleration: A New Theory of Modernity*, trans. Jonathan Trejo-Mathy (New York: Columbia University Press, 2013).

14. The first four components of the above "definition" of globalization refer to objective processes, what Roland Robertson has called "the compression of the world," and the last one to human awareness, in Robertson's terms "intensification of consciousness of the world as the whole" (see *Globalization: Social Theory and Global Culture* [London: Sage, 1992], 8).

15. David Singh Grewal, "The World Isn't Flat—It's Networked," accessed May 20, 2014, http://www.theguardian.com/commentisfree/2008/jul/29/globalisation .globaleconomy. For the full account of this position, see David Singh Grewal, *Network Power: The Social Dynamics of Globalization* (New Haven: Yale University Press, 2008).

16. See Nicholas Crafts, "Globalisation and Economic Growth: A Historical Perspective," *World Economy* 27, no. 1 (2004): 45–58. For discussions of trends in global income inequality, see Isabel Ortiz and Matthew Cummins, "Global Inequality: Beyond the Bottom Billion" (Social and Economic Policy Working Paper, UNICEF, April 2011); Branko Milanovi , "Global Income Inequality by the Numbers: In History and Now" (Policy Research Working Paper 6259, World Bank Development and Research Group Poverty and Inequality Team, November 2012).

17. See Jan Aart Scholte, *Globalization: A Critical Introduction*, 2nd ed. (Basingstoke, U.K.: Palgrave Macmillan, 2005), 279–315. On the relationship between globalization and peace and security, see Katherine Barbieri and Rafael Reuveny, "Economic Globalization and Civil War," *Journal of Politics* 67 (2005): 1228–47; Roger G. Blanton and Clair Apodaca, "Economic Globalization and Violent Civil Conflict: Is Openness a Pathway to Peace?" *Social Science Journal* 44 (2007): 599–619; Indra de Soysa and Hanne Fjelde, "Is the Hidden Hand an Iron Fist? Capitalism and Civil Peace, 1970–2005," *Journal of Peace Research* 47 (2010): 287–98; Indra de Soysa and Krishna Chaitanya Vadlamannati, "Does Being Bound Together Suffocate, or Liberate? The Effects of Economic, Social, and Political Globalization on Human Rights, 1981–2005," *Kyklos* 64 (2011): 20–53.

For globalization and international crime, see Willem van Schendel and Itty Abraham, eds., *Illicit Flows and Criminal Things: States, Borders, and the Other Side of Globalization* (Bloomington: Indiana University Press, 2005); H. Richard Friman, "The Great Escape? Globalization, Immigrant Entrepreneurship and the Criminal Economy," *Review of International Political Economy* 11 (2004): 98–131; Ralph Rozema,

"Forced Disappearance in an Era of Globalization: Biopolitics, Shadow Networks, and Imagined Worlds," *American Anthropologist* 113 (2011): 582–93.

18. For the complex relationship between globalization and cultural homogeneity, see Appadurai, *Modernity at Large,* 32–47; Luke Martell, *The Sociology of Globalization* (Cambridge: Polity, 2010), 89–104; Robert Holton, "Globalization's Cultural Consequences," *Annals of the American Academy of Political and Social Science* 570 (July 2000): 140–52.

Although a number of scholars have pointed to globalization as a key factor in the increasing extinction of languages (e.g., Daniel Nettle and Suzanne Romaine, *Vanishing Voices: The Extinction of the World's Languages* [Oxford: Oxford University Press, 2000]), globalization seems to have varied effects on local and endangered languages. See, for example, Salikoko S. Mufwene, "Language Birth and Death," *Annual Review of Anthropology* 33 (2004): 201–22; Nicholas Faraclas, "Globalization and the Future of Creole Languages," *Journal of Language and Politics* 4 (2005): 331–65.

19. See Appadurai, *Modernity at Large,* 43–45.

20. See James K. Boyce, "Green and Brown? Globalization and the Environment," *Oxford Review of Economic Policy* 20 (2004): 105–28; Robin M. Leichenko and Karen L. O'Brien, *Environmental Change and Globalization: Double Exposures* (Oxford: Oxford University Press, 2008); Arthur P. J. Mol, *Globalization and Environmental Reform: The Ecological Modernization of the Global Economy* (Cambridge, Mass.: MIT Press, 2001).

21. See Anthony Elliott and Charles Lemert, *The New Individualism: The Emotional Costs of Globalization,* rev. ed. (Abingdon, U.K.: Routledge, 2009). International concern for suffering is not, of course, a new phenomenon. In the first century, the Apostle Paul, for example, considered taking a collection among the Greek-speaking churches he helped found for "the poor among the saints in Jerusalem" an important part of his ministry (Romans 15:26; see Acts 11:27–30; 2 Corinthians 8–9). But it does presuppose some degree of interconnectedness (the Roman "globalization" of the Mediterranean world in Paul's case and contemporary globalization in ours), and there is evidence that it has been increasing in recent years. For instance, Americans' giving to international causes increased by approximately 15 percent in 2010. It remains, however, a small fraction of total U.S. charitable giving. See Susan Froetschel, "Global Causes Attract Growing Share of US Giving," *YaleGlobal Online,* January 10, 2012, accessed May 7, 2015, http://yaleglobal.yale.edu/content/global-causes-attract-growing-share-us-giving.

22. On businesses and data gathering, see Jaron Lanier, *Who Owns the Future?* (New York: Simon & Schuster, 2013). The revelations in May and June of 2013 that the U.S. National Security Agency was routinely gathering telephone "metadata" and accessing information from the servers of major Internet companies are indicative of the extent of state information-gathering capabilities.

23. See Daniele Archibugi and Simona Iammarino, "The Globalization of Techno-

logical Innovation: Definition and Evidence," *Review of International Political Economy* 9 (2002): 98–122, for a discussion of the various facets of globalization's impact on technological innovation. The threats include not only those resulting indirectly from technological innovation, such as climate change and, perhaps, genetically modified organisms, but also technologies that directly threaten human life, such as nuclear and biological weapons. For an overview of a wide variety of risks, see Nick Bostrom and Milan M. Ćirković, eds., *Global Catastrophic Risks* (Oxford: Oxford University Press, 2008).

24. Chanda, *Bound Together*, 23. On these four drivers of globalization, see also Appadurai, *Modernity at Large*, 28.

25. Immanuel Wallerstein, *Geopolitics and Geoculture* (Cambridge: Cambridge University Press, 1991), 223. On this, see Nicholas Boyle, *Who Are We Now? Christian Humanism and the Global Market from Hegel to Heaney* (Edinburgh: T&T Clark, 1998), 70–77. A fairly widely cited article (Kevin H. O'Rourke and Jeffrey G. Williamson, "When Did Globalization Begin?" *European Review of Economic History* 6 [2002]: 23–50) puts the "big bang" of globalization in the 1820s, when a sharp rise in international commodity trade began.

26. Chanda, *Bound Together*, 105–44.

27. Vinaya-Pitaka, Mahāvagga, I.11.1, in *Vinaya Texts*, trans. T. W. Rhys Davids and Hermann Oldenberg, vol. 13 of *The Sacred Books of the East*, ed. F. Max Müller (Oxford: Clarendon, 1881), 112–13.

28. Some argue that world religions—above all, monotheisms—incarnate the split between insiders and outsiders just because they operate within the categories of true and false in the realm of faith (see, for example, Jan Assmann, *The Price of Monotheism*, trans. Robert Savage [Stanford: Stanford University Press, 2010]). And yet precisely because they make universal truth claims and apply these to the moral realm as well—the moral realm being integral to faith—world religions operate with universal moral codes, the prime example of which is the Golden Rule. Central to the Golden Rule is the assumption that everyone is included.

29. The same sense of the unity of humanity is found in Greek philosophical systems, starting at least with Socrates and finding sophisticated expressions in Stoic writers like Seneca (see Lucius Annaeus Seneca, *Epistles*, vol. 3, trans. Richard M. Gummere [Cambridge, Mass.: Harvard University Press, 1925], esp. 95.51–53). For a good discussion, see Michelle Lee, *Paul, the Stoics, and the Body of Christ* (Cambridge: Cambridge University Press, 2006), 62–65.

30. See also Jonathan Sacks, *The Dignity of Difference: How to Avoid the Clash of Civilizations* (London: Continuum, 2002), 43. In the second edition, though, he limits the claim to "Biblical monotheism" ([London: Continuum, 2003], 43).

31. Jan Assmann distinguishes between globalization and universalism: "By globalization I understand a process of coalescence of various previously isolated zones into

one system of interconnections and interdependencies, where everything, that is, all nations, empires, tribes, and states cohere in some way or other by political, economic, or cultural relations. Universalism, on the other hand, refers to the rise of theories, ideas, or beliefs with a claim to universal validity. By universalism, therefore, I understand an intellectual and spiritual phenomenon; by globalization, a political, economic, and civilizational process (implying material rather than spiritual culture)" ("Cultural Memory and the Myth of the Axial Age," in *The Axial Age and Its Consequences,* ed. Robert N. Bellah and Hans Joas [Cambridge, Mass.: Belknap, 2012], 376). I, on the other hand, take it that globality and globalization properly understood include claims to universal validity and an awareness of humanity as one.

32. For a very brief discussion of the role of the state in making the economy the increasingly dominant end of society, see Charles Taylor, *Modern Social Imaginaries* (Durham: Duke University Press, 2004), 72–73. Over the course of centuries, the "nation-state," oriented as it was to the welfare of its people, could both support and push back against the forces of the market. But as the U.S. constitutional theorist Philip Bobbitt has argued convincingly, today the nation-state has given way to the "market state," which sees itself as a mechanism of enhancing opportunities through the market (see *The Shield of Achilles: War, Peace, and the Course of History* [New York: Random House, 2002]; *Terror and Consent: The Wars for the Twenty-First Century* [New York: Random House, 2008]).

33. See David Singh Grewal, *The Invention of Economy: The Origins of Economic Thought* (Cambridge, Mass.: Harvard University Press, 2014); David Singh Grewal, "From Love to Self-Love: Toward a Political Theology of *Homo Economicus*" (paper presented at the conference "Love in a Time of Capital: Relationality and Commodification as Subjects of Religion," Yale University, New Haven, Conn., May 9, 2014).

34. See Kathryn Tanner, "Is Capitalism a Belief System?" *Anglican Theological Review* 92 (2010), 623–27.

35. For an examination of the extent to which markets are shaped by beliefs about the fundamental character of human life and its moral values and ideals, see ibid., 617–35.

36. My point is not that human beings became insatiable on account of the dominance of the market. As I will note shortly, the writer of Ecclesiastes wrestled with human insatiability. Plato, too, thought "the love of wealth and the spirit of moderation cannot exist together"; the "desire to become as rich as possible" is "insatiable" (*Republic*, trans. Benjamin Jowett [New York: Random House, 1960], 555b–c). My point here is that insatiability directed toward consumer goods is neither inevitable nor morally desirable— and that the market stimulates consumer insatiability both by its competitive structure and by championing it as a virtue (see Eugene McCarraher's discussion of *pleonexia* in "The End of Capitalism and the Wellsprings of Radical Hope," *Nation,* June 27, 2011, http://www.thenation.com/article/161237/end-capitalism-and-wellsprings-radical-hope#).

37. See Robert Wuthnow, *Meaning and Moral Order: Explorations in Cultural Analysis* (Berkeley: University of California Press, 1987), 66–96; Christian Smith, *Moral, Believing Animals: Human Personhood and Culture* (Oxford: Oxford University Press, 2003), 23–24. As Karl Polanyi suggested in *The Livelihood of Man* (New York: Academic, 1977), 5–17, to take as a "natural" outworking of economic interest the embodiment of generic economic laws found in all human societies is to commit the "economistic fallacy."

38. See Michael J. Sandel, *What Money Can't Buy: The Moral Limits of Markets* (New York: Farrar, Straus & Giroux, 2012).

39. See Andrew Glyn, *Capitalism Unleashed: Finance, Globalization, and Welfare* (Oxford: Oxford University Press, 2006), 156–83; David Harvey, *A Brief History of Neoliberalism* (Oxford: Oxford University Press, 2005); George DeMartino, *Global Economy, Global Justice: Theoretical and Policy Alternatives to Neoliberalism* (London: Routledge, 2000). David Rueda and Jonas Pontusson have provided evidence that social market economies with significant welfare states, government regulation of employment conditions, and highly institutionalized collective bargaining tend to produce less wage inequality than do liberal market economies without these features ("Wage Inequality and Varieties of Capitalism," *World Politics* 52 [2000]: 350–83). In contrast, proponents of liberal capitalism argue that a *minimally* regulated market economy produces *less* inequality than other systems (e.g., Milton Friedman, *Capitalism and Freedom*, 3rd ed. [Chicago: University of Chicago Press, 2002], 169).

40. Tariq Ramadan, *Globalization: Muslim Resistances* (Lyon: Tawhid, 2003); *Alternative Globalization Addressing Peoples and Earth (AGAPE)* (Geneva: World Council of Churches, 2005).

41. In "Two Theories of Modernity," Charles Taylor argues both against purely "a-cultural" as well as against purely "cultural" accounts of modernity, suggesting instead that there are multiple modernities resulting from the intersection in a given social space of "a-cultural processes" (such as the market) and "cultural factors" (such as the available accounts of self, social relations, and the good). See Charles Taylor, "Two Theories of Modernity," in *Alternative Modernities*, ed. Dilip Parameshwar Gaonkar (Durham: Duke University Press, 2001), 172–96; here he builds on the thesis of multiple modernities—rather than a single secularizing modernity—formulated by Shmuel Eisenstadt ("Multiple Modernities," *Daedalus* 129.1 (2000): 1–29). Taylor's argument about modernity applies to globalization as well. Hence my phrase: single globalization in multiple registers. In whatever register we encounter globalization, however, it is a result of the intersection of the market and its embedded values on the one hand and the available cultural resources, shaped mainly by world religions, on the other. So by "globalization" I refer to the whole set of registers in which globalization is "played" at the intersection of the market and traditional cultural vectors.

42. Charles Taylor, *Sources of the Self: The Making of the Modern Identity* (Cam-

bridge, Mass.: Harvard University Press, 1989), 14, 211–302. See also Charles Taylor, *A Secular Age* (Cambridge, Mass.: Belknap, 2007), 370–74.

43. Adam Smith, *Lectures on Justice, Police, Revenue and Arms,* ed. E. Cannan (New York: Random House, 1896), 338. The debates in Marxism in the mid-twentieth century between those who highlighted "labor" (economic development) and those who stressed "praxis" (political and artistic activity broadly construed) were about this very issue: is the Marxian vision to be given primarily an "ordinary" or a "higher" life twist? (though, of course, in that debate the "higher life" was understood within the framework of materialism); see Joseph Femia, "Western Marxism," in *Twentieth-Century Marxism: A Global Introduction,* ed. Daryl Glaser and David M. Walker (New York: Routledge, 2007), 95–117.

44. Taylor, *The Sources of the Self,* 215. On Calvinism, Lutheranism, and their specific effects on the shape and exercise of state power, see Philip Gorski, *Disciplinary Revolution: Calvinism and the Rise of the State in Early Modern Europe* (Chicago: University of Chicago Press, 2003), 15–22, 114–55.

45. For a Christian condemnation of economic globalization, see the document of the World Council of Churches that the Justice, Peace and Creation team prepared for its 2006 General Assembly: *Alternative Globalization Addressing Peoples and Earth (AGAPE).* For a Muslim condemnation of globalization, see Ramadan, *Globalization.* For present-day critiques of globalization along the same lines, see Michael Hardt and Antonio Negri, *Empire* (Cambridge, Mass.: Harvard University Press, 2000); Naomi Klein, *No Logo* (New York: Picador, 2000); Luis Suarez-Villa, *Globalization and Technocapitalism* (Farnham, U.K.: Ashgate, 2012); and the essays in *Globalization, the State, and Violence,* ed. Jonathan Friedman (Walnut Creek, Calif.: AltaMira, 2003). Amish, Haredim, and Tablighi Jamaat are examples of religious communities that take the "enclavist" option, withdrawing into alternative communities (see Sara Heitler Bamberger, "Retaining Faith in the Land of the Free," in *The Impact of Globalization on the United States,* ed. Michelle Bertho [Westport, Conn.: Praeger, 2008], 1:231–32). Samuel Heilman has used the term *enclavist* to describe Jewish groups like the Haredim for their attempt to remain "protected within [Judaism's] parochial cultural enclaves" (*Sliding to the Right: The Contest for the Future of American Jewish Orthodoxy* [Berkeley: University of California Press, 2006], 4). Commenting on enclavist groups, Bamberger notes that while they "strive to deny or mute the impact of globalization, economic reality makes a fully impermeable barrier impossible" ("Retaining Faith in the Land of the Free," 234).

46. See Max Stackhouse, *Globalization and Grace: A Christian Public Theology for a Global Future,* vol. 4 of *God and Globalization,* ed. Max Stackhouse, Peter Paris, Don Browning, and Diane Obenchain (New York: Continuum, 2007). For a defense of globalization that is not done from a specifically religious standpoint, see Jagdish Bhagwati, *In Defense of Globalization* (Oxford: Oxford University Press, 2007).

47. For an argument for such a stance to any given culture from a Christian perspective, see Miroslav Volf, *A Public Faith: How Followers of Christ Should Serve the Common Good* (Grand Rapids, Mich.: Brazos, 2011), 77–97.

48. John Paul II, "Address of John Paul II to the Pontifical Academy of Social Sciences," April 27, 2001, no. 4, accessed July 15, 2014, http://www.vatican.va/holy_father/john_paul_ii/speeches/2001/documents/hf_jp-ii_spe_20010427_pc-social-sciences_en.html; John Paul II, "Address of His Holiness John Paul II (at the Fiftieth General Assembly of the United Nations Organization)," October 5, 1995, no. 7, accessed July 15, 2014, http://www.vatican.va/holy_father/john_paul_ii/speeches/1995/october/documents/hf_jp-ii_spe_05101995_address-to-uno_en.html.

49. John Paul II, "From the Justice of Each Comes Peace for All: Message of His Holiness, Pope John Paul II for the Celebration of the World Day of Peace," January 1, 1998, no. 1, no. 8, accessed July 15, 2014, http://www.vatican.va/holy_father/john_paul_ii/messages/peace/documents/hf_jp-ii_mes_08121997_xxxi-world-day-for-peace_en.html.

50. Ibid., no. 8.

51. John Paul, II, "Address of John Paul II," no. 2.

52. Ibid., no. 3.

53. Ibid., no. 4; John Paul II, "Address of His Holiness John Paul II," no. 13; John Paul II, "From the Justice," no. 3. I take it that by not treating a human being as "a means," John Paul II means not treating a human being as *mere* means, a formulation corresponding exactly to that of Immanuel Kant, on whom he implicitly leans (see Immanuel Kant, *Grounding for the Metaphysics of Morals: On a Supposed Right to Lie Because of Philanthropic Concerns,* trans. James W. Ellington [Indianapolis: Hackett, 1993]), for in social exchanges it is impossible not to treat a human being at all as a means.

54. The following analysis is based on Tenzin Gyatso's famous lecture "The Global Community and the Need for Universal Solidarity," *International Journal of Peace Studies* 7 (2002): 1–14.

55. Milan Kundera, *The Unbearable Lightness of Being,* trans. Michael Henry Heim (New York: Harper Perennial Classics, 1999).

56. Immanuel Kant, *Critique of the Power of Judgment,* trans. Paul Guyer and Eric Matthews (Cambridge: Cambridge University Press, 2000), #85; Plato, *Republic* 555b: the desire "to become as rich as possible . . . is insatiable." See also Georg W. F. Hegel, *Elements of the Philosophy of Right,* trans. H. B. Nisbet (Cambridge: Cambridge University Press, 1991), #190.

57. For an argument that an assessment of our mortality such as Qoheleth's is overly negative because desire and its satisfaction are predicated on the experience of mortal-

ity, see Martin Hägglund, *Dying for Time: Proust, Woolf, Nabokov* (Cambridge, Mass.: Harvard University Press, 2012). This is not the place to critically engage arguments in Hägglund's important book, except to indicate why I don't find them fully compelling. He rightly highlights the temporal structure of desire, debunking a widely held assumption in the West, from Socrates to Jacques Lacan, that desire aims at eternal fulfillment (a big difference between the two in this regard being that Socrates believed that eternal fulfillment is possible whereas Lacan didn't). But Hägglund fails to distinguish categorically between finitude and temporality on the one side and mortality on the other. Mortality, I would suggest, is not a condition of the possibility of desire and its satisfaction (though, of course, there are things we could not desire and satisfactions we could not have were we not mortal), but instead subverts without fully undoing our sense both of meaningfulness and of enjoyment. At the same time, he underplays the significance of the insatiability of human desire: the strange phenomenon that we always desire more and other than what the object of our desire happens to be. This feature of human desire connects with the claim—I do not say: entails the claim—that the desire of finite and temporal beings can find its dynamic rest in God, though not so much in God's eternity (eternal fulfillment, which, as Hägglund rightly notes, would be the cessation of humans as temporal beings and their desiring) as in God's infinity (everlasting movement of desire and fulfillment); see note 64. In the epilogue I will take a further step and argue that the relationship to God as the creator enhances finite and temporal beings' enjoyment of finite and temporal things and relationships.

58. On Qoheleth and the predicaments of insatiability and mortality, see Miroslav Volf, "Hunger for Infinity: Christian Faith and the Dynamics of Economic Progress," in *Captive to the Word of God: Engaging the Scriptures for Contemporary Theological Reflection* (Grand Rapids, Mich.: Eerdmans, 2010), 151–78.

59. John Kenneth Galbraith, *The Affluent Society* (Boston: Houghton Mifflin, 1958), 154.

60. Ibid., 155, 153. Robert Skidelsky and Edward Skidelsky (*How Much Is Enough? Money and the Good Life* [New York: Other Press, 2012]) argue that modern insatiability owes much to the fact that the acquisition of money is no longer subordinated to the pursuit of the good life.

61. See Gregory Clark, who notes, perhaps with exaggeration, that the level of human happiness has not increased since prehistoric times, all the economic progress notwithstanding (*A Farewell to Alms: A Brief Economic History of the World* [Princeton: Princeton University Press, 2007], 16). See also Barry Schwartz, *Paradox of Choice* (New York: Ecco, 2003): "Once a society's level of per capita wealth crosses a threshold from poverty to adequate subsistence, further increases in national wealth have almost no effect on happiness" (106).

62. Smith, *Lectures*, 160.

63. Galbraith, *The Affluent Society*, 158.

64. Gregory of Nyssa argued that the state of perfection was one of infinite progress (*Against Eunomius* I and VIII; see also Paul M. Blowers, "Maximus the Confessor, Gregory of Nyssa, and the Concept of 'Perpetual Progress,'" *Vigiliae Christianae* 46 [1992], 151–53). If there is progress, then the desire must remain, and if the desire remains, the problem of contentment surfaces immediately. Buddhism's extinction of desire is one way to address the problem (see Jacob N. Kinnard, *The Emergence of Buddhism: Classical Traditions in Contemporary Perspective* [Minneapolis: Fortress, 2011], 45). In the Christian tradition, one option is to think of eternal life not as everlasting but as timeless. Immanuel Kant put it this way: "[Man] cannot (even in the consciousness of the immutability of his disposition [to progress in doing good]) unite contentment with the prospect of his condition (moral as well as physical) enduring in an eternal state of change. For the condition in which man now exists remains ever an evil, in comparison to the better condition into which he stands ready to proceed" ("The End of All Things," in *Religion and Rational Theology*, ed. Allen W. Wood and George di Giovanni [Cambridge: Cambridge University Press, 1996], 217–32; see also Friedrich Schleiermacher, *The Christian Faith*, trans. H. R. Mackintosh and J. S. Stewart [Philadelphia: Fortress, 1978], §163). Gregory of Nyssa, in contrast, argued for life *everlasting* and suggested that the "enjoyment of the superior perfection erases all memory of that which was inferior" since "at each stage the greater and superior good holds the attention of those who enjoy it and does not allow them to look at the past" (*Song of Songs*, trans. Casimir McCambley [Brookline, Mass.: Hellenistic College Press, 1987], 128).

65. See Ludwig Feuerbach, *The Essence of Christianity*, trans. G. Eliot (New York: Harper & Row, 1957). Many others have followed in his trail.

66. See Albert Camus, *The Myth of Sisyphus*, trans. J. O'Brien (New York: Vintage, 1955).

67. In *Gorgias* Socrates, for instance, counseled temperance against Callicles' affirmation of the unbridled satisfaction of desires, which, in his view, is possible as a consequence of human attachment to the Good (see Plato, *Gorgias* 507a–508a).

68. Walter Benjamin, *Illuminations*, trans. Harry Zohn, ed. Hannah Arendt (New York: Schocken, 1968), 257. On the following, see Jürgen Moltmann, "Das Geheimnis der Vergangenheit: Erinnern—Vergessen—Enschuldigen—Vergeben—Loslassen—Anfangen," in *Das Geheimnis der Vergangenheit: Errinnern—Vergessen—Enschuldigen—Vergeben—Loslassen—Anfangen*, ed. Jürgen Moltmann (Neukirchen-Vluyn: Neukirchener Verlagsgesselschaft, 2012), 118–21.

69. Max Weber, *The Protestant Ethic and the Spirit of Capitalism*, trans. Stephen Kalberg (Los Angeles: Roxbury, 2002), 181.

70. Ibid.

71. Thomas L. Friedman, for instance, defines globalization as precisely "the *inexorable* integration of markets, nation-states and technologies to a degree never witnessed

before" (*The Lexus and the Olive Tree: Understanding Globalization*, rev. ed. [New York: Farrar, Straus & Giroux, 2000], 8; my emphasis).

72. Anthony Giddens, *Runaway World: How Globalization Is Reshaping our Lives* (New York: Routledge, 2010), 19.

73. For an argument that we in fact do not live in an iron cage, see Charles Taylor, *The Ethics of Authenticity* (Cambridge, Mass.: Harvard University Press, 1992), 93–108. See also Taylor, *Modern Social Imaginaries*, 31–48.

74. On ways in which the Christian faith was shaped by economic imagery and then legitimized certain economic practices in turn, see Devin Singh, "God's Coin: On Monetary and Divine Economies" (Ph.D. diss., Yale University, 2013).

2.
Religions and the Challenge of Globalization

1. Barack Obama, address at the National Defense University, May 23, 2013, accessed June 21, 2013, http://articles.washingtonpost.com/2013-05-23/politics/39467399_1_war-and-peace-cold-war-civil-war.

2. I present here a summary of the findings from multiple sources. I owe the compilation and merging of data from various sources to Ryan McAnnally-Linz. Data compiled from *The World Christian Encyclopedia*, 2nd ed., ed. David B. Barrett, George T. Kurian, and Todd M. Johnson (Oxford: Oxford University Press, 2001); Pew Forum on Religion & Public Life, *The Future of the Global Muslim Population*, January 27, 2011, accessed May 7, 2015, http://pewforum.org/The-Future-of-the-Global-Muslim-Population.aspx; and *The World Christian Database*, 2005, accessed May 19, 2011, http://www.worldchristiandatabase.org.

3. Because Confucianism has no institutional body or organized clergy, the number of its adherents is notoriously hard to ascertain. Adding to the difficulty is the ambivalence of many East Asians regarding whether Confucianism counts as a religion at all. Anna Sun notes that according to a 2007 study on Chinese religion, "among the 6,984 people surveyed, only 12 individuals considered themselves Confucians." Yet, "when questions about ancestral rites were asked . . . about 70 percent of people interviewed said that they visited their ancestors' graves in the past year." This leads Sun to suggest that examining the frequency of certain religious practices like visitations to ancestral sites would give scholars a more accurate accounting of Confucianism's membership, although the extent to which participating in ancestor worship unambiguously indicates a Confucianist is complicated. Sun asserts nonetheless that, with regard to the 2007 study, "there has been a great increase in the number of people making annual trips to their ancestral hometowns to perform rituals at the grave sites of their deceased family members." Koh Byong-ik notes similar dynamics in Korea (see Anna Sun, *Confucianism*

as a World Religion: Contested Histories and Contemporary Realities [Princeton: Princeton University Press, 2013], 112–19; and Koh Byong-ik, "Confucianism in Contemporary Korea," in *Confucian Traditions in East Asian Modernity: Moral Education and Economic Culture in Japan and the Four Mini-dragons*, ed. Tu Wei-ming [Cambridge, Mass.: Harvard University Press, 1996], 191–92). For the 2007 study analyzed by Sun, see the archived results at "Spiritual Life Study of Chinese Residents," *Association of Religion Data Archives*, June 2007, accessed May 7, 2015, http://www.thearda.com/ Archive/Files/Descriptions/SPRTCHNA.asp, as well as the analysis of Rodney Stark and Eric Y. Liu in "The Religious Awakening in China," *Review of Religious Research* 52, no. 3 (2011): 282–89.

4. This growth was driven in great part by a significant relative increase in the global Muslim population. Hinduism also saw a relative increase. Christianity, Judaism, and Buddhism all experienced (mostly relatively small) relative decreases.

5. See the results of the 2012 Pew study on the global religion landscape: "Religiously Unaffiliated," December 18, 2012, accessed May 7, 2105, http://www.pew forum.org/2012/12/18/global-religious-landscape-unaffiliated/.

6. In *Sacred and Secular: Religion and Politics Worldwide* (New York: Cambridge University Press, 2004), Pippa Norris and Ronald Inglehart present research that supports the assertion that the world as a whole is becoming more religious, but note that richer societies are becoming more secular (53–79, 215–39).

7. See Asra Nomani, "Amr Khaled," *Time*, May 3, 2007, http://www.time.com/ time/specials/2007/*tie100*/article/0,28804,1595326_1615754_1616173,00.html.

8. Feuggang Yang and Helen Rose Ebaugh, "Transformations in New Immigrant Religions and Their Global Implications," *American Sociological Review* 66, no. 2 (2001), 270.

9. In *God Is Back: How the Global Revival of Faith Is Challenging the World* (New York: Penguin, 2009), John Micklethwait and Adrian Wooldridge argue that Christianity will win over Islam in the game of numbers, mainly because of Christians' greater education and wealth and Islam's tensions with modernity, which values pluralism and religious freedom (265–96). But the effects on religion itself of its positive or negative relation to wealth, education, and modernity are hard to gauge and all predictions are risky. Islam itself is more likely to change than to simply collide with a globalized world. See Olivier Roy, *Globalized Islam: The Search for a New Ummah* (New York: Columbia University Press, 2004).

10. For a discussion of the epistemic significance of disagreement with informed and intelligent disputants, especially as applied to religious belief, see John Pittard, "Conciliationism and Religious Disagreement," in *Challenges to Moral and Religious Belief: Disagreement and Evolution*, ed. Michael Bergmann and Patrick Kain (Oxford: Oxford University Press, 2014), 80–97.

11. Monica Duffy Toft, Daniel Philpott, Timothy Samuel Shah, *God's Century: Resurgent Religion and Global Politics* (New York: Norton, 2011), 3.

12. For the distinction between prophetic and mystical types of religion, see Fredrich Heiler, *Prayer: A Study in the History and Psychology of Religion* (1932; repr., Oxford: Oneworld, 1997), chapter 6.

13. See Christopher S. Queen and Sallie B. King, ed., *Engaged Buddhism: Buddhist Liberation Movements in Asia* (Albany: State University of New York Press, 1996); Arnold Kotler, ed., *Engaged Buddhist Reader* (Berkeley, Calif.: Parallax, 1996); Christopher Queen, Charles Prebish, and Damien Keown, eds., *Action Darma: New Studies in Engaged Buddhism* (London: RoutledgeCurzon, 2003).

14. Gandhi motivated his social and political activism also in the view that God exists equally and identically in all. See Joan Valerie Bondurant, *Conquest of Violence: The Gandhian Philosophy of Conflict* (Berkeley: University of California Press, 1965), 109–12; Miriam Sharma and Jagdish P. Sharma, "Hinduism, Sarvodaya, and Social Change," in *Religion and Political Modernization,* ed. Donald Eugene Smith (New Haven: Yale University Press, 1974), 227–42; and Gene Sharp, "Gandhi's Political Significance," in *Gandhi as a Political Strategist* (Boston: Porter Sergeant, 1979), 8–14. For engaged Hinduism in the tradition of Swami Vivekananda (1863–1902), see Anantanand Rambachan, *A Hindu Theology of Liberation* (Albany: State University of New York Press, 2015); and Anantanand Rambachan, "Vivekananda: 'For One's Freedom and for the Well-Being of the World.'" *Huffington Post,* September 30, 2013, http://www.huffing tonpost.com/anantanand-rambachan/vivekananda-for-ones-free_b_4013859.html.

15. Anthony Giddens, *Runaway World: How Globalization Is Reshaping Our Lives* (New York: Routledge, 2010), 68.

16. On the spread of the democratic ideal, see Toft, Philpott, and Shah, *God's Century,* 48–120.

17. See José Casanova, *Public Religions in the Modern World* (Chicago: University of Chicago Press, 1994). See also José Casanova, "Rethinking Secularization: A Global Comparative Perspective," *Hedgehog Review* 8 (2006), 20.

18. See Alexis de Tocqueville, *Democracy in America,* trans. Arthur Goldhammer (New York: Library of America, 2004), 172–73.

19. See Miroslav Volf, *Allah: A Christian Response* (San Francisco: HarperOne, 2011), 221–31.

20. A high percentage of world Muslims favor making Islamic law (*sharia*) the official law of their country (99 percent in Afghanistan and 91 percent in Iraq), though less than half of these think it should apply to all citizens rather than to Muslims alone. Muslims whose religious practice is most vibrant—who pray, for instance, several times a day—are more likely to favor sharia as the law of the land (see Pew Forum on Religion & Public Life, *The World's Muslims: Religion, Politics and Society,* April 30, 2013,

http://www.pewforum.org/2013/04/30/the-worlds-muslims-religion-politics-society
-overview/. Clearly, embracing sharia and embracing religious freedom—freedom of
Islam—are not incompatible.

21. See Peter Berger, "The Desecularization of the World: A Global Overview,"
in *The Desecularization of the World: Resurgent Religion and World Politics,* ed. Peter L.
Berger (Grand Rapids, Mich.: Eerdmans, 1999), 1–18.

22. The inclusion of Hinduism, Confucianism, and Judaism among world religions
with the six features I analyze below might be contested. Some people resist describing
Hinduism as a single religion, let alone as a *world* religion. For what goes under the
term *Hinduism* is a primarily geographically identifiable set of very diverse religious
phenomena. "It is helpful," writes Anantanand Rambachan, "if we think of Hinduism
as a very ancient, extended and many-branched family, sharing many features but preserving rich uniqueness of its individual members" (personal communication, January
24, 2014). In some of its expressions (e.g., the work of Vinayak Damodar Savarkar), it
appears more as a local religion. In contrast, in the Advaita Vedanta tradition (e.g., the
work of Swami Vivekananda), for instance, it appears as a world religion (see Anantanand Rambachan, "Hinduism, Hindutva and the Contest for the Meaning of Hindu
Identity: Swami Vivekananda and V. D. Savarkar," in *The Cyclonic Monk: Vivekananda
in the West,* ed. S. Sengupta and M. Paranjape [New Delhi: Samvad, 2005], 121–28).

Whether Confucianism counts as a "religion," not to mention a "world religion," is
famously contested. In my engagement with Confucianism, however, not much rides on
the outcome of the scholarly debate on the matter. I am content to follow Joseph Adler
in calling it a "diffused religion" ("Confucianism as Religion/Religious Tradition/
Neither: Still Hazy After All These Years" [paper presented at Minzu University of
China, June 23, 2010]; on the debate regarding Confucianism's characterization as a
world religion, see Sun's study *Confucianism as a World Religion*). For me much rides,
however, on whether Confucianism—or, more precisely, some significant plausible interpretation of it—shares the six features of world religions I identify. In this regard,
Confucius may be closer to Socrates than he is to Jesus or Muhammad. Socrates' philosophy shares the six features and, were it a widespread philosophy of life today, it could
arguably have been included among the religions discussed in this book. In at least some
of its versions, Confucianism has a "two worlds" account of reality, albeit a decidedly
nondualistic one; heaven (*tian*) has endowed human nature with an innate goodness, the
cultivation and actualization of which is the ultimate aim of human life, giving humanity what Tu Wei-ming calls a "transcendental anchorage" (*Centrality and Commonality:
An Essay in Confucian Religiousness* [Albany: State University of New York Press, 1989],
69; see also Shu-Hsien Liu, "The Confucian Approach to the Problem of Transcendence
and Immanence," *Philosophy East and West* 22, no. 1 [1972], 48; Benjamin I. Schwartz,
"The Age of Transcendence," *Daedalus* 104, no. 2 [1975] , 2–3). Though it conceives of

the individual as "constituted by [his or her] social relations," Confucianism nonetheless addresses the individual, calling her or him into a process of "self-perfection" that is of a piece with the "perfection of society" (Joseph Adler, personal communication, February 9, 2014). From the transcendental anchorage of human life, it follows that Confucianism has a claim to truth and sees itself as valid for all human beings, as a way of life appropriate for the entirety of humanity; "the Confucian Way (*dao*) . . . was the highest and best way of life and was accessible to all humans" (Adler, personal communication; see also Hsu Cho-Yun, "Rethinking the Axial Age—The Case of Chinese Culture," in *Axial Civilizations and World History*, ed. Johann P. Arnason, S. N. Eisenstadt, and Björn Wittrock [Leiden: Koninklijke Brill, 2005], 457–58). It also conceives of a good beyond ordinary flourishing; while acknowledging the gravity of matters like health, wealth, and prosperity, Confucianism contends, nonetheless, that without an "inner change of consciousness," whereby one "transcend[s] beyond" matters of ordinary flourishing, "the dissatisfactions in [one's] heart will never come to an end" (Shu-Hsien, "Transcendence and Immanence," 51). Furthermore, though Confucianism has functioned as a "political religion," originally it did not emerge as a state religion and is a cultural system distinct from politics (on Confucianism's interface with politics, see chapter 5, note 68). Finally, becoming a Confucian sage is linked to the transformation of mundane realities; "the twin goals of classical Confucianism, in fact, are the perfection of the self and the perfection of society, and they are interdependent. The Sage, beginning with Mencius, is one who exerts a transforming (*hua*) influence on society and the world" (Adler, personal communication).

Some may question whether the cluster of six traits of world religions fits Judaism, especially given its organic ties to a specific people, the people of Israel. It would take us too far afield to discuss here the historical development of Judaism from its beginnings to its becoming a world religion. We can safely say, however, that at least since Isaiah's articulation of full-blown monotheism and after the fall of the Temple in Jerusalem centuries later, Judaism had all the relevant features of a world religion (for the role of the destruction of the Temple in the transformation of Judaism, see Guy G. Stroumsa, *The End of Sacrifice: Religious Transformations in Late Antiquity*, trans. Susan Emanuel [Chicago: University of Chicago Press, 2009], 56–83). First, as the original monotheistic religion marked by belief in the God who created the universe, Judaism clearly operates with what I have called here a "two realms account of reality." Second, as monotheism inevitably introduces the question of truth in the sphere of religions (the feature of monotheism Assmann called a "Mosaic distinction" [see *The Price of Monotheism*, trans. Robert Savage (Stanford: Stanford University Press, 2010)]), Judaism makes universal truth claims. Even if it differentiates between two covenants—Noahide and Abrahamic—Judaism still insists that Yahweh is the one true God and that the eschatological fate of all human beings is tied to their obedience to God's commands and their stance toward the God of Israel (see Jacob Neusner, "Theological Foundation of Tolerance in Classical Judaism," in *Religious Tolerance in World Religions*, ed. Jacob Neusner and Bruce Chilton [Conshohocken, Pa.: Templeton Foundation, 2008], 193–95, 213–16; Terrence L. Donaldson, *Judaism and the Gentiles: Jewish Patterns of Universalism (to 135 CE)* [Waco: Baylor University Press, 2007], 499–505). Third, even though biological lineage plays a crucial role in Judaism, still, as a religion Judaism should not be thought of primarily in ethnic terms. According to Neusner, "The Judaism that has set the norms from nearly the time of Paul to our own day conceives of its Israel as never ethnic, but solely transcendental" (*Children of the Flesh, Children of the Promise: A Rabbi Talks with Paul* [Cleveland: Pilgrim, 1995], vii). For the rabbis, "the convert becomes wholly, completely, Israel—without differentiation by reason of his or her ethnic past" (41). Correspondingly, the conversion of Gentiles to Judaism is not a collective but an individual act (see Donaldson, *Judaism and the Gentiles*, 483–92). Joseph Soloveitchik has insisted that "the man of faith has been a solitary figure throughout the ages," called the phenomenon "ontological loneliness," and tied it in Judaism to the relation to "God in His transcendental loneliness and numinous solitude" (*The Lonely Man of Faith*, rev. ed. [Jerusalem: Magid Books, 2012], 3–4). Fourth, from the three features discussed above, it follows that Judaism is not inextricably intertwined with a particular ethnic group and its political rule; as a religion, it is a cultural system distinct from ethnicity and politics and is therefore no less transplantable than other world religions. Fifth, even if one leaves aside the disputed question about the resurrection from the dead and immortality of the soul (see Jon D. Levenson and Kevin J. Mattigan, *Resurrection: The Power of God for Christians and Jews* [New Haven: Yale University Press, 2008], 201–20), keeping the Law is the higher good that trumps ordinary flourishing (health, wealth, longevity, and fertility). The book of Job, with its key challenge of whether Job will curse God in the face of extreme and undeserved suffering, offers a compelling illustration of such a stance. Finally, as a religion Judaism is deeply invested in the transformation of the self and the world; it is the original prophetic religion, and the practice of "mending the world" is its signature characteristic.

23. For a defense of the term *religion*, contested especially in the field of religious studies, see introduction, note 1.

24. For the categories of "primary" and "secondary" religions, see Theo Sundemeier, "Religion, and Religions," in *Dictionary of Mission: Theology, History, Perspectives*, ed. K. Müller et al. (Maryknoll, N.Y.: Orbis, 1997); Theo Sundemeier, *Was ist Religion? Religionswissenschaft im theologischen Kontext* (Gütersloh: Gütersloher Verlagshaus, 1999). Both of these distinctions—primary/local religions and secondary/world religions—build on Max Weber's distinction between "community cults" and "religions of salvation" ("The Social Psychology of the World Religions," in *From*

Max Weber: Essays in Sociology, ed. H. H. Gerth and C. Wright Mills (Abingdon, U.K.: Routledge, 1991), 272–73.

25. Today we associate the idea of "axiality" with German philosopher Karl Jaspers (1883–1969). Though he did not originate the term "axial period," he popularized it after World War II as a designation for an era, roughly spanning the fifth century BC, when analogous changes in religious landscapes of different parts of the world occurred and the world religions were founded (*The Origin and Goal of History,* trans. Michael Bullock [London: Routledge & Kegan Paul, 1953], 1–21). He considered these changes, all seemingly occurring simultaneously, a better candidate for the central dividing line in the world history, its axis, than was the birth of Christ, as thinkers in the West from Augustine to Hegel had maintained. Hence he called the period "axial." Alongside with many scholars recently (for instance, some of the authors in *The Axial Age and Its Consequences,* ed. Robert N. Bellah and Hans Joas [Cambridge, Mass.: Belknap, 2012]), I think that it is better to use the terms "axial breakthrough" and "axial transformation" then "axial period." For one, the synchronicity in appearance of the axial religions and philosophies is more apparent than real; arguably, an axial *period* never existed. The two most widespread axial religions (Christianity and Islam) stem from the first and seventh centuries CE, long after the axial period; similarly, long before the axial period we can clearly identify at least one axial breakthrough, Akhenaten's "monotheistic" revolution in the thirteenth century BC in Egypt (see Jan Assmann, *Moses the Egyptian: The Memory of Egypt in Western Monotheism* [Cambridge, Mass.: Harvard University Press, 1997], 23–55), even if, to the extent that in Akhenaten's case the political and the religious merge in the person of the pharaoh, that axial breakthrough was incomplete (see Eric Voegelin, *The Political Religions,* trans. T. J. DiNapoli and E. S. Easterly III [Lewiston, N.Y.: Edwin Mellen, 1986], 18). Second, I don't think that we can identify from an allegedly neutral standpoint the axis of world history. Jaspers himself illustrates my point. He termed the period he identified as "axial" because he believed that the key cultural features associated with modernity emerged at that time. But identifying a period with these features as "axial" amounts to privileging modernity as the goal of history. The term "axial transformation" is better, I think, insofar as it draws attention to shifts in the character of religions. But even that term is problematic; I use it sparingly, preferring to work with the contrast of "local" versus "world" (or, occasionally, "primary" versus "secondary") religions. My purpose behind the avoidance of "axial transformations" is the desire to leave open at the terminological level the question of whether there is anything like the axis of world history associated with religions and, if there is, where it is to be located.

26. For "old mold" having hold on axial spiritualities, see Charles Taylor, *Modern Social Imaginaries* (Durham: Duke University Press, 2004), 61. For one compelling

account of the transformation of religion in the critical period of late antiquity, see Stroumsa, *The End of Sacrifice.*

27. Friedrich Nietzsche, *Will to Power,* trans. Walter Kaufmann and R. J. Hollingdale (New York: Random House, 1968), #507. See Hans Joas, "The Axial Age Debate as Religious Discourse," in Bellah and Joas, *The Axial Age,* 11.

28. Charles Taylor, *A Secular Age* (Cambridge, Mass.: Belknap, 2007), 147. See also Charles Taylor, "What Was the Axial Revolution?" in Bellah and Joas, *The Axial Age,* 31.

29. For an example of a shift from a civic to individual character of religion in late antiquity, see Stroumsa, *The End of Sacrifice,* 84–109. "Individual" here isn't meant in the sense of modern individualism. In Louis Dumont's terminology, this is the "individual-outside-the-world," not yet the modern "individual-in-the-world" whose existence presupposes that the social world is constituted by individuals (see *Essays on Individualism* [Chicago: University of Chicago Press, 1986], 26).

30. When I say that world religions are addressed to individuals, I do not mean to reduce religious belonging to "choice," at least not in the sense we commonly use the word, implying a sovereign chooser between alternatives whose value the chooser determines for himself or herself. Though addressed to individual persons and taken on by individual persons, world religions are properly embraced not "as a matter of individual choice, but as a given to which allegiance is due in virtue of the intrinsic claims of the sacred" (Rowan Williams, *Faith in the Public Square* [London: Bloomsbury, 2012], 141).

31. See Taylor, *A Secular Age,* 150.

32. Ibid., 151.

33. Some world religions, like Judaism, developed fully into world religions in my sense of that term when they were thrust into situations in which their adherents were living as minorities within a state or an empire (Jonathan Sacks, "On Creative Minorities," the 2013 Erasmus Lecture, October 21, 2013, accessed May 7, 2015, http://www.rabbisacks.org/erasmus-lecture-creative-minorities). In an inverse development, Islam acquired elements of a political religion—or strengthened its original elements of a political religion, if it is true that "the political dimension of the *umma* of believers" was important from its beginnings (Stroumsa, *The End of Sacrifice,* 107)—when Muhammad moved from Mecca to Medina and established an Islamic state with a universal vision. Other world religions, like Buddhism and Christianity, were pulled into becoming political religions when they encompassed the majority of the population in cultural and political settings in which tight unity between religion and rule was prevalent. For instance, the Christianization of the imperial power meant turning Christianity into a state religion and therefore a certain "imperialization" of the Christian faith.

34. See Assmann, *The Price of Monotheism,* 2.

35. See Friedrich Nietzsche, "What I Owe to the Ancients," in *Twilight of the Idols*, trans. R. J. Hollingdale (London: Penguin, 1990), 4–5.

36. W. E. H. Stanner, "On Aboriginal Religion, II: Sacramentalism, Rite and Myth," *Oceania* 30 (June 1960), 276.

37. In the words of William James, central to all world religions is "the belief that there is an unseen order, and that our supreme good lies in harmoniously adjusting ourselves thereto" (*The Varieties of Religious Experience: A Study in Human Nature* [New York: Modern Library, 1929], 53).

38. In discussion of axial breakthroughs, Ingolf Dalfferth has rightly noted the complexity of the idea of transcendence (see "The Idea of Transcendence," in Bellah and Joas, *The Axial Age*, 147–88). For a discussion of the differences and similarities in accounts of transcendence—of the one God—between Christianity and Islam, see Volf, *Allah*.

39. See David Martin, *Does Christianity Cause War?* (Oxford: Oxford University Press, 1997). In chapter 5 I use his suggestion about a repertoire of motifs in discussion of the relation between religion and violence.

40. For these features of religions, see Clifford Geertz, "Religion as a Cultural System," in *The Interpretation of Cultures: Selected Essays* (New York: Basic, 1973), 91–125.

41. For Nietzsche's critique of nihilism, see the epilogue. See also Hubert Dreyfus and Sean Dorrance Kelly, *All Things Shining: Reading the Western Classics to Find Meaning in a Secular Age* (New York: Free Press, 2011), 118–33.

42. Compassion (*karuna*) is a prominent element in all schools of Buddhism. See Ruben L. F. Habito, "Wisdom into Compassion: Buddhism in Practice," in *Divine Love: Perspectives from the World's Religious Traditions*, ed. Jeff Levin and Stephen G. Post (Radnor, Pa.: Templeton, 2010), 108–30; Ruben L. F. Habito, "Compassion out of Wisdom: Buddhist Perspectives from the Past Toward the Human Future," in *Altruism and Altruistic Love: Science, Philosophy, and Religion*, ed. Stephen Post, Lynn G. Underwood, Jeffrey P. Schloss, and William B. Hurlbut (New York: Oxford University Press, 2002), 362–75; Samdhong Rinpoche, "On Compassion: The Buddhist Approach," and Geshe Lakh Dor, "Compassion—A Complement to Wisdom," both in *Compassion in the World's Religions: Envisioning Human Solidarity*, ed. Anindita Balslev and Dirk Evers (New Brunswick, N.J.: Transaction, 2010), 11–20, 21–40.

43. See, for example, Taittiriya Upanishad (1.11): "After teaching him the Veda, the teacher tells the student, 'Speak truth, follow righteousness, do not neglect study. After you have given a gift to the teacher, do not cut off your family line. Do not neglect truth; do not neglect righteousness. Do not neglect your health; do not neglect your wealth; do not neglect study and teaching. Do not neglect your duties to devas and ancestors. May you become one who honors and respects your mother; may you become one who honors and respects your father; may you become one who honors and

respects your teacher; may you become one who honors and respects the stranger.'" (I owe this reference to Anantanand Rambachan.)

44. Debates have gone on in the history of Christianity about how exactly to understand the relation between higher life and ordinary life, but these debates have been carried on for the most part within the parameters of a dual conviction that (1) the higher life has priority over ordinary life, but that (2) it does not invalidate the goodness of ordinary life. Among the most influential theological formulations of the order of priorities is Augustine's doctrine of "the order of love" (*ordo amoris*). In *De Doctrina Christiana* (*On Christian Doctrine*), Augustine distinguishes four types of things that are to be loved: that which is above us, ourselves, things that are on an equal level as us, and things beneath us (which for Augustine includes our bodies). Priority goes to that which is above us (namely, God), followed by ourselves and our neighbors, who are equal to us, then followed by things below us (1.23.22). Augustine summarizes: "Now he is a man of just and holy life who forms an unprejudiced estimate of things, and keeps his affections also under strict control, so that he neither loves what he ought not to love, nor fails to love what he ought to love, nor loves that more which ought to be loved less, nor loves that equally which ought to be loved either less or more, nor loves that less or more which ought to be loved equally. No sinner is to be loved as a sinner; and every man is to be loved as a man for God's sake; but God is to be loved for His own sake. And if God is to be loved more than any man, each man ought to love God more than himself. Likewise we ought to love another man better than our own body, because all things are to be loved in reference to God, and another man can have fellowship with us in the enjoyment of God, whereas our body cannot; for the body only lives through the soul, and it is by the soul that we enjoy God" 1.27.28) The idea that human loves must be properly ordered and that the love of God takes priority runs throughout Augustine's works (see, for example, *City of God* 15.22). Augustine's doctrine has generated an immense amount of commentary and debate. To name just a few notable examples: Hannah Arendt, *Love and St. Augustine,* ed. Joanna Vecchiarelli Scott and Judith Chelius Stark (Chicago: University of Chicago Press, 1996); Oliver O'Donovan, *The Problem of Self-Love in St. Augustine* (New Haven: Yale University Press, 1980); Raymond Canning, *The Unity of Love for God and Neighbor in St. Augustine* (Leuven: Augustinian Historical Institute, 1993); Eric Gregory, *Politics and the Order of Love: An Augustinian Ethic of Democratic Citizenship* (Chicago: University of Chicago Press, 2008).

45. Another example is Socrates (though it is somewhat disputed whether his axial breakthrough is to be described as religious; see José Casanova, "Religion, the Axial Age, and Secular Modernity in Bellah's Theory of Religious Evolution," in Bellah and Joas, *The Axial Age,* 205). He insisted on and embodied the primacy of universal ethical principles ("obeying God") over pursuing the goods of ordinary life, even over preserving his own life. He wasn't willing to sacrifice virtue even on pain of being

condemned to death for calling into question the gods of the state and thus, from the perspective of its representatives, undermining its thriving (see *Apology*). And even though he believed that he was condemned falsely, he was unwilling to escape from prison when offered the opportunity because his principles (which included obedience to the state, notwithstanding the denial of the then widespread ground of its legitimacy) would not allow it, and he would rather sacrifice his life than his ethical principles (see *Crito*). Socrates did not reject, however, "the pleasant"—food, wine, houses, ships, and such—but he insisted on the proper ordering of "the pleasant" and "the good": "The pleasant should be pursued for the sake of the good" and not "the good for the sake of the pleasant" (see *Gorgias* 506c). There is an alignment between Socrates and Jesus on the order of priority of transcendent over mundane goods. As can be illustrated in their respective stances toward death, there is also a significant misalignment between them with regard to valorization of the ordinary life. Socrates is persuaded that in dying he is "losing nothing of value"; death is a cure for life's illness. Not so for Jesus, at least in the Synoptic account; he drinks the bitter cup of suffering and death with agony and protest against God. Consequently, "Christian renunciation is an affirmation of the goodness of what is renounced" (Charles Taylor, *Sources of the Self: The Making of the Modern Identity* [Cambridge, Mass.: Harvard University Press, 1989], 219).

46. The story of Job is often read as an attempt to justify God in the face of the suffering of the innocent. Read in this way, the story is a manifest failure; it provides no good answer to why bad things happen to good people. Instead, the story sketches an account of the proper relation of transcendent commitments and ordinary flourishing.

47. For an analogous account in contemporary Judaism of the affirmation of the mundane realm in the context of the primacy of the transcendent realm, see Soloveitchik, *The Lonely Man of Faith*, 63–67.

48. Nicholas Wolterstorff, *Justice: Rights and Wrongs* (Princeton: Princeton University Press, 2008), 145–47. In addition to its active dimension (life being led well) and passive dimension (life going well), which Wolterstorff noted, I have argued that the good life has also an affective dimension (life feeling good). See Miroslav Volf, "The Crown of the Good Life: Joy, Happiness, and the Good Life—A Hypothesis," October 21, 2014, accessed October 22, 2014, https://www.bigquestionsonline.com/content/what-difference-between-joy-and-happiness, where I give a sketch of the integral relation of the three and argue that joy is the crown of the good life.

49. Christopher Hitchens, *God Is Not Great: How Religion Poisons Everything* (New York: Twelve, 2007).

50. In recent years, a number of Christian theologians have elaborated accounts of theology that give an important place to the internal critique of Christian practices (see, for instance, David Kelsey, *Eccentric Existence: A Theological Anthropology* [Louisville: Westminster John Knox, 2009], 12–27; Kathryn Tanner, *Theories of Culture: A New*

Agenda for Theology [Minneapolis: Fortress, 1997], 61–92). They build on a long history from which I name only two examples. Martin Luther's theology of grace, for example, was in great part a critique of and an alternative to the contemporary practices of the church (see, for example, "The Pagan Servitude of the Church," in *Martin Luther: Selections from His Writings*, ed. John Dillenberger [New York: Anchor, 1962], 249–362). Around the same time as Luther, Bartolomé de las Casas, a Dominican friar, protested in the name of properly functioning Christian faith against the practices of the Spanish colonists of the Americas (see *A Short Account of the Destruction of the Indies*, trans. Nigel Griffin [New York: Penguin, 1992]).

51. Two particularly publicized instances of such accusations came from Pat Robertson on the *700 Club* on February 12, 2005, accessed May 23, 2013, http://digitaljournal.com/article/343453; and Baptist minister Jerry Vines at the Southern Baptist Convention in June 2002 (see Jim Jones, "Baptist Pastor's Words Shock Muslim Leaders," *Fort Worth Star Telegram*, June 12, 2002; see also Richard Cimino, "'No God in Common': American Evangelical Discourse on Islam After 9/11," *Review of Religious Research* 47 [December 2005]: 162–74). For Judaism's appraisal of Christianity as an idolatrous religion, see Howard Kreisel, *Maimonides' Political Thought: Studies in Ethics, Law, and the Human Ideal* (Albany: State University of New York Press, 1999), 39. Kreisel cites *Laws of Idolatry* 9:4 and also *Laws of Forbidden Foods* 11:7 (MS Kushta); *Commentary on the Mishnah: Avodah Zarah* 1:3. Kreisel also notes that despite this view of Christianity, many of Maimonides' statements reflect the fact that he distinguishes between Christians and the idolaters of old. See Hugh Goddard, *A History of Christian-Muslim Relations* (Chicago: New Amsterdam, 2000), 27–28.

52. Alternative accounts of human flourishing exist also within a single tradition of a given religion. Among Protestants, to take an example from Christianity, advocates of the just war theory and pacifists, advocates of the free market and its opponents, those who insist on the moral language of "rights" and those who argue that the moral language of "duties" is far superior debate their positions fiercely. A pacifist opponent of market economy who rejects "rights" as morally corrupting will deem a coreligionist who advocates just war, free market economics, and human rights as distorting the religion and undermining true flourishing.

53. There are ways of bridging the gap between these two traditions, especially from the perspective of Sufi Islam (see Reza Shah-Kazemi, *Common Ground Between Islam and Buddhism: Spiritual and Ethical Affinities* [Louisville: Fons Vitae, 2010]).

54. On Confucianism, Joseph Adler writes, "The ultimate goal of human life in Confucian thought is to actualize [the] moral potential given by Heaven, thereby transforming oneself into a Sage. . . . The twin goals of classical Confucianism, in fact, are the perfection of the self and the perfection of society, and they are interdependent" (personal communication); on the Confucian self, see also Shu-Hsien Liu, "The Con-

fucian Approach to the Problem of Transcendence and Immanence," *Philosophy East and West* 22, no. 1 (1972), 47–50.

55. The divergent interpretations of reality and of human flourishing cannot be settled from a neutral perspective for the simple reason that no such neutral perspective exists. We are familiar with such perspectival rivalry between religions and exclusive humanism. From Nietzsche's perspective, to take one example, Christian pity for the weak appears as little more than the religiously stylized resentment of the weak against the strong (see Friedrich Nietzsche, *On the Genealogy of Morals*, rev. ed., ed. Keith Ansell-Pearson [Cambridge: Cambridge University Press, 2007]). From a Christian perspective, Nietzsche's "will to power" seems a callous disregard for the dignity of human life, deeply at odds with Jesus's commitment "not break a bruised reed or quench a smoldering wick until he brings justice to victory" (Matthew 12:20, quoting Isaiah 42:3) (see, for instance, Rene Girard, *I See Satan Fall Like Lightning* [Maryknoll, N.Y.: Orbis, 2001], 170–81). If you make a life for yourself in either a Nietzschean or a Christian intellectual home, each will seem sturdily built, functional, even beautiful; visit one after you've made your home in another, and it may seem to you badly designed, flimsy, and dangerous. Nietzsche has relentlessly attacked the Christian faith as irrational and detrimental to life; Christians have reacted in kind, accusing Nietzsche of being inconsistent and destructive. There may be a way to "settle the score" between the rival traditions, but it isn't a simple and conclusive procedure. On traditions broadly construed, their differences on matters of justice and rationality, and ways of comparing them, see Alistair MacIntyre, *Whose Justice, Which Rationality* (South Bend: University of Notre Dame Press, 1989) and *Three Rival Versions of Moral Inquiry: Encyclopedia, Genealogy, and Tradition* (South Bend: University of Notre Dame Press, 1991).

56. For the term *de-secularization,* see Berger, "The Desecularization of the World," 1–18.

57. Taylor, *A Secular Age,* 3.

58. See Casanova, "Religion, the Axial Age, and Secular Modernity," 214.

59. See Taylor, *A Secular Age,* 539–93.

60. See Charles Taylor, *Varieties of Religion Today: William James Revisited* (Cambridge, Mass.: Harvard University Press, 2002), 33–60. See also Peter Berger, *The Heretical Imperative: Contemporary Possibilities of Religious Affirmation* (New York: Anchor, 1980).

61. Stephen Jay Gould famously advocated a "nonoverlapping magisteria," or "NOMA" view, which argued that any debate on the relationship between science and religion is misguided because religion and science are two different domains that do not overlap, thus having no possibility of competition (see his "Nonoverlapping Magisteria," *Natural History* 106, no. 2 [1997]: 16–22). For discussion of the compatibility be-

tween science and religion, see Del Ratzsch and John Worrall, "Does Science Discredit Religion?" in *Contemporary Debates in Philosophy of Religion*, ed. Michael L. Peterson and Rayond J. Vanarragon (Malden, Mass.: Blackwell, 2004), 59–94. For discussion of divine causation and science, see Alvin Plantinga, "Divine Action in the World: The Old Picture," in *Where the Conflict Really Lies: Science, Religion, and Naturalism* (New York: Oxford University Press, 2011), 68–90; William P. Alston, "Divine Action: Shadow or Substance?" in *God Who Acts: Philosophical and Theological Explorations*, ed. Thomas F. Tracy (State College: Penn State University Press, 2010), 41–62.

62. Augustine, *Confessions* 1.1.1. For Judaism, see Psalms 42 and 63. For Islam, the parallel concept is *fitrah*, the basic inclination that God has placed in the hearts of all humans: "Verily in the remembrance of Allah do hearts find rest" (Ar-Ra'd 13:28; for the idea, see, for instance, Said Nursi, *The Damascus Sermon* [Istanbul: Sözler, 2012], 30–31). In Buddhism, with its emphasis on the extinction of desire, what Augustine calls "restlessness" is seen as present in all longing, which comes to rest in the complete cessation of craving. The second and third of the Four Noble Truths, in which all dharmas are included, read as follows: "What then is the Holy Truth of the Origination of Ill? It is that craving which leads to rebirth, accompanied by delight and greed, seeking its delight now here, now there, i.e., craving for sensuous experience, craving to perpetuate one-self, craving for extinction. What then is the Holy Truth of the Stopping of Ill? It is the complete stopping of that craving, the withdrawal from it, the renouncing of it, throwing it back, liberation from it, non-attachment to it" (quoted in *Buddhist Scriptures* [New York: Penguin, 2004], 186–87). Hinduism also sees the openness to transcendence as a structural orientation of human beings. For example, Chandogya Upanishad 7.21.3 indicates that human beings will be satisfied only by the Infinite, and Brhadaranyaka Upanishad 2.4.5 states that the final object of love and desire (behind all desires) is the Ultimate. In Confucianism, moral potential is given to human beings by heaven (*tian*) and "the ultimate goal of human life . . . is to actualize that moral potential . . . , thereby transforming oneself into a Sage"; this is human nature's "transcendental anchorage" (Adler, personal communication; the latter phrase is Tu Wei-ming's in *Centrality and Commonality*, 69).

63. The idea that the reference to the divine is fundamental to the character of human beings has implications for how we approach secularization. The theory of secularization is predicated on the account of human beings as basically a-religious. What needs explaining in this case is why people, who are by nature a-religious, embrace religion. But if openness to transcendence is a structural feature of human beings, then what needs explaining is not the persistence of religion but its absence.

64. The metaphor of a "cage" comes from Max Weber's comment at the end of *The Protestant Ethic and the Spirit of Capitalism*, trans. Stephen Kalberg (Los Angeles: Roxbury, 2002). The "hollow" metaphor comes from T. S. Eliot's critique of instrumental

reason and utilitarian calculation, which turn a human being into "shape without form, shade without color" ("The Hollow Men," in *Poems: 1909–1925* [London: Faber & Faber, 1934], 123–28). The metaphor of "lightness" comes from Friedrich Nietzsche via Milan Kundera's *Unbearable Lightness of Being,* trans. Michael Henry Heim (New York: Harper & Row, 1984).

65. Religion can leave to the sciences much of the explanation of reality and to technology much of the transformation of the world. Religion's main positive function is to connect humans to the transcendent realm which, by definition, is beyond the reach of science, and to give meaning and orientation to their lives in the mundane realm. Both of these functions of religion remain untouched by developments in science and technology.

66. If religions did not fulfill these roles, they would turn into "compassionate NGOs," as Pope Francis noted in regard to his own Catholic Church shortly after his election, March 14, 2013, accessed May 8, 2015, http://www.bbc.co.uk/news/world-europe-21793224. See also the comments of Rowan Williams, former archbishop of Canterbury, August 15, 2013, accessed May 8, 2015, http://www.theguardian.com/uk-news/2013/aug/15/rowan-williams-persecuted-christians-grow-up.

67. The effect of globalization on local religions might be different (see Lionel Obadia, "Globalization and the Sociology of Religion," in *The New Blackwell Companion to the Sociology of Religion,* ed. Bryan S. Turner [Malden, Mass.: Wiley-Blackwell, 2010], 487; and Carlos Gigoux and Colin Samson, "Globalization and Indigenous Peoples," in *The Routledge International Handbook of Globalization Studies,* ed. Bryan S. Turner [New York: Routledge, 2010], 301–3).

68. On varieties of the engagement of world religions with ecological issues, see Mary Evelyn Tucker, *Worldly Wonder: Religions Enter Their Ecological Phase* (Chicago: Carus, 2003), 27–54.

69. Among modern thinkers, Georg W. F. Hegel gave the most compelling articulation of this position. See especially his *Philosophy of Right,* trans. Alan White (Indianapolis: Hackett, 2002), and *Lectures on the Philosophy of History,* trans. Robert F. Brown and Peter C. Hodgson (Oxford: Oxford University Press, 2011). See Nicholas Boyle, *Who Are We Now? Christian Humanism and the Global Market from Hegel to Heaney* (Edinburgh: T&T Clark, 1998), 84–86.

70. See Joel Baden, *The Historical David: The Real Life of an Invented Hero* (San Francisco: HarperOne, 2014), 165–69.

71. See Thomas Banchoff, "Introduction: Religious Pluralism in World Affairs," in *Religious Pluralism, Globalization, and World Politics,* ed. Thomas Banchoff (New York: Oxford University Press, 2008), 13–17. By connecting minority groups with other like-minded people across the globe and providing them with means to articulate their stances, globalization is also making majorities more aware that, contrary to their perception, they live in pluralistic social environments (9–11).

72. On religious nationalism, see Philip Gorski and Gulay Türkmen-Dervişoğlu, "Religion, Nationalism and Violence: An Integrated Approach," *Annual Review of Sociology* 39 (2013), 193–210.

73. See Patrick Grant, *Buddhism and Ethnic Conflict in Sri Lanka* (Albany: State University of New York Press, 2009); Stanley J. Tambiah, "Buddhism, Politics, and Violence in Sri Lanka," in *Fundamentalisms and the State: Remaking Polities, Economies, and Militancy*, vol. 3 of *The Fundamentalism Project*, ed. Martin E. Marty and F. Scott Appleby (Chicago: University of Chicago Press, 1993), 589–619.

74. See Motti Inbari, *Messianic Religious Zionism Confronts Israeli Territorial Compromises* (New York: Cambridge University Press, 2012), 95–132; Aviad Rubin, "Religious Actors in a Democratic Civil Society: Turkey and Israel Compared," in *Secular State and Religious Society: Two Forces in Play in Turkey*, ed. Berna Turam (New York: Palgrave Macmillan, 2012), 181–87.

75. See Christian Smith, *Christian America: What Evangelicals Really Want* (Berkeley: University of California Press, 2000), 21–60, for a discussion of the nuances of evangelicals' talk about a "Christian nation"; see also Daniel K. Williams, *God's Own Party: The Making of the Christian Right* (Oxford: Oxford University Press, 2010).

76. Sayyid Qutb, *Milestones* (Chicago: Kazi, 2007), 14.

77. See Toft, Philpott, and Shah, *God's Century*, 48–120.

78. For this, in relation to the Christian faith, see Nicholas Wolterstorff, *The Mighty and the Almighty: An Essay in Political Theology* (Cambridge: Cambridge University Press, 2012), 83–104.

79. Williams, quoting Karl Barth, in *Faith in the Public Square*, 4.

80. Friedrich Nietzsche, "The Anti-Christ," #16 in *Twilight of Idols*, 138. Nietzsche himself was highly critical of such a cosmopolitan god as he sought a return to the "pagan" self-assertions of both individuals and whole communities.

81. Increasingly, every world religion has a significant number of adherents living in a "diaspora," existing as a minority, and occasionally even as a majority, in a religiously pluralistic setting outside its "native habitat." This is the consequence of globalization —of the global migration of people and the transnational acceptance of religious ideas (see Mark Juergensmeyer, "Thinking Globally about Religion," in *Global Religions: An Introduction*, ed. Mark Juergensmeyer [Oxford: Oxford University Press, 2003], 5–7).

82. Olivier Roy, *Globalized Islam: The Search for a New Ummah* (New York: Columbia University Press, 2004), 99.

83. Max Weber, *Economy and Society: An Outline of Interpretive Sociology* (Oakland: University of California Press, 1978), 541–44.

84. See David Singh Grewal, "From Love to Self-Love: Toward a Political Theology of *Homo Economicus*" (paper presented at the conference "Love in a Time of

Capital: Relationality and Commodification as Subjects of Religion," Yale University, New Haven, Conn., May 9, 2014).

85. Jeremiah Burroughs, *The Rare Jewel of Christian Contentment* (Scotts Valley, Calif.: CreateSpace, 2013), 1. See Weber, *The Protestant Ethic and the Spirit of Capitalism*, 103–25.

86. See Theodore Roosevelt Malloch, *Doing Virtuous Business: The Remarkable Success of Spiritual Enterprise* (Nashville: Thomas Nelson, 2008); Michael Novak, *The Catholic Ethic and the Spirit of Capitalism* (New York: Free Press, 1993), xiv–xvii, 1–14.

87. See Kenneth Copeland, *The Laws of Prosperity* (Fort Worth: Kenneth Copeland, 1974); Gloria Copeland, *God's Will Is Prosperity* (Tulsa: Harrison House, 1989); John Avanzini, *The Wealth of the World: The Proven Wealth Transfer System* (Tulsa: Harrison House, 1989). Similarly, various forms of New Age spirituality teach "the art of creating your life as you want it" (David Gerschon and Gail Straub, *Empowerment: The Art of Creating Your Life as You Want it* [New York: Dell, 1989]).

88. This is the thrust of Susan Curtis's critique of the social gospel movement—namely, that "social gospelers, reformers though they were, created, not a critique of modern capitalism, but rather a consuming faith in the material abundance it promised" (*A Consuming Faith* [Baltimore: Johns Hopkins University Press, 1991], 278). Curtis may or may not have Rauschenbusch right, but she captures the ironic potentialities latent in a critique of economic inequality should it fail to challenge the value ascribed to material goods.

89. Many years ago, Alexis de Tocqueville noted in *Democracy in America* that Americans "adhere to their religion out of self-interest" and that they often "locate the kind of self-interest that might cause a person to adhere to religion in this world rather than in the next." In contrast to the Middle Ages, when priests spoke "only of the other life" without much concern about how a Christian "can be a happy man here below," American preachers "refer to this world constantly and, indeed, can avert their eyes from it only with the greatest difficulty. Seeking to touch their listeners all the more effectively, they are forever pointing out how religious beliefs foster liberty and public order, and in listening to them it is often difficult to tell whether the chief object of religion is to procure eternal happiness in the other world or well-being in this one" (616). Tocqueville has noted the tendency in American religion to make providing integration for society ("foster liberty and public order") and enhancing ordinary flourishing ("well-being in this one [world]") its primary goals. These are the two great malfunctions of religion that I have identified above. The integrative function of religion—its relation to the social order and the state—has become difficult, given the multiplicity of religions, but globalization has increased the temptation to see religion as merely a support for ordinary flourishing.

90. See Tariq Ramadan, *Globalization: Muslim Resistances* (Lyon: Tawhid, 2003).

91. See Lamin Sanneh, *Whose Religion Is Christianity? The Gospel beyond the West* (Grand Rapids, Mich.: Eerdmans, 2003). He stresses respect for cultural differences—indeed, celebration and strengthening of particular cultures—as crucial to world Christianity, in contrast to the homogenizing thrust of both Islamic globalization (no translation of the Holy Book in indigenous languages) and economically driven globalization (McDonaldization).

92. In *Globalization and Grace*, Max Stackhouse *aligns* the Christian faith and the processes of globalization: globalization, he thinks, can be viewed as the realization of the Christian vision. Since "a major part of the impetus for globalizing developments derive[s] from the ways in which Christian thought has shaped cultural and social institutions and given rise to transforming patterns of life" (*Globalization and Grace: A Christian Public Theology for a Global Future*, vol. 4 of *God and Globalization*, ed. Max Stackhouse, Peter Paris, Don Browning, and Diane Obenchain [New York: Continuum, 2007], 2), the Christian faith, which he considers "the most valid worldview or metaphysical moral vision available to humanity" (7), should "form or reform the inner moral fabric driving the globalization process" (2). The universalism of today's globalization and the universalism of the Christian faith, ideally, merge. The two would, obviously, at least partly clash with other universalisms. To mitigate the clash, Stackhouse may have to argue that "the historically Christian message, if it is to continue to gain global influence, may well have to remain disguised in a host of 'secular' ideologies and religions, maintaining a distinct separation from the original Christian language and institutional settings," as Robert H. Nelson has suggested in a friendly review of Stackhouse's work ("A Covenant for Globalization?" *Review of Faith and International Affairs* 6, no. 4 [2008], 74). Stackhouse's position echoes that of Arend van Leeuwen, who argued in the middle of the last century not only that the sociohistorical forces of technology, urbanization, democracy and human rights are worldly effects of prophetic Christian presuppositions (Stackhouse, in fact, explicitly endorses van Leeuwen's position; see Max Stackhouse, "The Theological Challenge of Globalization," Religion-online, accessed July 12, 2014, http://www.religion-online.org/showarticle. asp?title=60), but also that Christianity is thereby leading all religions into a global secularism that would transcend the limitations of all particular creeds (see Arend T. van Leeuwen, *Christianity in World History* [London: Edinburgh House, 1964]). In contrast, I think that the relation of the Christian faith to globalization is much more ambiguous. There are alignments, tensions, and incompatibilities between the two, just as there are alignments, tensions, and incompatibilities between the Christian faith and other world religions.

93. Samuel Huntington, famous for his work on the clash of civilizations, does see the need to develop a deeper understanding of other civilizations and identify "ele-

ments of commonality" among them, but on the whole he sees civilizations and the religions that underpin them as mutually exclusive ("The Clash of Civilizations?" *Foreign Affairs* 72, no. 3 [1993]: 22–49). His work echoes that of Oswald Spengler, who argued for the incommensurability and untranslatability of world civilizations (*The Decline of the West*, trans. Charles Francis Atkinson, abridged ed. [Oxford: Oxford University Press, 1991]).

94. Wilfred Cantwell Smith, *Towards a World Theology* (Philadelphia: Westminster, 1981), 124. See also N. Ross Reat and Edmund F. Perry, *A World Theology: The Central Spiritual Reality of Humankind* (Cambridge: Cambridge University Press, 1991).

95. In one of the last texts he produced, Ninian Smart argued that "in addition to a congeries of different religions in the world it will be essential for there to be some overarching sense of order and respect." He speculated that this emerging higher order would become "the global worldview" ("The Global Future of Religion," in Juergensmeyer, *Global Religions*, 130). From a Muslim perspective, Abdulaziz Sachedina has similarly argued that democratic pluralism at local and global levels requires "general religion," a religion beyond "exclusionary and consequently intolerant institutional religiosity" (*The Islamic Roots of Democratic Pluralism* [Oxford: Oxford University Press, 2001], 7).

96. See S. Mark Heim, *Salvations: Truth and Difference in Religion* (Maryknoll, N.Y.: Orbis, 1995).

97. Miroslav Volf, Ghazi bin Muhammad, and Melissa Yarrington, eds., *A Common Word: Muslims and Christians on Loving God and Neighbor* (Grand Rapids, Mich.: Eerdmans, 2010). For a discussion of the proposal, see Volf, *Allah*.

98. On this verse, see Mun'im Sirry, "'Compete with One Another in Good Works': Exegesis of Qur'an Verse 5.4 and Contemporary Muslim Discourses on Religious Pluralism," *Islam and Christian-Muslim Relations* 20 (2009): 423–38. In *Nathan the Wise*, Gotthold Ephraim Lessing bases the whole program for the reconciliation of monotheistic religions on this verse. See *Nathan the Wise: A Dramatic Poem in Five Acts* (Leipzig: Bernhard Tauchnitz, 1868): 89–93.

99. On "coerciveness" (imposition of one's religion vision on others) and "idleness" (retreat into privacy) as malfunctions of religion, see Volf, *A Public Faith*, 3–54.

3.
Mindsets of Respect, Regimes of Respect

1. See Chris Seiple and Denis R. Hoover, "Religious Freedom and Global Security," in *The Future of Religious Freedom: Global Challenges*, ed. Allen D. Hertzke (New York: Oxford University Press, 2013), 315–30.

2. U.S. Commission on International Religious Freedom, *Annual Report 2013*, April

2013, accessed May 8, 2015, http://www.uscirf.gov/sites/default/files/resources/ 2013%20USCIRF%20Annual%20Report%20(2).pdf. See also the Pew report *Global Restriction on Religion*, December 2009, accessed May 8, 2015, http://www.pewforum .org/uploadedFiles/Topics/Issues/Government/restrictions-fullreport.pdf; the Pew report *Rising Tide of Restrictions on Religion*, September 20, 2012, accessed May 8, 2015, http://www.pewforum.org/Government/Rising-Tide-of-Restrictions-on-Religion -findings.aspx; and *Article 18: An Orphaned Right; A Report of the All Party Parliamentary Group on International Religious Freedom*, June 2013, accessed May 8, 2015, https:// freedomdeclared.org/media/Article-18-An-Orphaned-Right.pdf.

3. Brian J. Grimm, "Restrictions on Religion in the World: Measures and Implications," in Hertzke, *The Future of Religious Freedom*, 89.

4. On persecution of Muslims, see Ibrahim Kalin, "Islamophobia and the Limits of Multiculturalism," in *Islamophobia: The Challenge of Pluralism in the 21st century* (New York: Oxford University Press, 2011), 3–20.

5. *Article 18*, 2. For a fuller treatment, see Rupert Shortt, *Christianophobia: A Faith under Attack* (London: Rider, 2012).

6. See Pierre Bourdieu, *Firing Back: Against the Tyranny of the Market 2* (London: Verso, 2003), 86; Pierre Bourdieu, *Pascalian Meditations* (Stanford: Stanford University Press, 2000), 71.

7. See Pope Benedict XVI, "Lecture of the Holy Father—Faith, Reason and the University: Memories and Reflections," September 12, 2006, accessed August 14, 2013, http:// www.vatican.va/holy_father/benedict_xvi/speeches/2006/september/documents/ hf_ben-xvi_spe_20060912_university-regensburg_en.html.

8. Mahathir Mohamad, May 4, 2001, accessed May 8, 2015, http://www.mahathir .com/malaysia/speeches/2001/2001-05-04.php. See also Naveed Sheikh, *Body Count: A Quantitative Review of Political Violence across World Civilizations* (Amman: Royal Islamic Strategic Studies Centre, 2009).

9. For Burma, see Mikael Gravers, "Spiritual Politics, Political Religion, and Religious Freedom in Burma," *Review of Faith and International Affairs* 11, no. 2 (2013): 46–52. For Sri Lanka, see Bradley S. Clough, "A Policy of Intolerance: The Case of Sinhala Buddhist Nationalism," in *Religious Tolerance in World Religions*, ed. Jacob Neusner and Bruce Chilton (Conshohocken, Pa.: Templeton Foundation, 2008), 331–59.

10. Charles Taylor, *Varieties of Religion Today: William James Revisited* (Cambridge, Mass.: Harvard University Press, 2002), 89. If "soft relativism" is a moral ideal, then tolerance does not go all the way down; it must stop somewhere. Alasdair MacIntyre, whose moral assessment is much bleaker than Taylor's, argues rightly that "in practice every group sets a limit to its tolerance and in one way or another enforces that limit" ("Toleration and the Goods of Conflict," in *Ethics and Politics: Selected Essays* [Cambridge: Cambridge University Press, 2006], 2:206).

11. Karl Marx and Friedrich Engels, *The Communist Manifesto,* in *Karl Marx: Selected Writings,* ed. David McLellan (Oxford: Oxford University Press, 1977), 224.

12. See Joseph Ratzinger, "Mass for the Election of the Roman Pontiff," homily, Vatican Basilica, April 18, 2005, accessed May 8, 2015, http://www.vatican.va/gpII/documents/homily-pro-eligendo-pontifice_20050418_en.html.

13. John Locke, *A Letter Concerning Toleration,* in *Two Treatises of Government and a Letter Concerning Toleration,* ed. Ian Shapiro (New Haven: Yale University Press, 2003), 215. About Locke's emphasis on mutual rather than unilateral toleration, see Richard Vernon, ed., *Locke on Toleration* (Cambridge: Cambridge University Press, 2010), xxxi.

14. For theologians concerned with exposing how the modern liberal state subverts a full-orbed practice of Christian faith, John Locke is a villain. In their view, his intertwined accounts of toleration, of church as a voluntary association, and of the separation of church and state underwrite dominance of the state over the church (see John Milbank, *Theology and Social Theory* [Oxford: Basil Blackwell, 1990], 13; William Cavanaugh, "The Wars of Religion and the Rise of the State," *Modern Theology* 11 [1995], 407; William Cavanaugh, *The Myth of Religious Violence: The Secular Ideology and the Roots of Modern Conflict* [Oxford: Oxford University Press, 2009], 78–80). I bring to the reading of Locke different sensibilities. As will be clear further below, following Nicholas Wolterstorff and Charles Taylor, I advocate a particular kind of political liberalism as a responsible form of Christian political philosophy and suggest that some such political liberalism can be shown to be in sync with important impulses in other world religions as well. I also make my own the main thrust of Jennifer Herdt's arguments against Cavanaugh's and Milbank's readings of Locke (see "Locke, Martyrdom, and the Disciplinary Power of the Church," *Journal of the Society of Christian Ethics* 23 [2003]: 19–35).

15. "Revocation of the Edict of Nantes," in *The Huguenot Connection: The Edict of Nantes, Its Revocation, and Early French Migration to South Carolina,* ed. Richard M. Golden (Dordrecht: Springer Netherlands, 1988), 137.

16. For the history of persecution and toleration in England, see John Coffey, *Persecution and Toleration in Protestant England, 1558–1689* (Harlow, U.K.: Pearson Education, 2000).

17. Mark Goldie, introduction to *Letter Concerning Toleration and Other Writings,* by John Locke (Indianapolis: Liberty Fund, 2010), ix.

18. Locke, *A Letter* in *Two Treatises of Government,* ed. Shapiro, 215.

19. See Augustine, "Concerning the Correction of the Donatists," in *The Works of Saint Augustine: Letters 156–210,* trans. Roland Teske (Hyde Park, N.Y.: New City, 2004), 185. For Augustine, coercion in matters of religion was to be educative, not purely punitive, and entailed "moderately severe discipline" (195); the deployment of "cruelty" depended on bringing about the good of those coerced (see Peter R. L. Brown, "St. Augustine's Attitude to Religious Coercion," *Journal of Roman Studies* 54

[1964], 114). Moreover, coercion had to be out of love and was justified in terms of love for the *one being coerced*—a difference between Augustine and many in the Middle Ages, who justified the killing of non-Christians during the Crusades by appealing to a fraternal love for endangered fellow Christians *only* (see Jonathan Riley-Smith, "Crusading as an Act of Love," in *Medieval Religion: New Approaches,* ed. Constance H. Berman [New York: Routledge, 2005], 49–67). As John Bowlin has argued, Augustine was also concerned—fundamentally mistakenly, if the argument of this book is correct—about the connection between the membership of the church and the civic community: "The Donatists want out; they want no standing in a church they considered defiled. At the same time, they want membership in the political community, and they want the benefits that membership affords, above all tolerance of their religious dissent" ("Tolerance among the Fathers," *Journal of the Society of Christian Ethics* 26, no. 1 [2006], 30).

20. There was, of course, more to the scriptural argument than this oft-invoked parable (saddled as it was also with the debate on whether the proper Latin translation for the key word is *cogo* [gather] or *compelle* [force]). People argued also from the conversion of the Apostle Paul: did he not come to his senses only after the divine light had thrown him off the horse and afflicted him with temporary blindness? Such interpretations of the New Testament passages, strained as they seem when considered on their own, made sense in the context of the analogy between the church and Israel: the church is the new Israel and therefore ought to follow the highly intolerant Old Testament pattern of prophetic and kingly defense of pure religion (on religious intolerance in the Old Testament, see Jacob Neusner, "Theological Foundation of Tolerance in Classical Judaism," in Neusner and Chilton, *Religious Tolerance,* 193–95; on the church modeling itself in this regard on Israel, see Eric Nelson, *The Hebrew Republic* [Cambridge, Mass.: Harvard University Press, 2010], 88–137; and Joan Lockwood O'Donovan, "Nation, State, and Civil Society in the Western Biblical Tradition," in *Bonds of Imperfection: Christian Politics, Past and Present,* ed. Oliver O'Donovan and Joan Lockwood O'Donovan [Grand Rapids, Mich.: Eerdmans, 2004], 276–95).

21. Locke, *A Letter,* 216.

22. Ibid., 219.

23. See Jonas Proast, *The Argument of the "Letter Concerning Toleration" (1690), "A Third Letter Concerning Toleration" (1691), "A Second Letter to the Author of the Three Letters for Toleration" (1704)* (New York: Garland, 1984).

24. Locke, *A Letter,* 219.

25. John Locke, *Two Treatises of Government,* ed. Peter Laslett (Cambridge: Cambridge University Press, 1989), 271.

26. John Locke, *A Third Letter for Toleration: To the Author of the Third Letter Concerning Toleration,* in *Works of John Locke* (Aalen: Scientia, 1963), 6:212.

27. Locke, *A Letter,* 215–17, 220–23. Locke states clearly, "The arms by which the

members of this society [the church] are to be kept within their duty, are exhortations, admonitions, and advice" (223).

28. Ibid., 217–20. Examples of the latter include "confiscation of estate, imprisonment, torments," none of which "can have any such efficacy as to make men change the inward judgment that they have framed of things" (219).

29. Ibid., 239.

30. Ibid., 249–50. Roman Catholics, Muslims, and atheists don't fare as well in Locke's commonwealth as do pagans and Jews. The stated reason is not religious intolerance but concern for social stability, partly on account of divided political allegiance. Catholics owe allegiance to an external authority (the pope in the Vatican) and therefore have divided loyalties: "That church can have no right to be tolerated by the magistrate, which is constituted upon such a bottom, that all those who enter into it, do thereby, *ipso facto*, deliver themselves up to the protection and service of another prince." Muslims, Locke believed, have similarly divided loyalties, as they are beholden to "the mufti of Constantinople" or "the Ottoman emperor" (245–46). As to atheists, "promises, covenants, and oaths, which are the bonds of human society, can have no hold upon" them (245–46). All three positions are problematic, at least in today's context.

31. United Nations, *The Universal Declaration of Human Rights*, December 10, 1948, accessed August 14, 2013, http://www.un.org/en/documents/udhr/index.shtml#a18.

32. See, for example, Kant's treatment of religion in his famous "What Is Enlightenment?" Having defined "enlightenment" as "man's release from his self-incurred tutelage" and defined "tutelage" as "man's inability to make use of his understanding without direction from another," Kant commends the monarch who does not infringe on religious freedom, clarifying that "I have placed the main point of enlightenment—the escape of men from their self-incurred tutelage—chiefly in matters of religion because our rulers have no interest in playing guardian with respect to the arts and sciences and also because religious incompetence is not only the most harmful but also the most degrading of all." The state ought to "[find] it to its advantage to treat men, who are now more than machines, in accordance with their dignity" (*Practical Philosophy: The Cambridge Edition of the Works of Immanuel Kant*, ed. Mary J. Gregor [Cambridge: Cambridge University Press, 1996], 11–22).

33. Locke, *A Letter*, 246.

34. See chapter 1, in which I suggest that the present market-driven phase of globalization had its beginnings in the fifteenth century.

35. See C. B. Macpherson, *The Political Theory of Possessive Individualism: Hobbes to Locke* (Oxford: Clarendon, 1962). For a critical theological account of the emergence of possessive individualism with its stress on inherent rights, see Joan O'Donovan, "Rights, Law and Political Community: A Theological and Historical Perspective," *Transformation* 20, no. 1 (2003): 30–38.

36. For an argument against the prevalent reading of early Christianity as anti-introspective, see Michal Beth Dinkler, "'The Thoughts of Many Hearts Shall Be Revealed': Listening in on Lukan Interior Monologues" (paper presented at the annual meeting for the Society of Biblical Literature, San Diego, November 22–25, 2014). For an argument against emphasizing external corporeal aspects of the self at the expense of inner, immaterial dimensions of the self in early Christianity, see François Bovon, "The Soul's Comeback: Immortality and Resurrection in Early Christianity," *HTR* 103 (2010): 387–406.

37. Tertullian, *Ad Scapulum* II (as quoted by Bowlin, "Tolerance among the Fathers," 27). Around AD 300, during the Diocletian persecution, Christian apologist Lactantius insisted that "nothing is so much a matter of free-will as religion; . . . if the mind of the worshipper is disciplined to it, religion is at once taken away, and ceases to exist" (*Divine Institutes,* v. 20, as quoted in Bowlin, "Tolerance among the Fathers," 18). On toleration in antiquity and the Middle Ages, see Rainer Forst, *Toleration in Conflict: Past and Present,* trans. Ciaran Cronin (Cambridge: Cambridge University Press, 2013), 36–95.

38. See Robert Louis Wilken, *The Christian Roots of Religious Freedom* (Milwaukee: Marquette University Press, 2014), 12–14.

39. In the official teaching of the Catholic Church, freedom of religion was embraced in 1965 (see Vatican Council II, *"Dignitatis Humanae* [Declaration on Religious Freedom, Promulgated by Pope Paul VI]," December 7, 1965, accessed August 14, 2013, http://www.vatican.va/archive/hist_councils/ii_vatican_council/documents/vat-ii_decl_19651207_dignitatis-humanae_en.html.) For an early Protestant advocacy of religious freedom, see Thomas Helwys, *A Short Declaration of the Mystery of Iniquity,* ed. Richard Groves (Macon: Mercer University Press, 1998); and Roger Williams, *The Bloudy Tenent of Persecution, for Cause of Conscience,* ed. Richard Groves (Macon: Mercer University Press, 2001).

40. For an argument for freedom of religion from the Hindu perspective, see Anantanand Rambachan, "Hinduism and Dialogue" (unpublished MS, 2014).

41. *"Kalama Sutta* (To the Kalamas)," in *Anguttara Nikaya: Discourses of the Buddha: An Anthology,* trans. Nyanaponika Thera and Bhikkhu Bodhi (Kandy: Buddhist Publication Society, 2010), 32–33.

42. See Vincent J. Cornell, "Theologies of Difference and Ideologies of Intolerance in Islam," in Neusner and Chilton, *Religious Tolerance,* 288–90. In fact, some Muslim teachers argue for coercion *just on the basis of the claim that Islam's truth is evident.* Those who don't embrace what is evident must be obstinate and can therefore be forced: "Such use of force is not really coercion according to [Dr. al-Shaykh Muhammad] al-Sadiqi; rather it is bringing people into line with their own nature and sound rationality (*al-'aqliyya al-saliha*); and in any case, what they believe in their hearts is not open to

coercion at all" (Patricia Crone, "'No Compulsion in Religion': Q. 2:256 in Mediaeval and Modern Interpretation," in *Le Shi'isme imamite quarante ans après: Hommage à Etan Kohlberg*, ed. Mohammad Ali Amir-Moezzi, Meir M. Bar-Asher, and Simon Hopkins [Turnhout: Brepols, 2009], 152). In Christianity, Augustine used similar arguments to justify compulsion: heretics and schismatics have poor reasons for their position and civil penalties can nudge them out of listlessness, pride, and sloth, providing them with incentive to rethink their position and see the truth of the orthodox faith (see Augustine, "Letter 93," in *The Works of Saint Augustine: Letters 1–99*, trans. Roland Teske [Hyde Park, N.Y.: New City, 2001], 376–409; also Coffey, *Persecution*, 34–35).

43. As quoted in Ibrahim Kalin, "Sources of Tolerance and Intolerance in Islam: The Case of the People of the Book," in Neusner and Chilton, *Religious Tolerance*, 263. Crone notes, however, that this may be al-Razi quoting Abu Muslim and disputes whether al-Razi's Mu'tazilite interpretation of al-Baqarah 2:256 actually concerns *human* coercion, arguing instead that the coercion to which al-Razi refers is a *divine* one, rendering al-Baqarah 2:256 a refutation of determinism (see "No Compulsion in Religion," 134).

44. In interpreting al-Baqarah 2:256, Gülen makes this statement by Hamdi Yazir his own: "Any religious act done through compulsion does not bring any reward; and an act of worship which is not done through free will is not counted as worship" (Fethullah Gülen, "Islam as the Embodiment of Divine Mercy and Tolerance," in *Abraham's Children: Liberty and Tolerance in an Age of Religious Conflict*, ed. Kelly James Clark [New Haven: Yale University Press, 2012], 248).

45. For ambivalence with regard to toleration of other religions in the Hebrew Scriptures, see Baruch A. Levine, "Tolerance in Ancient Israelite Monotheism," in Neusner and Chilton, *Religious Tolerance*, 15–28. Jacob Neusner sees little ambivalence in the Torah, though, only condemnation (see "Theological Foundation of Tolerance in Classical Judaism," 193–95).

46. James Madison, one of the founding fathers of the United States, grounded religious freedom in the "duty of every man to render to the Creator such homage, and such only, as he believes to be acceptable to him" ("A Memorial and Remonstrance Against Religious Assessments," in *The Selected Writings of James Madison*, ed. Ralph Ketcham [Indianapolis: Hackett], 22.) On this, see Michael W. McConnell, "Why Is Religious Liberty the 'First Freedom?'" *Cardozo Law Review* 21 (1999–2000): 1247–48. Cardinal Newman put the position succinctly and precisely: conscience "has rights because it has duties" (John Henry Newman, *A Letter Addressed to His Grace the Duke of Norfolk* [New York: Catholic Publication Society, 1875], 75). See also Allen D. Hertzke, "Advancing the First Freedom in the 21st Century," in Hertzke, *The Future of Religious Freedom*, 6. My contention is not that it is mistaken to deduce religious freedom from personal dignity and autonomy and conceive of it as a human right, but that we can argue for religious freedom plausibly by appealing to the "rights of God."

47. Abu Zaid Abdullah ibn Umar ibn Isa al-Dabusi, *Taqwim al-Adillah fi Usul al-Fiqh* (Beirut: Dar al-Kutub al-Ilmiyyah, 2001), 417, as quoted by Recep Şentürk, "Human Rights in Islamic Jurisprudence: Why Should All Human Beings Be Inviolable?" in Hertzke, *The Future of Religious Freedom*, 296. In the essay, Şentürk develops the inviolability of personhood as a foundation of human rights in Islam on the same principle.

48. For freedom of religion and coercion during the Reformation and after, see Coffey, *Persecution*, 21–46.

49. On the possibility and impossibility of toleration under such conditions, see Bernard Williams, "Tolerating the Intolerable," in *The Politics of Toleration: Tolerance and Intolerance in Modern Life*, ed. Susan Mendus (Edinburgh: Edinburgh University Press, 1999), 72–73.

50. See G. W. F. Hegel, *Phenomenology of Spirit*, trans. A. V. Miller (Oxford: Clarendon, 1977), 111–19.

51. See Jan Assmann, *The Price of Monotheism*, trans. Robert Savage (Stanford: Stanford University Press, 2010), 2; see also Jan Assmann, *Herrschaft und Heil: Politische Theologie in Altägypten, Israel und Europa* (Munich: Carl Hanser Verlag, 2000).

52. This is one example of how the effects of axial transformations were held in check because the "old mold" religious sensibilities have for centuries continued to exert influence on world religions (see Charles Taylor, *Modern Social Imaginaries* [Durham: Duke University Press, 2004], 61).

53. On the identity of religious and political communities in Israel as grounding coercive intolerance, see Levine, "Tolerance in Ancient Israelite Monotheism."

54. Augustine, who decisively shaped the tradition of religious coercion in Christianity, stressed the centrality of inner conviction for religion. The last sentence of the only surviving sermon Augustine preached on the "compel them in" passage in the Gospel of Luke reads: "Let compulsion be found outside, the will arise within" (see Brown, "St. Augustine's Attitude to Religious Coercion," 112). Sayyid Qutb, one of the main thinkers of the Muslim Brotherhood, makes an analogous argument. Islam, he writes, "forbids the imposition of its belief by force." At the same time, Islam commands people to engage in aggressive jihad, attempting "to annihilate all those political and material powers which stand between people and Islam" (*Milestones* [New Delhi: Millat Book Centre, n.d.], 57). Force is, ultimately, in the service of inner conviction. But there is a problem with this position. To assert that it is legitimate to force conformity of practice is in fact to presuppose an account of religion in which inner convictions but *not* outer practices are the proper response to the transcendent call. If practices were construed as a response to a transcendent call, they could not be legitimately forced upon those who don't understand them as such. Now, advocating that one can legitimately *force* conformity of practice because it is expected to lead to inner conviction is categorically

different from advocating that engaging in practices required by faith is conducive to the inner embrace of faith. In the second case, both practices and inner convictions are embraced *freely*, whereas this is not the case in the first. For an argument that practices of faith lead to convictions in Islam, see Ghazi bin Muhammad, *What Is Islam and Why?* (Amman: Mabda, 2012), 32–34.

55. Presently, Muslims worldwide overwhelmingly support criminalizing apostasy, whereas Christians overwhelmingly oppose it. See Ann Black, Hossein Esmaeili, and Nadirsyah Hosen, *Modern Perspectives on Islamic Law* (Northampton, U.K.: Edward Elgar, 2013), 268–74; see Abdulaziz Sachedina, *The Islamic Roots of Democratic Pluralism* (New York: Oxford University Press, 2001), 97–101. For the criminalization of apostasy in various religious traditions around the world, see Pew Forum on Religion & Public Life, *Laws Penalizing Blasphemy, Apostasy and Defamation of Religion Are Widespread*, November 21, 2012, accessed May 8, 2015, http://www.pew forum.org/2012/11/21/laws-penalizing-blasphemy-apostasy-and-defamation-of -religion-are-widespread/. For large swaths of their history, Christians too have believed that apostasy was a crime that deserves fierce punishments (see B. J. Oropeza, *Paul and Apostasy: Eschatology, Perseverance, and Falling Away in the Corinthian Congregation* [Tübingen: Mohr Siebeck, 2000], 1–33).

56. Ghazi bin Muhammad, "On 'A Common Word Between Us and You,'" in *A Common Word: Muslims and Christians on Loving God and Neighbor,* ed. Miroslav Volf, Ghazi bin Muhammad, and Melissa Yarrington (Grand Rapids, Mich.: Eerdmans, 2010), 6.

57. For Sayyed Hossein Nasr, both Christian evangelism and Muslim *da'wa* are attempts by the two religions to "destroy each other" ("We and You: Let Us Meet in God's Love," [paper presented at the Common Word meeting with Pope Benedict XVI, Rome, November 6, 2008], 14). As ultimate allegiance is more important than worldly goods, the loss of souls to another religion might be seen as worse than the loss of sovereignty to another nation, a destruction worse than the loss of possessions and even life.

58. So Şentürk, "Human Rights in Islamic Jurisprudence," 306. On apostasy in Islam, see Mohammad Hashim Kamali, "Freedom of Religion in Islamic Law," *Capital University Law Review* 21 (1992): 70–74.

59. On bearing witness in an interfaith context from a Christian standpoint, see Miroslav Volf, *A Public Faith: How Followers of Christ Should Serve the Common Good* (Grand Rapids, Mich.: Brazos, 2011), 99–117.

60. For a Christian ecumenical account of bearing witness in a religiously pluralistic world, see the document issued in 2011 by the World Council of Churches, the Pontifical Council for Interreligious Dialogue, and the World Evangelical Alliance titled "Christian Witness in a Multi-religious World: Recommendations for Conduct," June 28, 2011,

accessed July 23, 2013, http://www.oikoumene.org/en/resources/documents/wcc
-programmes/interreligious-dialogue-and-cooperation/christian-identity-in-pluralistic
-societies/christian-witness-in-a-multi-religious-world. See also J. Dudley Wood-
berry, "Comparative Witness: Christian Mission and Muslim Da'wa," *Review of Faith
and International Affairs* 7 (2009), 71.

61. For elaboration of these, see Miroslav Volf, *Allah: A Christian Response* (San
Francisco: HarperOne, 2011), 201–18.

62. My distinction here between "respect for freedom of religion" and "respect for
a religion" maps well onto the two last senses of toleration in Forst's *Toleration in Conflict*, 27–32. In addition to the "permission conception" of toleration (an authority or
a majority tolerates a minority) and the "coexistence conception" (groups of roughly
equal strength practice toleration), he distinguishes between the "respect conception"
(tolerating parties respect each other as autonomous or equally entitled members of a
political community) and the "esteem conception" (people esteeming other persons'
convictions and practices as ethically valuable).

63. Explicating Kant's position on human dignity, Allen Wood writes: "The worst
human being (in any respect you can possibly name) has the same dignity or absolute
worth as the best rational being in that respect (or any other)" (*Kant's Ethical Thought*
[Cambridge: Cambridge University Press, 1999], 132).

64. William Shakespeare, *Measure for Measure*, in *Riverside Shakespeare*, ed. G. Blakemore
Evans (Boston: Houghton Mifflin, 1974), 560.

65. On the distinction between person and work in Luther, see Gerhard Ebeling, *Luther:
An Introduction to His Thought*, trans. R. A. Wilson (Philadelphia: Fortress, 1970), 148–58.

66. Ghazi bin Muhammad, *Love in the Holy Qur'an* (Chicago: Kazi, 2010), 71.
Ghazi's formulation is similar to Augustine's in *De Doctrina Christiana:* "No sinner is to
be loved as a sinner" (1.27.28).

67. Ibid. Those familiar with both Christianity and Islam will note that in important
variants of each, love (Christianity) and mercy (Islam) function in analogous ways.

68. Ibid., 78.

69. On objection, acceptance, and rejection with regard to toleration, see Forst, *Tolerance in Conflict*, 18–25.

70. Jonathan Sacks, *The Dignity of Difference: How to Avoid the Clash of Civilizations*
(London: Continuum, 2002), 20.

71. Jonathan Sacks, *The Dignity of Difference: How to Avoid the Clash of Civilizations*, 2nd ed. (London: Continuum, 2003), 21. In the first edition, Sacks made a stronger
claim that religions themselves have dignity and deserve respect.

72. The answer depends also on how adherents of world religions make the claim to
truth. Two issues are crucial in this regard. One is the modality in which those claims
are made: provisionally or absolutely, humbly or arrogantly, for instance. The other

issue is the significance ascribed to existing overlaps in truth claims among religions, for no world faith, even when it asserts its own exclusive superiority, can claim that all other faiths are *entirely* false (so already Friedrich Schleiermacher, *The Christian Faith*, trans. H. R. MacKintosh and J. S. Stewart [Philadelphia: Fortress, 1928], §7.3).

73. Robin S. Dillon, "Respect: A Philosophical Perspective," *Gruppendynamik und Organisationsberatung* 38, no. (2007), 203.

74. Ibid., 204.

75. For "appraisal respect," see Stephen L. Darwall, "Two Kinds of Respect," *Ethics* 88, no. 1 (1977), 38–39, 41–47.

76. Charles Taylor, *Multiculturalism: "The Politics of Recognition,"* ed. Amy Gutmann (Princeton: Princeton University Press, 1994), 72–73. People of faith somehow find it more difficult to respect other religions than a-religious interpretations of reality. For instance, apostasy laws in many countries mistakenly, I believe, treat atheism—exclusive humanism—not as another "religion" but as a neutral territory between religions.

77. On prejudice and understanding with regard to other religions, see Volf, *Allah,* 203–5.

78. On Luther and Islam, see ibid., 60–76.

79. Rowan Williams, *Faith in the Public Square* (London: Bloomsbury, 2012), 141.

80. For the seven Noahide laws, see Babylonian Talmud, Sanhedrin 56a.

81. HC Q/A 100; see "The Heidelberg Catechism" in *Book of Confessions,* part 1 of *The Constitution of the Presbyterian Church (U.S.A.)* (Louisville: Office of the General Assembly, 1999), 4.100 (p. 46).

82. *The Charter Granted by Their Majesties King William and Queen Mary, to the Inhabitants of the Province of the Massachusetts-Bay in New-England* (Boston: S. Kneeland, 1759), 72.

83. Quoted in Paul Marshall and Nina Shea, *Silenced: How Apostasy and Blasphemy Codes Are Choking Freedom Worldwide* (Oxford: Oxford University Press, 2011), 86.

84. See ibid., 177–226.

85. See http://www.buddhisma2z.com/content.php?id=40#sthash.quyiAe00.dpuf (accessed May 8, 2015).

86. See Tom Heneghan, "Thai Buddhists Seek Blasphemy Law to Punish Offences Against Their Faith," October 25, 2007, accessed May 11, 2015, http://blogs.reuters.com/faithworld/2007/10/25/thai-buddhists-seek-blasphemy-law-to-punish-offences-against-their-faith/.

87. T. W. Rhys Davids and J. Estlin Carpenter, eds., *Digha-Nikaya* (Oxford: Pali Text Society, 1995), 1:1–3.

88. See Gerd Theissen and Annete Merz, *The Historical Jesus: A Comprehensive Guide,* trans. John Bowden (Minneapolis: Fortress, 1998), 464.

89. See, for instance, Nasr Hamid abu-Zayd, "Renewing Qur'anic Studies in the Contemporary World," in Marshall and Shea, *Silenced*, 293.

90. The connection between legitimacy and blasphemy laws is visible in cases where legitimacy needs to be established rather than only protected. Take the case of General Zia ul-Haq, who came to power by deposing Zulfiqar Ali Bhutto in 1977 by a military coup. Since he lacked democratic legitimacy, he accelerated the Islamization of Pakistan, doing so, he claimed, in response to a charge received from God in a dream to create an Islamic state in Pakistan. It was he who introduced Pakistan's notorious blasphemy laws (Marshall and Shea, *Silenced*, 85).

91. In Judaism, however, even after the destruction of the Temple and the loss of Jewish political rule, the penalty of death continued to be inflicted upon a blasphemer "as long as the Jewish courts exercised criminal jurisdiction" ("Blasphemy," in *The Jewish Encyclopedia* [New York: Funk & Wagnalls, 1907], 3:237).

92. Marshall and Shea, *Silenced*. See also Abdurrahman Wahid, "God Needs No Defense," in Clark, *Abraham's Children*, 212.

93. Richard Webster, *A Brief History of Blasphemy: Liberalism, Censorship and the Satanic Verses* (Southwold, U.K.: Orwell, 1990), 129.

94. Williams, *Faith in the Public Square*, 147.

95. Michael Walzer analyzes five distinct types of "political arrangements that make for toleration," five historically prominent Western "models of a tolerant society." His walk through the landscape of these models reminds us that there are more ways than one of institutionalizing toleration. The same applies analogously to institutionalizing respect. See *On Toleration* (New Haven: Yale University Press, 1997), 8–13.

96. Nicholas Wolterstorff, "The Role of Religion in Decision and Discussion of Political Issues," in *Religion in the Public Square: The Place of Religious Convictions in Political Debate*, ed. Robert Audi and Nicholas Wolterstorff (Lanham, MD: Rowman & Littlefield, 1997), 73.

97. For the phrase, see Thomas Jefferson, "To Messrs. Nehemiah Dodge, Ephraim Robbins, and Stephen S. Nelson, a Committee of the Danbury Baptist Association, in the State of Connecticut," in *Thomas Jefferson: Political Writings*, ed. Joyce Appleby and Terence Ball (Cambridge: Cambridge University Press, 1999), 397.

98. See Locke, *Two Treatises of Government and a Letter Concerning Toleration;* John Rawls, *Political Liberalism* (New York: Columbia University Press, 2005).

99. http://www.independent.co.uk/news/world/middle-east/isis-declares-new-islamic-state-in-middle-east-with-abu-bakr-albaghdadi-as-emir-removing-iraq-and-syria-from-its-name-9571374.html (June 30, 2014, accessed May 11, 2015).

100. Jocelyn MacLure and Charles Taylor, *Secularism and Freedom of Conscience*, trans. Jane Marie Todd (Cambridge, Mass.: Harvard University Press, 2011), 5.

101. Ibid., 19–26.

102. See Wolterstorff, "The Role of Religion in Decision and Discussion of Political Issues," 67–120; Forst, *Toleration in Conflict*, 539–40. See also the conversation between Jürgen Habermas and Charles Taylor on the issue: http://blogs.ssrc.org/tif/2009/11/20/rethinking-secularism-jurgen-habermas-and-charles-taylor-in-con versation/ (November 20, 2009, accessed May 11, 2015).

103. Williams, *Faith in the Public Square*, 61.

104. Ibid., 27.

4.
Religious Exclusivism and Political Pluralism

1. Many Christians would say that outside of *Jesus Christ*—as distinct from Christian convictions about Jesus Christ—there is only the darkness of falsehood. This follows from the Christian belief that Jesus Christ is divine and that, as the eternal Word, he is the creator; as God, the creator, he is the source of all truth and the original embodiment of it. From the time of the early church father Justin Martyr, many Christians have believed that, because the eternal Word is the life and light of all people, all truth found in any philosophy or any religion derives from the eternal Word. In Christ, the eternal Word is incarnate; sages, like Socrates, possess the "seeds" of the Word and in those seeds other religions and philosophies have access to aspects of truth (for a brief discussion of this view and its implications, see Miroslav Volf, *A Public Faith: How Followers of Christ Should Serve the Common Good* [Grand Rapids, Mich.: Brazos, 2011], 112–13).

2. The religious exclusivism I describe here is of a moderate kind. Some people, a minority, espouse a stronger form of exclusivism (see, for example, the teaching of John MacArthur, "Nothing but the Truth," *Grace to You*, January 2015, accessed May 11, 2015, http://www.gty.org/resources/articles/A213/Nothing-but-the-Truth). They believe that they alone possess the truth; whatever truth other religions and philosophies may contain, it has been turned into falsehood because it has been twisted and employed to wrong ends. In the overlaps in convictions between their faith and others, they see signs of the craftiness of the demons that inspired these religions (for more recent claims that Islam is demonically inspired, see Joel Richardson, *The Islamic Antichrist: The Shocking Truth about the Real Nature of the Beast* [Los Angeles: WorldNetDaily, 2009]; and Terry Jones, *Islam Is of the Devil* [Lake Mary, Fla.: Creation House, 2010]).

3. Friedrich Schleiermacher, *The Christian Faith*, trans. H. R. Mackintosh and J. S. Stewart (Philadelphia: Fortress, 1978), §10, postscript.

4. See Frithjof Schuon, *The Transcendent Unity of Religions* (Wheaton, Ill.: Quest, 1984); John Hick, *An Interpretation of Religion* (New Haven: Yale University Press, 1991).

5. For Frithjof Schuon, different religious traditions reflect the inherent diversity of human beings; each tradition is the manifestation of the one unique Truth as instantiated among a certain type of human (see *The Essential Frithjof Schuon*, ed. Seyyed Hossein Nasr [Bloomington, Ind.: World Wisdom, 2005], 149–53).

6. On Nazism and Stalinism, see Hannah Arendt, *The Origins of Totalitarianism* (New York: Harcourt, 1951).

7. These statistics are based on analysis of the following sources: Ipsos MORI Global @dvisor survey: "Views on Globalization and Faith," April 2011, accessed June 20, 2014, http://www.fgi-tbff.org/randp/casestudies/religion-globalisation; Pew Global Attitudes Project, "Chapter 3: Views of Democracy and the Role of Islam," in *Arab Spring Fails to Improve U.S. Image*, May 17, 2011, accessed May 11, 2015, http://www.pewglobal.org/2011/05/17/chapter-3-views-of-democracy-and-the-role-of-islam; Pew Global Attitudes Project, *Egyptians Embrace Revolt Leaders, Religious Parties and Military, as Well*, April 25, 2011, accessed May 11, 2015, http://www.pewglobal.org/2011/04/25/egyptians-embrace-revolt-leaders-religious-parties-and-military-as-well; Pew Global Attitudes Project, *Public Opinion in Pakistan: Concern about Extremist Threat Slips*, July 29, 2010, accessed May 11, 2015, http://www.pewglobal.org/2010/07/29/concern-about-extremist-threat-slips-in-pakistan; Gallup, *Importance of Religion among Predominantly Islamic Countries*, April 16, 2002, accessed May 11, 2015, http://www.gallup.com/poll/5821/Importance-Religion-Among-Predominantly-Islamic-Countries.aspx?utm_source=Importance%20of%20Religion%20among%20Predominantly%20Islamic&utm_medium=search&utm_campaign=tiles; Pew Forum on Religion & Public Life, *Tolerance and Tension: Islam and Christianity in Sub-Saharan Africa*, April 15, 2010, accessed May 11, 2015, http://www.pewforum.org/2010/04/15/executive-summary-islam-and-christianity-in-sub-saharan-africa; Gallup, *Iranians, Egyptians, Turks: Contrasting Views on Sharia*, July 10, 2008, accessed May 11, 2015, http://www.gallup.com/poll/108724/Iranians-Egyptians-Turks-Contrasting-Views-Sharia.aspx?utm_source=Iranians,%20Egyptians,%20Turks:%20Contrasting%20Views%20on%20S&utm_medium=search&utm_campaign=tiles; Gallup, *Majorities See Religion and Democracy as Compatible*, October 3, 2007, accessed May 11, 2015, http://www.gallup.com/poll/28762/Majorities-Muslims-Americans-See-Religion-Law-Compatible.aspx?utm_source=Majorities%20See%20Religion%20and%20Democracy%20as%20Compatibl&utm_medium=search&utm_campaign=tiles; World Public Opinion Surveys, 2008, 2009, 2010, accessed May 11, 2015, www.worldpublicopinion.org/.

8. See Jan Assmann, *The Price of Monotheism*, trans. Robert Savage (Stanford: Stanford University Press, 2010), 1–2.

9. In the Gospels Jesus, however, consistently favored a positive version of this command based on Deuteronomy 6:5. In response to the question, "Which commandment is the first of all?" Jesus said: "The first is, 'Hear, O Israel: the Lord our God, the

Lord is one; you shall love the Lord your God with all your heart, and with all your soul, and with all your mind, and with all your strength'" (Mark 12:28–30). The rejection of false gods and false religion is implied, but not stated.

10. John Hartley, "Religious Exclusivists Taking Inclusive Action" (Ph.D. diss., Yale University, forthcoming 2015).

11. Peter Berger, *A Far Glory: The Quest of Faith in an Age of Credulity* (New York: Free Press, 1992), 39. More recently, Berger has amended his theory. According to the quote above, the situation of pluralism changes the "what" of one's belief: a person who believed in the truth of one religion first comes to see the truth of them all and finally abandons claims to truth for relativism. In an interview in 2006 Berger suggested that concern with the "what" of belief was a mistake. Referring to his original position, Berger said: "What I did not understand when I started out—my God, it's now almost forty years ago—is that [in the context of pluralism] what has changed is not necessarily the what of belief but the how of belief. Someone can come out with an orthodox Catholic statement of belief—'I believe everything that the Pope would approve of'— but how that person believes is different. What pluralism and its social and psychological dynamics bring about is that certainty becomes more difficult to attain. That's what I mean by the how of belief. It's more vulnerable. The what can be inherently unchanged, but the how is different, and I think the difference is that certainty becomes more difficult to attain or can only be attained through a very wrenching process, of which fundamentalism is the main expression" (Charles T. Mathewes, "An Interview with Peter Berger," *Hedgehog Review* 8 [2006], 153).

12. See Berger, *A Far Glory*, 39–40.

13. For a brief summary of this argument, see Hans Joas, *Do We Need Religion? On the Experience of Self-Transcendence*, trans. Alex Skinner (Boulder: Paradigm, 2008), 26–27.

14. Berger, *A Far Glory*, 45.

15. See Gavin d'Costa, *Meeting of Religions and the Trinity* (Maryknoll, N.Y.: Orbis, 2000); Jung H. Lee, "Problems of Religious Pluralism: A Zen Critique of John Hick's Ontological Monomorphism," *Philosophy East and West* 48 (1998): 453–77; Paul R. Eddy, "Religious Pluralism and the Divine: Another Look at John Hick's Neo-Kantian Proposal," *Religious Studies* 30 (1994): 467–78.

16. For a distinction between the programmatically secular state and the procedurally secular state, see Rowan Williams, *Faith in the Public Square* (London: Bloomsbury, 2012).

17. Karl Popper, *The Open Society and Its Enemies II: Hegel and Marx* (Princeton: Princeton University Press, 1971), 225.

18. Ibid., 243.

19. Ibid., 235.

20. Karl Popper, *The Open Society and Its Enemies I: Plato* (Princeton: Princeton University Press, 1966), 200–201.

21. Anthony Kronman makes the same point in *Education's End: Why Our Colleges and Universities Have Given up on the Meaning of Life* (New Haven: Yale University Press, 2007), 199.

22. Popper's great hero is Socrates. And one of Socrates' key insights, according to Popper, is to connect the love of reasoned argument with the love of human beings and, conversely, the hatred of reasoned arguments with the hatred of human beings (Plato, *Pheado* 89d—a likely misreading of what Socrates says there: "For as there are misanthropists or haters of men, there are also misologists or haters of ideas, and both spring from the same cause, which is ignorance of the world"). Plato, Socrates' more genial student, is Popper's great villain. For Plato took Socrates' original egalitarian and democratic position favoring an open society and distorted it until it could serve as a justification for his vision of a closed and nonegalitarian society.

23. Popper, *Open Society II*, 23.

24. Jan Assmann offers an alternative explanation. Though egalitarian, early Christianity was intolerant. Like the original intolerance of all secondary, exclusivist religions, Christianity's intolerance was at the beginning a negative one—willingness to die on account of one's faith rather than to embrace convictions and practices incompatible with the true faith; it was an intolerance of victims who saw compromise as an abandonment of God and a form of assimilation. When Christians found themselves in the center of power and Christianity became the state religion of the Roman Empire, negative intolerance turned into positive intolerance. "Their fastidious refusal to eat the meat of animals sacrificed to pagan deities then became a ban on carrying out such sacrifices" (Assmann, *The Price of Monotheism*, 21). Descriptively, Assmann may be right or nearly right, but he seems not to note that in the process later Christian theologians suppressed some significant motifs prominent in early Christianity (such as commitment to nonviolence and tolerance) and reconfigured others (such as the relation to the state). On "motifs" in Christianity, their highlighting, suppressing, and reconfiguring, see chapter 5.

25. Jean-Jacques Rousseau, *The Social Contract*, ed. Lester G. Crocker (New York: Washington Square, 1989), 146.

26. Ibid., 146.

27. Berger, *A Far Glory*, 37.

28. Rousseau, *The Social Contract*, 146–47.

29. Whether this is in fact the case—whether religious pluralism has affinity to political pluralism or what forms of religious pluralism have affinity to political pluralism —would require a careful examination. Ancient Rome, for instance, was religiously pluralistic while at the same time imperialistic; religious pluralism was placed in the service of imperialism (see Jörg Rüpke, "Roman Religion—Religions of Rome," in *A Companion to Roman Religion*, ed. Jörg Rüpke [Malden, Mass.: Wiley-Blackwell, 2007];

Janet Huskinson, *Experiencing Rome: Culture, Identity and Power in the Roman Empire* [New York: Routledge, 2000]).

30. John Barry, *Roger Williams and the Creation of the American Soul: Church, State, and the Birth of Liberty* (New York: Viking Penguin, 2012), 389.

31. Izaak Walton, *The Life of Mr. Richard Hooker* (Ann Arbor, Mich.: Text Creation Partnership, 2003), 47, accessed May 11, 2015, http://quod.lib.umich.edu/e/eebo/A67470.0001.001/1:26?rgn=div1;view=fulltext.

32. Roger Williams, *The Bloudy Tenent of Persecution*, in *The Complete Writings of Roger Williams* (Eugene, Ore.: Wipf & Stock, 2007), 3:321.

33. Together with John Smyth (1554–1612), with whom he was in exile in Amsterdam, Thomas Helwys composed the Baptist *Declaration of Faith* (1611). Around the same time he finished a book that contains the first formulation of the principle of religious liberty, *A Short Declaration of the Mystery of Iniquity* (1611–12), and sent it to King James. Its basic thesis was bad news for the king, who rewarded Helwys for the gift with imprisonment. The thesis read as follows: "The king is a mortal man and not God, therefore he has no power over the immortal souls of his subjects, to make laws and ordinances for them, and to set spiritual lords over them" ([Macon: Mercer University Press, 1998], xiv). The thesis was revolutionary: each "immortal soul"—whether of a "heretical" Christian or a Jew, a Muslim or an atheist—is free from the state's interference with regard to its faith. It is likely that Williams derived his views from these first English Baptists, as Williams's recent biographer, John Barry, suggests. For they "had worshiped near Williams' home—and many had been sent to Newgate prison, a few hundred yards away from his home, where at least one of them, Thomas Helwys, died" (Barry, *Roger Williams*, 152). But if Helwys was the first to articulate the individual's religious liberty in a political sense, Williams was the first to create a government informed by this belief.

34. Rainer Forst, *Toleration in Conflict: Past and Present*, trans. Ciaran Cronin (Cambridge: Cambridge University Press, 2013), 183.

35. Roger Williams, "Queries of Highest Consideration," query 12, in *Complete Writings*, 2:273.

36. Williams, *The Bloudy Tenent*, 3:421; see also *The Bloudy Tenent Yet More Bloudy*, in *Complete Writings*, 4:154.

37. Williams, *The Bloudy Tenent Yet More Bloudy*, 4:154.

38. Barry, *Roger Williams*, 394.

39. Williams never undertook to show how, from within his own religious framework, an argument could be made for *reciprocal* toleration among different religions and a-religions.

40. See Emil Oberholzer Jr., *Dominion and Civility: English Imperialism and Native America* (Ithaca: Cornell University Press, 1999), 218 (Oberholzer finds Williams in this

regard inferior to Jefferson who, in his judgment, was a true Enlightenment man and therefore a "secular" figure).

41. John Plamenatz, *Man and Society: A Critical Examination of Some Important Social and Political Theories from Machiavelli to Marx* (London: Longmans, 1963), 51.

42. See, for example, "Vast Right-Wing Conspiracy," *American Prospect* 14 (June 2003): 9; E. L. Doctorow, "Why We Are Infidels," in *Reporting the Universe* (Cambridge, Mass.: Harvard University Press, 2004), 83–88; Kevin Phillips, *American Theocracy: The Peril and Politics of Radical Religion, Oil, and Borrowed Money in the 21st Century* (New York: Penguin, 2007), 99–263. Jon Shields offers a brief summary and numerous examples of the tendency to vilify the Christian Right (*The Democratic Virtues of the Christian Right* [Princeton: Princeton University Press, 2009], 13–15).

43. See, for example, Randall H. Balmer, *Thy Kingdom Come: How the Religious Right Distorts the Faith and Threatens America* (New York: Basic, 2006), 181. Among supporters of the Christian Right, the conservative pastor and activist D. James Kennedy muses that "in a sense," Winthrop's "city on a hill" remark "helped create the template for a uniquely free and Christian America"—the sort of America he calls his readers to help rebuild (D. James Kennedy and Jerry Newcombe, *What if America Were a Christian Nation Again?* [Nashville: Nelson, 2003], 15).

44. Shields, *The Democratic Virtues*, 1.

45. Ibid., 5.

46. Ibid., 2.

47. Ibid.

48. Ibid., 3.

49. Ralph Reed, "A Strategy for Evangelicals," *Christian American*, January 1993, 14.

50. Shields, *The Democratic Virtues*, 24.

51. Ibid., 68–99.

52. In addition to Karl Popper, whom I discussed above, see John Dewey, *Logic: The Theory of Inquiry*, vol. 12 of *The Later Works of John Dewey*, ed. JoAnn Boydston (Carbondale: Southern Illinois University Press, 2008), 481–505.

53. Shields, *The Democratic Virtues*, 2.

54. On personal responsibility for a human life, see Ronald Dworkin, *Is Democracy Possible Here?* (Princeton: Princeton University Press, 2006), 17.

5.
Conflict, Violence, and Reconciliation

1. Steven Pinker, *The Better Angels of Our Nature: Why Violence Has Declined* (New York: Penguin, 2011), xxi.

2. In contrast to Thomas Hobbes, who famously contended that the state of na-

ture is a state of war of all against all (*Leviathan*, ed. C. B. MacPherson [New York: Penguin, 1968], 185–86), Rousseau argued that in the state of nature "the care for our own preservation interferes least with the preservation of others" and that the state of nature is consequently "most favorable to peace" (Jean-Jacques Rousseau, *Discourse upon the Original and Foundation of Inequality among Mankind*, ed. Lester G. Crocker [New York: Washington Square, 1967], 200). He thought—or rather conjectured, for he had no reliable information to speak of—that it is "ridiculous to represent savages constantly murdering each other to glut their brutality" (206). Modern archaeological investigation has shown that pre- and nonstate humans were just as violent, if not *more* so, than moderns (see Lawrence H. Keeley, *War Before Civilization: The Myth of the Peaceful Savage* [New York: Oxford University Press, 1997]).

3. Pinker, *Better Angels*, 52.

4. Richard Dawkins, *The Selfish Gene* (Oxford: Oxford University Press, 1976).

5. Pinker, *Better Angels*, 32–33.

6. On the humanitarian revolution and the escalator of reason, see ibid., 647–57, 690–92.

7. Others have called into question at least some of his statistics (see John Gray, "Delusions of Peace," *Prospect*, September 21, 2011, accessed April 28, 2013, http://www.prospectmagazine.co.uk/magazine/john-gray-steven-pinker-violence-review/).

8. As Sarah Coakely noted in her 2012 Gifford Lectures, there is a revolution under way in evolutionary biology—something "imploding distractingly within it"—that reintroduces *cooperation* into evolutionary explanation ("Stories of Evolution, Stories of Sacrifice" [2012 Gifford Lectures at Aberdeen University, April 17, 2012], 5, accessed May 11, 2015, http://www.abdn.ac.uk/gifford/about/2012-giff/). This has everything to do with a new tendency to permit discussion of group-level selective pressures and adaptations (David Sloan Wilson, "Altruism and Organism: Disentangling the Themes of Multilevel Selection Theory," *American Naturalist* 150 [1997]: S122-S133; Martin A. Nowak and Roger Highfield, *Supercooperators: Altruism, Evolution and Why We Need Each Other to Succeed* [New York: Free Press, 2011]; Edward O. Wilson, *The Social Conquest of Earth* [New York: Liveright, 2012]).

9. For the phrase and its justification, see Christian Smith, *Moral, Believing Animals: Human Personhood and Culture* (New York: Oxford University Press, 2003).

10. Granted, Pinker and others who reduce morality to a cost-benefit calculus will translate deeply held moral convictions, such as the command to be compassionate or to love one's enemies, into "benefits." The debate is whether such translations account adequately for these moral convictions. Charles Taylor, for instance, rejects the homogenization of goods that these translations presuppose. There are goods, which Taylor calls "hypergoods," that cannot be placed on the same scale as others. See *Sources of the Self: The Making of Modern Identity* (Cambridge, Mass.: Harvard University Press, 1989), 63–75.

11. With regard to the motivation for violence, "the case study evidence generally

suggests a mix of material and symbolic motives amongst both leaders and followers" (Philip S. Gorski and Gulay Türkmen-Dervişoğlu, "Religion, Nationalism and Violence: An Integrated Approach," *Annual Review of Sociology* 39 [2013], 193–210.).

12. Bruce Russett and John Oneal, *Triangulating Peace: Democracy, Interdependence, and International Organizations* (New York: Norton, 2001).

13. In Pinker's case, Kant's conditions for peace are filtered through the seminal work of Norbert Elias published in Germany in 1939 and translated into English as *The Civilizing Process: Sociogenetic and Psychogenetic Investigations*, trans. Edmund Jephcott (Malden, Mass.: Blackwell, 2000). Pinker also gives Kant's conditions a more contemporary spin and supplements them with a theory of the human mind based on evolutionary biology and recent developments in the sciences of human nature.

14. Immanuel Kant, *Toward Perpetual Peace*, in *Immanuel Kant, Practical Philosophy*, trans. and ed. Mary J. Gregor (Cambridge: Cambridge University Press, 1996), 322. In this regard, Kant is close to Hobbes, who insisted that "the nature of War, consisteth not in actuall fighting; but in the known disposition thereto, during all the time there is no assurance to the contrary" (*Leviathan*, 186). But Kant's position is not exactly contrary to Rousseau's idea of a "noble savage," either. Rousseau imagined a human being in the state of nature as an asocial individual and connected peace in the natural state directly to the absence of social ties. Humans were made wicked by becoming sociable, he believed (*Discourse*, 210). In Rousseau's (admittedly not very plausible) opinion, "primitive man" was "an equal stranger to war and every social tie, without any need for his fellows, as well as without any desire of hurting them" (207–8). Absence of need for fellow human beings and absence of need to hurt them are here directly related.

15. Kant was not the first to use "perpetual peace" in a title dealing with issues of war. Abbé St. Pierre published in 1713 a much-discussed book titled *Project surrender la paix perpetualle en Europe*.

16. Kant, *Toward Perpetual Peace*, 323, 336. There is a long political tradition, of course, of enforcing laws within a community but practicing lawlessness without (see Paul W. Kahn, *Political Theology: Four New Chapters on the Concept of Sovereignty* [New York: Columbia University Press, 2011], 43–45).

17. Kant, *Toward Perpetual Peace*, 328.

18. Ibid., 333, 336–37. For Kant himself, the spirit of commerce is not a condition of peace to be established by human beings but an effect of the purposiveness of nature, which makes "concord arise by means of discord between human beings even against their will" (331). Since few today think of economic systems as effects of nature's purposiveness (or, as Marx did, as results of the dialectic of historical progress), considering them instead as cultural artifacts that human beings create and shape, political scientists inspired by Kant (such as Russett) have recast the spirit of commerce from an effect of nature into a humanly shaped condition for peace.

19. See Political Instability Task Force, "Polity IV Individual Country Regime Trends, 1946–2013," June 6, 2014, accessed July 15, 2014, http://www.systemicpeace .org/polity/polity4.htm.

20. Immanuel Kant, *Toward Perpetual Peace*, 326.

21. Daniel Philpott, *Just and Unjust Peace: An Ethic of Reconciliation* (Oxford: Oxford University Press, 2012), 1–2.

22. See, for instance, the case studies in *Handbook of Ethnic Conflict: International Perspectives*, ed. Dan Landis and Rosita D. Albert (New York: Springer, 2012).

23. Commentators strongly influenced by Catholic social teaching who consider abortion an act of lethal violence against a person argue that we have to include the estimated 42 million abortions a year worldwide (see World Health Organization, *Unsafe Abortion: Global and Regional Estimates of the Incidence of Unsafe Abortion and Associated Mortality in 2008*, 2011, accessed May 11, 2015, http://whqlibdoc.who.int/publi cations/2011/9789241501118_eng.pdf) in the assessment of the prevalence of violence in the contemporary world. See Dallas A. Blanchard, *Religious Violence and Abortion: The Gideon Project* (Gainesville: University of Florida Press, 1993), 250–72.

24. On the entanglement of violence and peace in the fundamental logic of liberalism, see brief comments by David Martin, "Axial Religions and the Problem of Violence," in *The Axial Age and Its Consequences*, ed. Robert N. Bellah and Hans Joas (Cambridge, Mass.: Belknap, 2012), 298–300.

25. For Foucault (drawing on Nietzsche), this is a dynamic fundamental to the nature of "law" itself (Michel Foucault, "Nietzsche, Genealogy, History," in *The Foucault Reader*, ed. Paul Rabinow [New York: Pantheon, 1984], 85).

26. See http://www.oxfam.org/en/pressroom/pressreleases/2015-01-19/richest -1-will-own-more-all-rest-2016 (January 19, 2015, accessed May 11, 2015).

27. See World Bank, World Development Indicators, May 2011, accessed May 11, 2015, http://chartsbin.com/view/1114; and Charles A. S. Hall and John W. Day Jr., "Revisiting the Limits to Growth After Peak Oil," *American Scientist* 97 (2009): 230–37.

28. The data are contested. Take such a vital resource as water. The most recent U.S. intelligence report sees global water conflicts rising, especially three decades from now (Intelligence Community Assessment, "Global Water Security," February 2, 2012, 3, accessed April 29, 2013, http://www.dni.gov/files/documents/Special%20Report_ ICA%20Global%20Water%20Security.pdf). Others consider such conflicts unlikely; for example, Meredith A. Giordano and Aaron T. Wolf, "Sharing Water: Post-Rio International Water Management," *Natural Resources Forum* 27, no. 2 (2003): 163–71.

29. For a comparative overview of the place of contentment within Hinduism, Buddhism, Judaism, Christianity, and Islam, see Peggy Morgan and Clive Lawton, eds., *Ethical Issues in Six Religious Traditions* (Edinburgh: Edinburgh University Press, 2007), 27–29, 80–82, 181–82, 238–40, 307–10.

30. I agree with Daniel Philpott in both affirming key elements of the "liberal peace" and seeing them as insufficient (*Just and Unjust Peace*, 70–73). He sketched his own ethic of reconciliation in a critical dialogue with the theory of liberal democratic peace and incorporated into his ethic the key features of the liberal peace, notably the importance of human rights.

31. I owe this observation to Fr. Michael Casagram of the Abbey of Gethsemani, Kentucky.

32. That holds true even if courts have ruled in our favor. For courts often don't provide sufficient satisfaction to the wronged, and the wrongdoers often deem their verdicts unjust. It is hard to agree on matters of justice.

33. For a list of political apologies that shows a clear increase in past decades, see Graham G. Dodds, "Political Apologies: Chronological List," April 28, 2013, accessed May 11, 2015, http://reserve.mg2.org/apologies.htm.

34. Daniel Philpott's *Just and Unjust Peace* is an example of an exploration of political reconciliation.

35. My own *Exclusion and Embrace: A Theological Exploration of Identity, Otherness and Reconciliation* (Nashville: Abingdon, 1996) explores primarily such reconciliation.

36. Lewis Smedes's *Forgive and Forget* (San Francisco: HarperSanFrancisco, 1996) may serve as an example.

37. For a fuller treatment of the subject, see Miroslav Volf, *The End of Memory: Remembering Rightly in a Violent World* (Grand Rapids, Mich.: Eerdmans, 2006); Miroslav Volf, "Remembering Wrongs Rightly: On Memories of Victims and Perpetrators," in *Das Geheimnis der Vergangenheit: Erinnerne—Vergessen—Enschuldigen—Vergeben—Loslassen—Anfangen,* ed. Jürgen (Neukirchen-Vluyn: Neukirchener Verlagsgesellschaft, 2012), 29–47.

38. On the contested nature of memory's truth in Rwanda, for instance, see Ervin Staub, *Overcoming Evil* (Oxford: Oxford University Press, 2011). He writes: "However, establishing truth and having it be accepted by all the parties is difficult. Survivors of intense violence are focused on their suffering. They usually see themselves as innocent and the other group as completely responsible and evil. . . . For reconciliation the truth has to recognize the injuries that each side has suffered at the hands of the other. In Rwanda, part of the truth is the harsh rule by Tutsis over Hutus before 1959, under Belgian colonial rule. Another part is that Hutus, when they took power in 1959, and then officially in 1962 when the country became independent, did not create a more equal society but instead discriminated against the Tutsis and engaged in frequent violence against them, repeatedly on a scale of mass killings. A major part of the truth is the horror of the genocide. For reconciliation the truth must also recognize the killings of Hutus by the Rwandan Patriotic Front (RPF) during the civil war and the Rwandan Patriotic Army (RPA) afterward; the killing of Hutu civilians as the Rwandan army

fought infiltrators from the Congo in the second half of the 1990s; the killing of Hutu refugees by the Rwandan army in the Congo. All this was not comparable to the genocide, but it is highly significant and part of the truth" (442–43).

39. Richard von Weizsäcker, "Speech in the Bundestag on 8 May, 1985 During the Ceremony Commemorating the 40th Anniversary of the End of War in Europe and of National-Socialist Tyranny," *MediaCulture Online*, accessed April 29, 2013 http://www.mediaculture-online.de/fileadmin/bibliothek/weizsaecker_speech_may85/weizsaecker_speech_may85.html.

40. See Barber Bevernage, *History, Memory, and State-Sponsored Violence: Time and Justice* (New York: Routledge, 2011), 8.

41. See Desmond Tutu, *No Future Without Forgiveness* (New York: Doubleday, 1999).

42. See Volf, *Exclusion and Embrace*, 120–22.

43. Pinker, *Better Angels*, 537.

44. Hannah Arendt, *The Human Condition: A Study of the Central Dilemmas Facing Modern Man* (Garden City, N.Y.: Doubleday, 1959), 212–13.

45. Miroslav Volf, *Free of Charge: Giving and Forgiving in a Culture Stripped of Grace* (Grand Rapids, Mich.: Zondervan, 2006), 129–30. For a similar definition of forgiveness, see Nicholas Wolterstorff, *Justice in Love* (Grand Rapids, Mich.: Eerdmans, 2011), 169.

46. Arendt, *Human Condition*, 216.

47. On the relation between forgiveness, punishment and retribution, see Volf, *Free of Charge*, 169–71.

48. On punishment as backward looking and rehabilitation, deterrence, and protection as forward looking, see Wolterstorff, *Justice in Love*, 198. The two main rationales for punishment strictly understood are retribution and reprobation. Forgiveness is incompatible with retribution because, by definition, to forgive is to forego retribution. But forgiveness is not incompatible with reprobation, for to forgive is to implicitly condemn the forgiven deed.

49. Other traditions, notably Jewish and Islamic, generally make repentance and apology a condition of forgiveness (see Yehudith Auerbach, "Forgiveness and Reconciliation: The Religious Dimension," *Terrorism and Political Violence* 17 [2005]: 479–81). In recent years, however, some prominent Christian philosophers have argued that in Christian thought as well repentance is a condition of forgiveness (see, for instance, Woltertorff, *Justice in Love*, 171–75).

50. On this see Aaron Lazare, *On Apology* (Oxford: Oxford University Press, 2004), 163.

51. On two aspects of the removing of the consequences of wrongdoing, apology and reparation (one dealing with the harm done by the purposive attitude of the wrong-

doer toward the victim and the other by the act itself), see Richard Swinburne, *Responsibility and Atonement* (Oxford: Clarendon, 1989), 80–81.

52. John Hare, *The Moral Gap: Kantian Ethics, Human Limits, and God's Assistance* (Oxford: Clarendon, 1996), 231.

53. Jürgen Moltmann, "Das Geheimnis der Vergangenheit: Erinnern—Vergessen—Enschuldigen—Vergeben—Loslassen—Anfangen," in Moltmann, *Das Geheimnis der Vergangenheit*, 109–10.

54. Hobbes, *Leviathan*, 185.

55. Ibid.

56. So, for instance, Pinker, *Better Angels*, 678. But as I have argued in chapters 3 and 4, early and formative formulations of tolerance, such as those by Thomas Helwys, Roger Williams, and John Locke, advocated the stance on explicitly religious grounds. On Christian origins of religious freedom, see Robert Wilken, *The Christian Roots of Religious Freedom* (Milwaukee: Marquette University Press, 2014).

57. See Keith Ward, *Religion and Human Nature* (Oxford: Clarendon, 1998), 1–9; "Sin," in *The Concise Oxford Dictionary of World Religions*, ed. John Bowker (New York: Oxford University Press, 2003), 545.

58. Mark Juergensmeyer (*Terror in the Mind of God: The Global Rise of Religious Violence* [Berkeley: University of California Press, 2003]) thinks that images of the "cosmic war" against the forces of "chaos" and "evil" (148–66) are present in all religions and contribute to their propensity toward violence.

59. See Miroslav Volf, *A Public Faith: How Followers of Christ Should Serve the Common Good* (Grand Rapids, Mich.: Brazos, 2011), 37–45.

60. David Martin's formulation on which I build here goes as follows: "My own procedure is to treat Christianity as a specific repertoire of linked motifs, internally articulated in a distinctive manner, and giving rise to characteristic extrapolations, but rendered recognizable by some sort of reference back to the New Testament and 'primitive tradition'" (*Does Christianity Cause War?* [Oxford: Oxford University Press, 1997], 32).

61. Ibid., 120.

62. Hobbes, *Leviathan*, 168, 173. The famous belligerent response to this misuse of religion by rulers was the exclamation, attributed to Diderot: "Man will not be free until the last king is hung with entrails of the last priest!" On the state's tendency to take over religion, see Monica Duffy Toft, Daniel Philpott, and Timothy Samuel Shah, *God's Century: Resurgent Religion and Global Politics* (New York: Norton, 2011), 48–81.

63. Kant, *Toward Perpetual Peace*, 336. This is not all Kant has to say about religion, of course. Kant contrasts "the single religion" and "historically different *creeds*." As there can be no different morals but only one (according to Kant), so there can be, properly speaking, no different religions but only "one single *religion* holding for all

human beings and in all times." Historical creeds, which differ "according to differences of time and place," are at best vehicles of that one religion. It is these historical creeds that separate people and contain propensity toward hatred and war. Forces of separation and motivators of conflict, they stand in contrast not only to the single religion as a source of unification but also to "the power of money" or "the spirit of commerce," which "cannot coexist with war" (336).

64. On religion as a marker of identity in the war in the former Yugoslavia, see Miroslav Volf, *Allah: A Christian Response* (San Francisco: HarperOne, 2011), 189. On religion as a marker of identity in Ayodhya, see Ragini Sen and Wolfgang Wagner, "History, Emotions and Hetero-Referential Representations in Inter-group Conflict: The Example of Hindu-Muslim Relations in India," *Papers on Social Representation* 14 (2005): 2.

65. Martin, *Does Christianity Cause War?* 134.

66. See Émile Durkheim, *Elementary Forms of Religious Life,* trans. Carol Cosman (Oxford: Oxford University Press, 2001). On the Durkheimian perspective on religious violence, see Philip S. Gorski, "Religious Violence and Peace-Making: A Meso-Level Theory," *Practical Matters Journal* (2012), accessed May 11, 2015, http://practical mattersjournal.org/issue/5/centerpieces/critical-responses-to-the-essays-on-reli gious-violence-and-religious-peacebuild#gorski.

67. For a survey of issues and approaches to the relation between religion, nationalism, and violence, see Gorski and Türkmen-Dervişoğlu, "Religion, Nationalism and Violence," 19.

68. In its self-representation in sacred texts, Judaism was from the beginning associated with an ethnic group and political power (Moses, David) and was a religion in which war—religious war—played a significant role. Once the entanglement with (or the aspiration to proximity to) political power was given up during exile and in diaspora, Judaism was reconfigured and became a much more peaceable religion (see Ron E. Hassner and Gideon Aran, "Religion and Violence in the Jewish Traditions," in *The Oxford Handbook of Religion and Violence,* ed. Mark Juergensmeyer, Margo Kitts, and Michael Jerryson [Oxford: Oxford University Press, 2013], 78–99; Michael S. Berger, "Taming the Beast: Rabbinic Pacification of Second-Century Jewish Nationalism," in *Belief and Bloodshed: Religion and Violence across Time and Tradition,* ed. James K. Wellman Jr. [Lanham, Md.: Rowman & Littlefield, 2007], 47–62). In some of its versions today— particularly those that embrace a religious version of Zionism—Judaism is again associated with violence (see Robert Eisen, *The Peace and Violence of Judaism: From the Bible to Modern Zionism* [New York: Oxford University Press, 2011], 141–204).

The history of Christianity shows a similar pattern, just with inverse sequence. Christianity, born as a socially marginal religious movement, was at its beginnings peaceable. Once it got entangled with political power after the conversion of Constantine, it was reconfigured; its central symbol, the cross, became not only a sign of God's identification with sinners and sufferers but also, as in Constantine's vision, a sign in which a ruler would conquer his enemies (Roland H. Bainton, *Christian Attitudes Toward War and Peace: A Historical Survey and Critical Re-evaluation* [New York: Abingdon, 1960]). Recently, the claim that there is a sturdy pre-Constantinian tradition of pacifism that gave way to a sanctioning of violence and identification with political power has been contested (e.g., Alan Kreider, "Military Service in the Church Orders," *Journal of Religious Ethics* 31 [2003]: 415–42; Louis J. Swift, "Early Christian Views on Violence, War, and Peace," in *War and Peace in the Ancient World*, ed. Kurt A. Raaflaub [Malden, Mass.: Blackwell, 2007], 279–96). What is uncontested and still makes my larger point (though weakening it somewhat) is that there are no elaborations of just war theory or any trace of embracing the doctrine of holy war before the fourth century (see Jonathan Riley-Smith, *The Crusades: A History*, 2nd ed. [London: Continuum, 2005]; Frederick H. Russell, *The Just War in the Middle Ages* [Cambridge: Cambridge University Press, 1977]; Paul Stephenson, "Imperial Christianity and Sacred War in Byzantium," in Wellman, *Belief and Bloodshed*; Christopher Tyerman, *God's War: A New History of the Crusades* [Cambridge, Mass.: Belknap, 2009]).

Islam has both distance and proximity to political power in its origin. While in Mecca, with a band of believers constituting a persecuted minority, Muhammad urged his followers to practice nonretaliation, for instance. It was in Medina, where Muhammad's followers were formed into a people with him as their spiritual and political leader, that his revelations not only provided the elements of "constitution" for the people but shifted from advocating nonretaliation to urging struggle against the enemies of Islam in God's name (see Bruce B. Lawrence, "Muslim Engagement with Injustice and Violence," in Juergensmeyer, Kitts, and Jerryson, *Oxford Handbook of Religion and Violence*, 126–52; Reuven Firestone, "Conceptions of Holy War in Biblical and Qur'ānic Tradition," *Journal of Religious Ethics* 24 [1996], 108–9).

Confucianism has come into close proximity and even near identification with state power at various points in its history; indeed, it was instated as the state ideology during the Han dynasty and following its Song revival (the so-called Neo-Confucianism). In each case, state power twisted what Tu Wei-ming has called "Confucianism as a way of life" into "political Confucianism," pressing Confucianism into the service of legitimating authoritarian regimes (see Tu Wei-ming, *Centrality and Commonality: An Essay in Confucian Religiousness* [Albany: State University of New York Press, 1989], 24; and Joseph A. Adler, "Confucianism in China Today" [paper presented at Pearson Living Religions Forum, New York, April 14, 2011]; Sor-hoon Tan, *Confucian Democracy: A Deweyan Reconstruction* [Albany: State University of New York Press, 2003], 7–8). Contrary to the common view that Confucianism's pacifism created a militarily docile Chinese state, Don Wyatt has shown that, once Confucianism was aligned with the state, the paternalism intrinsic to its hierarchical worldview extended to justify the military aggression of the Chinese against neighbors whom they saw as subordinates, explaining this violence away as "punitive": "This hierarchical outlook . . . became superimposed from the realm of human relations onto that of interstate relations. It thus provided the basis for what became . . . the imperial tribute system, through which subordinate neighboring states paid spiritual homage to the Chinese sovereign as overlord. . . . [When] one side in the relationship . . . committed some ungrateful offense such as defaulting [this justified] some form of redress by the superior power—ranging from a mild diplomatic reproof to a full-scale armed invasion" ("Confucian Ethical Action and the Boundaries of Peace and War," in *The Blackwell Companion to Religion and Violence,* ed. Andrew R. Murphy [Malden, Mass.: Blackwell, 2011], 237–48).

69. Michael K. Jerryson and Mark Juergensmeyer, *Buddhist Warfare* (Oxford: Oxford University Press, 2010).

70. Stanley J. Tambiah, "Buddhism, Politics, and Violence in Sri Lanka," in *Fundamentalisms and the State: Remaking Polities, Economies, and Militancy,* vol. 3 of *The Fundamentalism Project,* ed. Martin E. Marty and F. Scott Appleby (Chicago: University of Chicago Press, 1993), 616.

71. Ibid., 600, 601.

72. A similar dynamic was at work in Rwanda in the years prior to the outbreak of violence. During Hutu rule (1961–94), church leadership was closely intertwined with the Hutu ethnic and state power structures (see Timothy Longman, *Christianity and Genocide in Rwanda* [New York: Cambridge University Press, 2011]). Cardinal Roger Etchegaray famously wondered whether "the blood of tribalism" ran "deeper than the waters of baptism" (quoted in Chris McGreal, *Chaplains of the Militia* [London: Guardian, 2014], chapter 2, Kindle edition).

73. Volf, *A Public Faith,* 40.

74. We need not enter here into complicated philosophical debates about the meaning of "same." It is an ancient problem. The Greek philosophers entertained themselves trying to puzzle out whether the famous ship of Theseus, whose decayed planks were gradually replaced by new ones, had remained the same ship throughout the process. In the same vein but more radically, Thomas Hobbes inquired whether a ship made entirely of the replaced planks would be the same ship as the original one (see Roderick M Chisholm, *Person and Object: A Metaphysical Study* [London: Routledge, 2002], 89–92).

75. See chapter 2. As indicated there, this account of religion builds on Ninian Smart's definition of religion as "worldview" understood as a system "of belief which, through symbols and actions, mobilize[s] the feelings and wills of human beings" (*Worldview: Cross-Cultural Explorations of Human Beliefs* [New York: Scribner's, 1983], 2–3).

76. See chapter 3 on the effect of social pluralism on the vibrancy of religious convictions.

77. It is sometimes claimed that one more feature of globalization exacerbates such conflicts. Though modern means of communication have put the world on our screens, they frequently have the effect opposite from broadening our knowledge of people different than ourselves. The Internet and media outlets that cater to particular audiences make it possible for people to cocoon themselves in virtual communities of elective affinities without having their perceptions ever challenged by real knowledge of people who espouse different religion, belong to a different political group, or are shaped by a different subculture. This holds true, the argument goes, even when people in fact share the same geographic and urban space. Spatially close and interdependent, they often live in alternative virtual realities and distort each other's positions and behaviors. Consequences seem to be both that conflicts are deepened and potential solutions to them are rendered more difficult to achieve. But empirical evidence calls such conflict-generating self-segregation on the Internet into question (see Matthew Gentzkow and Jesse M. Shapiro, "Ideological Segregation Online and Offline," *Quarterly Journal of Economics* 126 [2011]: 1799–1839).

78. Philpott, *Just and Unjust Peace*, 97–167.

Epilogue

1. See Osama bin Laden, "Letter to America," *Guardian*, September 24, 2002, accessed March 13, 2015, http://www.theguardian.com/world/2002/nov/24/theobserver.

2. Klaus Schwab, preface to *The Global Agenda 2009* (Geneva: World Economic Forum, 2009), 9, accessed March 12, 2015, http://www.weforum.org/pdf/global agenda.pdf.

3. Pedro Nicolaci da Costa, "Bernanke: 2008 Meltdown Was Worse Than Great Depression," *Wall Street Journal*, August 26, 2014, accessed March 13, 2015, http://blogs.wsj .com/economics/2014/08/26/2008-meltdown-was-worse-than-great-depression-ber nanke-says/?mod=WSJ_hp_Europe_EditorsPicks.

4. See Plato, "Phaedrus," in *Gorgias and Phaedrus*, trans. James H. Nichols Jr. (Ithaca: Cornell University Press, 1998), 184–88. For Jesus, consider Matthew 6:33 and 5:27–28. For the Buddha, of course, desire is central. On desire in modern philosophy, see George Wilhelm Friedrich Hegel, *The Philosophy of History* (New York: Dover, 1956), 23; and David Hume, *A Treatise of Human Nature*, ed. L. A. Selby-Bigge, 2nd ed. revised by P. H. Nidditch (Oxford: Clarendon, 1978), 415.

5. Friedrich Nietzsche, *On the Genealogy of Morality*, ed. Keith Ansell-Pearson, trans. Carol Diethe (Cambridge: Cambridge University Press, 2007), 27–31.

6. Hubert Dreyfus and Sean Dorrance Kelly, *All Things Shining: Reading the Western Classics to Find Meaning in a Secular Age* (New York: Free Press, 2011), 131. Their argument is that if we look past ordinary things to find "something deeper" behind

them, we will find nothing behind them and miss the joy that is in them. This reading of the *Paradiso* is, arguably, mistaken. My colleague at Yale Peter Hawkins, who has studied and taught Dante his entire career, objects strenuously to the claim of Beatrice's irrelevance: "The beatific vision does not make either earth or earthly affections irrelevant. In *Paradiso* 14 Solomon tells Dante that the souls of the blessed long for the end of time when they are reunited with their flesh (glorified flesh, whatever that means). This desire is not only for their own completion; they long for the 'reclad flesh' of their 'mammas, their fathers, and all they held dear' . . . the whole poem argues for an alignment of loves that envisions a fulfillment rather than a cancellation of the earthly. When Dante sees Beatrice unveiled in *Purgatorio* 31 he looks into her eyes but reflected in them be beholds 'la viva Luce eternal,' God's light. She, and things of earth, aren't cancelled out; they become translucent" (personal communication, May 2, 2015).

7. See Friedrich Nietzsche, *The Will to Power*, trans. Walter Kaufmann and R. J. Hollingdale (New York: Random House, 1968), 17–18, 38.

8. Friedrich Nietzsche, *Thus Spoke Zarathustra*, trans. Walter Kaufmann (New York: Viking, 1966), 17–18.

9. Dreyfus and Kelly, *All Things Shining*, 20, 71, 133, 142.

10. The phrase "wiping the horizon" comes from the famous "death of God" passage in Nietzsche's *The Gay Science*, trans. Walter Kaufmann (New York: Vintage, 1974), 181.

11. Slavoj Žižek, "Are the Worst Really Full of Passionate Intensity?" *New Statesman*, May 2015, accessed May 11, 2015, http://www.newstatesman.com/world-affairs/2015/01/slavoj-i-ek-charlie-hebdo-massacre-are-worst-really-full-passionate-intensity.

12. Nietzsche, *Thus Spoke Zarathustra*, 137–40.

13. For the novel method of interreligious engagement that underlies this book, see the introduction.

14. See Margaret Farley, *Just Love* (London: Bloomsbury, 2006), 239–40; see also Philip Zimbardo, "The Demise of Guys?" TEDTalk, August 5, 2011, accessed March 13, 2015, http://www.youtube.com/watch?v=FMJgZ4s2E3w&feature=youtube_gdata_player; and Gary Wilson, "The Great Porn Experiment," TEDxGlasgow, May 16, 2012, accessed March 13, 2015, http://www.youtube.com/watch?v=wSF82AwSDiU&feature=youtube_gdata_player.

15. Maurice Merleau-Ponty, *Phenomenology of Perception*, trans. Colin Smith (London: Routledge, 1962), 405. He writes: "In the cultural object, I feel the close presence of others beneath a veil of anonymity." See Komarine Romdenh-Romluc, *Routledge Philosophy Guidebook to Merleau-Ponty and Phenomenology of Perception* (London: Routledge, 2011), 130–31.

16. Paul Bloom, *How Pleasure Works: The New Science of Why We Like What We Like* (New York: Norton, 2010), 24.

17. Ibid., 3.

18. Ibid., xxi.

19. For a theological account of gift giving, see Miroslav Volf, *Free of Charge: Giving and Forgiving in a Culture Stripped of Grace* (Grand Rapids, Mich.: Zondervan, 2006).

20. I am not describing here an "epiphanic" experience of the kind, for instance, Václav Havel had while in prison. Here is how he describes it: "I was flooded with a sense of ultimate happiness and harmony with the world and with myself, with that moment, with all the moments I could call up, and with everything invisible that lies behind it and has meaning" (*Letters to Olga* [New York: Knopf, 1988], 332). I am thinking of the ordinary experience we have of the world and things in it in the light of our awareness of them as gifts of God, the kind of experience that doesn't just come and overcome us but that we can nurture and integrate into our daily life, indeed, that *is* our daily life.

21. In the course of a Shabbat meal, Alon Goshen-Gottstein reported to me this perspective on Shabbat founded on the teachings of the Jerusalem-based Rebbe of Slonim. Rabbi Shmuel Berezovsky writes (translation of the excerpt from Hebrew by Alon Goshen-Gottstein): "Though there is no commandment to be joyful on the Sabbath, joy comes of its own, without our intentionality. The very reality of Sabbath in which the Jew dwells in perfect restfulness brings him happiness and joy. For joy there is no need for a cause or a particular action, it is sufficient that a person has no burdens for peace of the soul to take hold and for him to feel good, which makes him happy. After all—God created the world in such a way that the reality of creation in and of itself elicits joy in a person's heart. . . . In a state of calm and peacefulness, the soul fills of itself with joy and gladness from the joy of creation" (*Darche Noam* [Jerusalem, 2014], 1:61–62).

22. For joy as unity between things being good and being experienced as good, see Miroslav Volf, "The Crown of the Good Life," in *Joy and Human Flourishing*, ed. Miroslav Volf and Justin Crisp (Minneapolis: Fortress, forthcoming 2015).

Index

Buddhism (*continued*)
   life, 72; blasphemy as viewed in, 128; violence associated with, 188–89
Buddhists, 60, 61; and public responsibility, 65; and religious intolerance, 100; in Sri Lanka, 84, 100, 188–89

caliphate, 86–87, 133. *See also* Islam
Calvin, John, 44
capitalism, 209n6; ambivalence toward, 6; and globalization, 5–6, 11; and world religions, 88–90. *See also* market economy; markets, world
Casanova, José, 65
Catholic Church, 84; in Yugoslavia, 8. *See also* Benedict XVI, Pope; Francis, Pope; John Paul II, Pope
Chanda, Nayan, 36–37, 212–13n1
China: Christianity in, 142; sweatshops in, 33. *See also* Confucianism
Christian Coalition, 158
Christianity, 3, 67, 140, 230n33, 265–66n68; and affirmation of ordinary life, 44, 73–74, 202–6, 232n44; apostasy as viewed by, 114–15; blasphemy as viewed by, 127–28, 129; and the capitalist economy, 88–89; and components of a good life, 75; debates within, 70; divisions within, 84, 103; and globalization, 11, 14–18, 25–26, 240n92; and Islam, 93, 99–100, 114–15, 224n9; Nietzsche's view of, 235n55; and other world religions, 19–20, 70; and reconciliation, 179, 183; and religious intolerance, 99–100, 256n24; and revelation, 139, 148; waiting as aspect of, 10–12. *See also* Catholic Church; Christian Right; Episcopal Church; Pentecostalism; religious exclusivism; religious pluralism

Christian Right, 258n43; as religious exclusivists, 156–59; as political pluralists, 156–59
Christians, 61; conflicts involving, 187; persecution of, 98, 108; as religious exclusivists, 137–39, 142. *See also* Jesus Christ; Williams, Roger
church and state, separation of, 105–6, 131–32, 134–35, 151, 243n14
Churchill, Winston, 4
Cistercian monastery, 173
civil rights movement, 183
Clark, Gregory, 221n61
cognitive contamination, 143–44
Cold War: end of, 3–5
commandments. *See* Ten Commandments
Common Word, A, 93
communism, 57; and globalization, 5–6, 42; religion under, 8. *See also* Marx, Karl
Communist Manifesto, The (Marx and Engels), 30–32, 37
compassion, 37, 38, 53; in Buddhism, 72, 171, 231n42; importance of, 49
conflict: and alternative visions of flourishing, 172, 190–92; in a diverse society, 172; as exacerbated by technology, 268n77; Hobbes's perspective on, 183–84; and reconciliation, 172–74. *See also* reconciliation; violence
Confucianism, 3, 67, 70, 75, 223–24n3, 226–27n22, 234–35n54, 236n62, 266–67n68
Confucius, 67, 82
Congo, Democratic Republic of, 33
conscience, freedom of, 106, 107, 155
consumerism, 82, 170, 199–200
contentment, 170–71, 172, 222n64
conversion, 114–17
Corinthians, Paul's first epistle to the, 18, 202